From Elvis to Elvira:

My Life On Stage

Richard Sterban

with Steven Robinson

Library of Congress Control Number: 2012940683

ISBN 978-0-9856601-0-9 (Paperback)
ISBN 978-0-9856601-1-6 (Electronic Book)

Published by: Richards & Southern, Inc.
P.O. Box 37 Goodlettsville, TN 37070

Executive Producer - Terry Calonge
Project Coordinator - Jeremy DeLoach
Project Design - Dennis Davenport

Printed in United States of America

FROM ELVIS TO ELVIRA: MY LIFE ON STAGE

"I have been a huge fan of Richard Sterban and the Oak Ridge Boys
for as long as I can remember. So it was great fun for me to discover
Richard's path to stardom in this delightfully written story of his life. I
knew about "Elvira" of course, but not about Elvis!"

The Hon. George H. W. Bush
41st President of the United States

෨

"Richard Sterban's book covers not only the journey from Elvis to Elvira,
but also the way in which The Oak Ridge Boys became both a cohesive
performing group and individual men of strength and character. It is an
inspirational story of lives well lived and songs well sung."

The Hon. Marsha Blackburn
Member, United States House of Representatives

෨

"Richard Sterban is a LOW DOWN SON OF A GUN; one of the very best
bass singers in the world, and one of the best ole' boys you could ever
hope to meet. I love my old friend RS, and I love this book. I am grateful
to God that Richard crossed my path a long time ago. What I really want
to say is OOM POPPA MAU MAU...That means "GOD BLESS YOU" in the
outer galactic language that Richard speaks fluently!"

Larry Gatlin

HIGHLIGHTS:

—Spend a day behind the walls of Graceland as Elvis hosts friends in an unforgettable experience that ends speeding through the streets of Memphis!

—Hear the encouragement offered by the Man in Black, Johnny Cash, and experience the heartbreak surrounding the death of his beloved wife, June.

—Sit at the control board and experience the recording process of a great song and watch as it becomes a worldwide hit.

—Learn never-before-heard, behind-the-scenes details of The Oak Ridge Boys through their unparalleled successes, their devastating split, and their triumphant reunion.

—Witness the bravery and showmanship of legends as varied as Sammy Davis Jr., Glen Campbell and Roy Clark.

—Hear the never-before-told details of the last time Richard and Elvis were together, in 1975, and what Elvis asked him.

—What is the one song Richard wishes The Oaks had never sung?

—Take a memorable look inside Air Force One, the White House and private times spent with four Presidents of the United States.

—Listen in as Elvis rehearses for concert appearances, recording sessions and for his Golden Globe winning documentary.

—Who is considered the fifth Oak Ridge Boy? Fans have heard him sing, and probably never knew it!

—Ronald Reagan was known as the "Great Communicator." Which Oak Ridge Boy does Richard consider the best communicator?

—Which Oak Ridge Boy does Richard think is the best singer?

—Watch a young Garth Brooks transform overnight into the showman that changed the face of country music.

—Read about the record producer who nearly ruined the singing career of his most famous bass singer, and the regimens the singer has practiced to overcome lifelong vocal challenges.

CONTENTS

FROM ELVIS TO ELVIRA: MY LIFE ON STAGE

Author's Note:

I have been blessed with a career that has found me peripherally associated with perhaps the greatest music star in history, and intimately involved with a singing group that has maintained a certain amount of popularity for a number of years. Much has been written about both subjects. I really haven't played a major role in any of the earlier written material. This book is, by no means, meant to be a comprehensive history of either Elvis Presley or The Oak Ridge Boys. In fact, within these pages I have tried not to retell too much that has been covered by others; however, some things demanded to be told again. Even when I cover topics that have been written about before, I hope I've been able to add something that will come as news and be interesting. More than anything, these pages represent my perspective on the things I've witnessed. I had a great time living the life on these pages; I hope you'll enjoy reading about it.

Richard Sterban

Hendersonville, Tennessee

PROLOGUE: *Stage Left*

"Ladies and gentlemen...Elvis has left the building. Thank you and good night." It wasn't the first time that Elvis's stage announcer had made that announcement—in fact he said it every night—and it wasn't the first time that countless fans refused to believe it. Just moments ago, he had been before them, arms outstretched revealing a jeweled cape, jumpsuit drenched with sweat, wet hair matted to his face.

For the previous hour, he had sung their favorite songs; he had carried them across the years and through their fantasies, back to a better time and forward to a happier place. It hadn't been just a concert to most of them, and he wasn't just a singer. He was the personage of their youth, the very reflection of their vitality. He had provided the background music to their lives. He had been their friend, their idol, their king; and now, he was gone. He had left the building. And like so many nights before, for so many different audiences in so many other towns, they simply sat in their seats refusing to believe that it could be over so soon.

It didn't matter if it had been the first time they had ever seen him, or the tenth, or the hundredth. They couldn't believe he was gone. It had happened so quickly. It had been all they hoped—exactly what they needed—but now it was over. While some sat in silence, others filed out of the arena or the showroom—whether on the way to their cars and homes, or their hotel rooms and the casino slot machines. They were on the way back to their lives, taking with them the memories of the night— for many, a life-changing experience.

Still, others remained, unwilling to let the experience end so abruptly. They stood several deep at the edge of the stage. Some pointed cameras, taking pictures. Some held concert programs or photos or scarves, asking for autographs. Elvis had left the building, but the next best thing remained: people who actually knew him, people who worked with him. They didn't have to be convinced of the association for they had just witnessed it first hand. They had seen this group surrounding him, performing behind him, singing with him. He had talked with them, joked and laughed. He had introduced them to the audience. He, Elvis, had thought so highly of these few people that he had taken the time away from singing to introduce them to his throng of fans. It was as if he were saying: "These people are good...these people are friends of mine... you should know them too."

The TCB Band was the rhythm section that had backed him since he began his comeback some three years before. The Sweet Inspirations, the Atlantic Records trio who had enjoyed chart success backing artists as varied as Dusty Springfield and Jimi Hendrix before becoming Elvis's female vocalists and opening act. Kathy Westmoreland, usually introduced as the "little girl with the beautiful high voice:" was a classically trained soprano who had backed him since he had resumed touring the country. His conductor, leading the orchestra, was Joe Guercio, also known as "the Maestro." And, the five men in matching suits who comprised one of the leading gospel groups in the nation, were The Stamps Quartet, under the leadership of J.D. Sumner. For the last year, The Stamps had stood, stage left, every night and blended their voices with the *King of Rock 'n' Roll*.

The fans knew their names, knew their faces. They wanted a handshake or an autograph. "What is he like?" "Is he really as nice as he seems?" "Are you married?" "It must be so exciting!" "He looked tired tonight. Does he get enough rest?" "How do you like the traveling?" "Doesn't it get lonely?" "Can I have your towel?" "Is he really gone or is he still backstage?" "Could I see you later?" "How does it feel to be a star?"

The members of the entourage answer the questions. Some pose for pictures. Some make dates for later. They all pack up their own gear. There's no bus to catch tonight, no flight to the next town; nowhere to go except to a lonely hotel room; the stand ends tonight. Another month in Vegas complete: this time, sixty-four shows in thirty-two days. The King of Rock won't step on stage to begin another tour for almost two months. When he does hit the road again, these same players will be there, on another stage in another town doing what they've chosen to do. And, likewise, the fans will play their part. They will stand in line and buy the tickets, then scream for their idol once again. Elvis will provide the heart and the soul, and these people—the band, the musicians, the background singers—they will provide the sounds, the backbeat, and the vehicle to deliver this spectacle to the masses.

I could not have known I would find my way to Elvis's stage. I couldn't even say that I'd always been a fan. I'd always wanted to sing, that's for sure, but I could not have predicted that I would end up singing on stage with the *King of Rock*. It hadn't been a conscious dream, but it certainly could have been seen as the pinnacle for a background singer like me. Gospel singers sang because they loved it—or felt called—not necessarily because they could make a living doing it, and certainly not to become a star. Gospel singers traveled in cars, vans or buses, not airplanes. They sang in churches or auditoriums, at all-night sings or Sunday morning services, often in exchange for love-offerings, not for standing-room-only crowds at the likes of Madison Square Garden. They didn't appear in award-winning movies. They didn't experience life on the road in quite the same way that I did, with one of the top touring acts in the world. We were the envy of many. Certainly this was the pinnacle. What could be better than this?

In many ways, for us, it was a surreal existence for, like his fans—while Elvis would be off the road, living his life at Graceland or beyond—we would return to our lives away from Elvis. For the Stamps, in this instance, that meant that, for the next two months, we would get on our own bus and travel the country singing gospel music. We would play our "normal shows" at churches and auditoriums for crowds large and small, only to reconnect with Elvis, this time on November 8, for a tour beginning in Lubbock, Texas that would, again, play before audiences in excess of 12,000 people per night. This particular tour would end in Hawaii for what promised to be an unprecedented record-setting worldwide television broadcast. How's that for surreal?

We each had our reasons to eagerly anticipate this next tour: the camaraderie of life on the road, an opportunity to witness, again, the mastery of Elvis on stage, the chance to get paid to travel to Hawaii—no small thing in our lives at that time. It promised to be a highlight for us all, and yet for me, it didn't quite happen that way.

I loved being a member of The Stamps Quartet. As a bass singer, I'd long idolized their leader, J.D. Sumner. I loved touring with Elvis and yet somehow it wasn't quite enough; I felt as if there was something more for me. Without the opportunity provided by Elvis, I might have never found the courage to follow bigger dreams, but just like he did for those fans, Elvis had given me exactly what I needed: a life-changing experience. This kid from Camden, New Jersey, grew up wanting to be a singer, loving gospel music, believing he could make a living doing it, dreaming of the day it might happen, but also being aware that he might want more than a life spent as a back-up singer. Many around me didn't understand, but I knew that "stage left" wasn't where I wanted to spend the rest of my life. As it turned out, what I was really waiting for—though I didn't know it at the time—was a phone call: one that would change my life in ways I could have only imagined.

CHAPTER ONE: *Dolce Vita*

C amden, New Jersey was never considered a hotbed for Southern gospel music, but somehow I found it—or rather, it found me. In the generation before I arrived, like so many cities in the Northeast, Camden had become a city divided geographically into ethnic neighborhoods: German, Polish, Irish, Jewish, Italian and others. Occasionally those neighborhoods blended. Such was the case in the home of Edward and Victoria Sterban. Vickie was a native of Salandra, a rural town in the Basilicata region of southern Italy. In 1920, at the age of two, she and her parents immigrated to America, first touching its shores at Ellis Island in the shadow of the Statue of Liberty.

Edward was a first-generation American born in Camden to Polish parents. He and Victoria met working at the Giant Tiger grocery store in Camden. She was a cashier, and he was a commercial electrician. They were married in Camden and then on April 24, 1943, I was born: Richard Anthony Sterban.

The first house I can remember living in was in Fairview, New Jersey, a suburb of Camden. That was the town where both sets of grandparents also lived—conveniently, within walking distance. As most Italians can boast, my earliest memories are from the kitchen, though it wasn't always my mother's. I spent a lot of time growing up with my maternal grandmother. She lived across the street from my elementary school in Fairview, so, almost every day, I would walk across the street to have lunch with her. Many were the days that she would babysit me, in part just because of the convenience of being so close to my school, but also because I enjoyed, so much, being with her. She never learned English—and I never learned Italian—but somehow we communicated all throughout my childhood.

In her home, my love for Italian cooking was born, and there it thrived. My mom was also a good cook, but as the dutiful wife, had to blend her own Italian tastes with my father's Polish tastes. The result was a combination that didn't always satisfy their firstborn son! Perhaps that was another reason I was drawn to my grandmother's kitchen. I still remember the first taste of pizza I ever had. It, too, came from my grandmother's oven. Despite being in the Northeast, back in those days there wasn't a pizza parlor on every block like there seems to be now.

One Italian tradition that thrived in our house involved the holidays. All of my aunts and uncles and cousins—and, often, friends—would gather around the table for a traditional Italian feast. Even on Thanksgiving, before the turkey and stuffing and sweet potatoes and vegetables would be served, we all had to eat our way through giant bowls of pasta.

My early days were pretty normal fare for that time in America's history. It was that familiar story of growing up in and around "rough areas" where trouble could be easily found—or could come and find you—but that was balanced with the innocence of the era. Though my parents taught me to be wary, they also trusted me. At an early age—as young as seven or eight years old—I would take the city bus by myself through the roughest areas of Camden to the YMCA. There I would take swimming lessons or play basketball with my friends—or with kids I didn't know—kids who actually lived in those poor sections I'd see through the bus windows. Such was the enigma of the early 1950's in America.

Contrary to the idyllic suburban life epitomized on classic television, both of my parents worked. Looking back on it, I realize it was probably necessary in order for them to make ends meet. When I was three, they had another son, Joe, and then seven years later a daughter, Susan, filled out our happy family. Dad continued his work as an electrician, and my mother worked a few different jobs, my personal favorite of which was the time she worked at the *A. N. Stollwerck Chocolate Factory* in Camden. In addition to making candy, they would also provide the chocolate and other products for *Whitman's Candy Company, Tastykakes* and others. That was a child's dream-come-true, as many evenings she would bring candy home to us kids. It was our own version of a *Whitman's Sampler*!

My family's first move took us to the outskirts of Camden, just off what is known as the Black Horse Pike, in a town called West Collingswood Heights. Geographically it was only a couple of miles away, but, demographically, it seemed much farther. It was definitely a step up from the house in which I was born. Though located in a neighborhood, the new house was situated on a pretty good-sized piece of land—well over an acre. Despite my young age, it became my job to do all of the yard work. While other kids might have complained about that, for some reason I not only enjoyed it, I excelled at it. Every week, throughout the warm months, I could be found pushing that big manual push mower with all of the strength I could muster. Then I would get on my hands and knees, and trim around the sidewalk, the hedges and trees, and also around the perimeter of the house. I really took pride in keeping the place looking good. I even grew a vegetable garden: lots of tomatoes, onions, radishes and corn. I can't explain why I had the interest, and I can't even remember how I knew how to grow a garden, but somehow I had learned, and we had lots of vegetables on our table throughout the summer.

The Black Horse Pike and the White Horse Pike were part of a highway system that led down to Atlantic City on the New Jersey shore. (In New Jersey, we never referred to it as the beach; it was always the shore, as in: "Let's go down the shore.") Even though it was sixty miles or so to Atlantic City, I remember thinking how cool it was that, from our house, you only had to make one right turn—onto the Black Horse Pike—in order to get to the shore. It was a straight shot.

On the Pike between Camden and Atlantic City was a little town called Clementon. One of the fondest memories of my childhood was going there to an amusement park called *Clementon Lake Park*. They had a big swimming pool and also lots of rides. It was a great place for kids, and my family enjoyed many days there. It's still there today though now it's called *Clementon Park Splash World*.

Despite the deep Polish and Italian influences on my childhood, one area where we did not follow tradition was religion. I was raised a Protestant. My mother had been converted from her Catholic upbringing as a young girl. Later, after she and my father began dating, he agreed to become Protestant also, after which my mother agreed to marry him.

The First Assembly of God Church was located on Walnut Street in the middle of the poor section of Camden. It was the first place, outside of my home, where I was taught the Bible, taught right from wrong. For all of my years spent living at home it was where my family went to church—and, believe me, we went virtually every time the doors opened. Our lives really revolved around it. As with most kids, as I got older, it was also a place I'd come to resent, somewhat, as it dominated so much of our lives. But for the most part—and certainly in retrospect—I'm grateful to have been given such a strong moral and religious base on which to build my life, as it would serve me well later on.

Mine was a fairly strict upbringing. I remember when televisions first started appearing on our street. Like all of the other kids, I wanted us to get one, but back in those days, some preachers considered televisions to be evil. Some even said that they were the eye through which Satan could see right into your house. Not wanting to take the chance, my parents chose not to have one. Fortunately for me, my paternal grandparents, though fervent in their Catholicism, weren't as strict—or maybe just weren't as worried about what the devil might see in their home—so they bought a television. After that, I began to enjoy visiting them more and more, if only to see the images come across that small black-and-white screen.

As I got a little older, things remained pretty strict. I wasn't allowed to do a lot of seemingly harmless things. For example, I wasn't allowed to go bowling with my friends because the bowling alleys had bars in them—and near a bar was no place for a good, church-going boy to be. I wasn't allowed to go see movies because of unknowns that I might see or learn about within those dark walls. (To this day, my mother still won't go to see movies. Not because she thinks they're evil but just because she's not comfortable in the theaters. Many years ago, however, she did decide that the mere presence of a television wasn't inherently a bad thing, so she got one—and she will watch movies on that.)

I was not allowed to go to dances—because everyone knows that dancing could lead to all sorts of evils—so traditional dating was tough for me. I was allowed to go out occasionally but only with girls from church. And more often than not, a date back then meant either hanging around the house with my parents or hers, or going to church. So, many of my earliest innocent flirtations were made all the more innocent because they occurred either in direct view of our parents, or walking to or from the church house.

In addition to some of those frustrations, however, that First Assembly of God church was also the site of two of the most significant moments in my young life; neither of which has lost importance with the passing of years. For there, in front of God and the entire congregation, I made my first public performance and sang in front of an audience. Though it was life changing for me, it was about as different as it could have possibly been from the performances that would follow years later. Even though it should probably be expected, in my particular case it always seems to surprise people to learn that, as a six-year old, I was a boy-soprano.

I wish I could say I remember the song that I sang, but I can't. That's a detail that has been lost in so many other songs sung. I can say, however, that I remember the experience itself as vividly as ever. Not only can I still visualize what I saw that morning: the church house, the congregation, the pastor, my parents smiling as their little man sang about Jesus; but, almost like an out-of-body experience, I can also see myself standing there, as if another person, so small and so young but also somehow so sure that this was to be his calling in life. I knew that I liked the feeling of standing on a stage and singing to an audience. I liked how it seemed to make them feel, and I definitely liked how it made me feel.

The other significant event occurred three years later—when I was nine years old. This time I was sitting in the pew of the very same sanctuary one Sunday morning when the preacher's words reached my heart, and I made my decision to become a Christian. Just as singing there that first time changed my life by putting me on the path that I'm still following all these years later, this decision, made in that same church house, in front of many of the same friends and family, also changed my life forever. It, too, set me on a path—and it's one that I've never regretted walking.

And just as I've undergone many transformations on my spiritual journey, I was in for some major changes in my singing. Until I was about twelve-years-old, I maintained my high voice. As late as the seventh grade, as a member of the Glee Club, I was still singing first tenor. Then in the summer between seventh and eighth grade, in what seemed like an overnight development—though I realize it wasn't—my voice dropped considerably. I never went through that awkward squeaky phase that plagued so many of my friends; my voice just sort of naturally kept sliding lower and lower, settling into a nice bass for a young man. When I returned to school in the fall, my choir teacher was shocked, but rather than fight nature, she just smiled and immediately moved me from first tenor to second bass. And there I stayed, though junior high and high school.

By my high school years, our family of five moved a couple of miles further down the road to Oaklyn, New Jersey. The yards were even bigger, the houses nicer, and the "rough sections" farther away. I attended Collingswood High School, just four years after its soon-to-be-famous alumnus, Michael Landon, had graduated. I remained active in the music department.

At various times, I played several different instruments. As a child, I had been drawn, for some inexplicable reason, to the trumpet so I'd begun taking trumpet lessons and, later, baritone horn. Those soon led to the French horn, which I played in the orchestra. Later, I picked up the E-flat Tuba and also the Sousaphone, which I began playing in the marching band. I loved it. So much so that, around this time, I helped organize a Pep Band for the basketball team. We would perform at all of the games, home and away. It was a great way for me to do things I loved even at that age: watch sports, play music, and hang around girls.

For the most part, being at all of the football and basketball games with the band was my outlet for satisfying an interest in team sports. I wasn't, however, always just an entertaining spectator; I did participate on some teams. I was a runner, competing in Track-and-Field in the spring, and Cross Country in the fall. I loved distance running—and I even got pretty good at it. The track coach also coached the wrestling team, so at his request, I wrestled one year, but I never really enjoyed that. As much as I loved baseball—both watching it and playing it with my friends in the neighborhood—I learned pretty early that my love of the game far exceeded my skills. I played up until junior high, most often as a catcher. As for my talent, I can say that what I lacked in ability, I made up for in enthusiasm. The coach used to put me in when the games were out of reach—with us either way out in front or so far behind that I couldn't hurt our chances. More often than not, though, because of my winning spirit and go-get-'em attitude, I was designated as the first base coach.

In addition to band, of course, I continued to sing all through my high school years. In fact, I actually did pretty well at it. My choir teacher, Edgar Wallace, was very good. He made it fun but at the same time really pushed us to make us better. We would sing a lot of classical acapella songs. We even recorded a couple of long-playing albums during my time there. I made All-State Choral twice, and for three years, I was named All-South Jersey Chorus. For each, I won a trip to perform at the Convention Center in Atlantic City—my first "road trip" with a band.

~~~

For thirty years, just after the turn of the century, Enoch "Nucky" Johnson was the undisputed "boss" of Atlantic City. He was the county treasurer and a political leader in the state, and guided Atlantic City through the Depression era and Prohibition, transforming it from a sleepy coastal town to a vacation destination and year-round convention city. He accomplished this, in large measure, by ignoring the laws that banned alcohol. He proudly proclaimed that his vision of Atlantic City was open for business and pleasure, for all to enjoy. In 1929, he opened the state-of-the-art

Convention Center, which, for its time, was modern and gargantuan. This soon attracted even more conventions and events, and became the home of the *Miss America Pageant.* Through the 1950s and into the 1960s, the pageant was the biggest show on television. And even though my TV-viewing was limited, the fact was not lost on me that Atlantic City and the Convention Center were each important to the American entertainment scene. When I got the chance to go there and sing, I was very excited.

The group was taken to Atlantic City and put up in a hotel right on the Boardwalk. We were there for the better part of a week, rehearsing and sightseeing. It was a very big deal to us. One of the things I remember most about those weeks—even more than the performances themselves—was walking down the boardwalk with some of my friends and other participants I had just met, and harmonizing with each other as the waves crashed just steps away from us. Though we were singing music that was a little more classical than classic, it was our own version of those doo-wop groups that hung out under lampposts harmonizing.

That was a great time to be a kid in America—and in South Jersey. Though Atlantic City had the nickname of "America's Playground," and there was, no doubt, plenty of debauchery that could be found for anyone who was looking for it, the fact is, I can't remember any of us actually looking for it. I might be idealizing some in my own memory, but I have to say I don't recall any of the kids I was hanging out with getting into trouble on those trips.

❧ ❧ ❧

Music had become more and more important to me over the years. My parents always had the radio on at home, but more often than not we listened to religious broadcasts. It seems Billy Graham was always on, or gospel music. There was a gospel music program that originated out of WCMB in Harrisburg, Pennsylvania, that I could sometimes tune in after dark on the old Philco radio in my parents' front room. In fact, that's probably the first place I ever heard quartet singing. Any time we were in the car, the radio was on, and it was almost always on gospel music. I would hear groups like the Blue Ridge Quartet, from Spartanburg, South Carolina, with Burl Strevell, singing bass. I remember hearing a great black gospel group called The Harmonizing Four, from Richmond, Virginia. Their spirituals were mesmerizing: "Only Believe," "Farther Along" and "In Jerusalem" with that big booming bass lead of Jimmy Jones. When quartets would come on, I just thought that was the coolest thing I'd ever heard. At some point, my mom's sister, Flossie, gave me a Blackwood Brothers Quartet record called *Hymn Sing*—with J.D. Sumner singing bass—and I was hooked. Sure, I loved other bass singers, but from that moment on, J.D. was my guy. The irony is not lost on me that I was attracted to J.D.'s big booming bass before my own voice changed.

When you think about it, even the most popular music of that day was not really suggestive, so eventually my parents would allow me to listen to whatever I wanted to on the radio but early on, even the radio was somewhat restricted. Of course, my parents had no problem with me listening to gospel music so that made it easier for me to indulge in my tastes.

And listen to it, I did! I can remember my brother Joe and me playing that Blackwood Brothers record over and over again on a record player in our bedroom and pretending we were singers in the quartet. Our twin beds each had four posts, and the posts at the foot of each bed served as our microphone stands. We would stand and jump around them just like the Blackwood Brothers on the cover of that record album. Sometimes I "appeared" solo in that room, but the best times were when we could pretend together. I know now that Joe never had the same desire I did to be a singer; I think his desire was to have something in common just so he could hang out with his big brother. Joe was the athlete of the family, playing high school football. He was much bigger than I, and could really put the hurt on those running backs. He's lived in South Florida for many years, and we see each other whenever possible. Almost anytime The Oaks perform near him, he comes to see us in concert. It's always good to see him, and catch up.

࿐࿐࿐

As I mentioned, I was ten years old when my sister, Susan, came along so our age difference kept us from being close as children. By the time she was seven years old, I was out of the house, living on my own. It's really just been as grown-ups that we've become very close. She still lives in New Jersey, and we get together as often as possible and enjoy being adult siblings in a way we never could as children.

࿐࿐࿐

Ironically, the only time the "religious only" radio rule seemed to be loosened was once a month during the summer months when the men's group at our church sponsored father/son deep-sea fishing trips. Dad and I would pile into his car and "go down the shore" where we would get on a boat and head out to the blue water and fish all day. This was a lot of fun for me—the chance to spend quality leisure time with my father—but it also afforded me the chance to listen to the popular songs on the radio. Occasionally, we would hear stations like WWVA out of Wheeling, West Virginia—the Wheeling Jamboree. That's also around the time I remember first hearing Elvis Presley. But while other kids were listening to him for the release or rebellion that rock-and-roll offered, I was drawn to him because he had a quartet, The Jordanaires, singing behind him. It was the kind of music that I liked, and it made me like him.

One Sunday morning our church hosted a singing service that featured a visiting quartet from Harrisburg, called "The Couriers." My family went and, while I think they all enjoyed it, I can say with certainty that it didn't affect anyone else the way it did me. I was immediately taken by them: the way they dressed, their stage presence, and the way their voices—Neil Enloe singing lead; Don Baldwin, baritone; and Duane Nicholson singing tenor—blended in that four-part harmony anchored by their bass singer, Dave Kyllonen. From then on I lived and breathed gospel quartets. I just couldn't get enough.

Later that same week, The Couriers were performing at a nearby church. Though it sounds like a story our grandparents might have told us about the "old days," the fact is I walked about two miles in the rain to go see their show. I'll never forget, I had saved up enough money to buy one of their albums. I walked all the way home after the show in a driving rainstorm. I cradled the album under my jacket in an attempt to keep it dry. Shortly after I got home, the inadequacy of my attempt became clear as the album cover all but disintegrated. Fortunately, the record itself still played.

Later that summer, the family had a vacation planned at the shore. I had just gotten my first car, a 1953 Ford. My parents were already at the shore, and I was supposed to drive there immediately after work. On my way there, I saw a church sign advertising that The Couriers were going to be performing there that night, and then I saw their bus parked around to the side. Well I couldn't pass up the chance to see my favorite singers, so I pulled in beside their bus to wait for the service to begin. Shortly, I saw their bass singer, Dave, getting off the bus. By that time, they were getting used to seeing me hanging around their shows, and I think Dave had a pretty good idea, based on my voice as well as my enthusiasm, that I was especially fond of his singing and that I aspired to be a bass singer as well. They were very nice to me that day and their singing that night was as good as ever. So good, in fact, that it made me forget where I was supposed to be at that time. Immediately after the service ended, I dutifully, though belatedly, drove to meet my parents as planned—only I would be several hours late. Of course this was long before the existence of cell phones so I had no way of letting them know that I was fine, just enjoying the good, clean fun of a gospel sing. When I arrived at the shore my mother was worried sick, and my father was furiously pacing. As soon as they saw me and realized I wasn't hurt or dead, they were ready to kill me!

They forgave me, of course. Though they were upset with me, I think, deep down, they were happy that my "rebellion" was over something as tame as gospel music. In fact, another time, not long after that, when The Couriers came back to sing at my church, my parents helped me get to know my favorite group even better. At the service, The Couriers accepted our invitation to come to our house for dinner afterwards. One of my favorite Italian things that my mom made was a meatball sandwich. They were outstanding. I was in Heaven. I couldn't believe that these singers were actually in my house eating at our kitchen table. And they raved about my mother's sandwiches, which made me even more proud. It was a big day for me.

So, while it's common knowledge that the Couriers deserve much of the credit for introducing and furthering southern gospel music in the northeast United States, it's also safe to say that The Couriers were, at least indirectly, very instrumental in my becoming a singer. If not for them, this flame inside me might have never had the chance to burn. Who knows, as my high school years were drawing to a close, I might have been drawn to some other dream to chase. I'll never know, but I'm glad I don't have to wonder. I will forever be grateful to those four guys from central Pennsylvania for unknowingly starting me down the path that would become my life.

CHAPTER TWO: *Black Coffee*

In addition to being great singers, The Couriers were also "in the business" of gospel music. That meant that while they worked shows for other promoters and buyers, they would also promote their own gospel sings all around the region that, in addition to themselves, would feature other local and even national groups. Once, when I was about seventeen, they promoted a show in Philadelphia. Of course, I was among the first ones there when the doors opened. Joining The Couriers on the bill that night was The Blackwood Brothers Quartet. Though I had never met them before, I was very familiar with The Blackwoods and their music. They, along with The Statesmen, recorded for RCA Records. As a result, record stores would carry their releases. Most quartets weren't on major labels so the only way to get one of their records was to see them at a gospel sing and buy one from the record table (as I had done with my rain-soaked Couriers album not too much earlier.) The Blackwood Brothers, at that time, were comprised of James and Cecil Blackwood; tenor singer, Bill Shaw; keyboard player Wally Varner; and the bass singer was a giant of a man named J.D. Sumner.

It was at this show that I first met J. D. I can still remember walking up to the record table to speak to him. Across the lobby I saw him standing there, tall and lanky, hair slicked back in that high pompadour; he was holding a cup of coffee in his hand. I approached and told him that I was an aspiring bass singer. He was very friendly to me, and we talked for a long time. At one point, I asked him if he had any tricks of the trade that he might share with me; some secret that would help me nurture my bass voice to be more like his. He smiled and looked down at the cup in his hand. After an extended pause, he raised the cup and said "Black coffee, son. That's the secret. You have to drink lots of coffee—always black. It helps the vocal chords and makes your voice lower."

I couldn't believe it. Here was a hero to me—the man who would be listed in the *Guinness Book of World Records* with the lowest bass voice—and he was sharing his secrets with me. I was just a kid with lofty dreams and a somewhat low-register voice. The fact that he would entrust me with the formula for success was so exciting for me.

Years later, after I'd started working for him as a member of The Stamps, I reminded J.D. about that day. He smiled and told me that of course he remembered. He went on to say "I had no idea what to say to you. Here you were this young guy obviously turned on by gospel quartet singing. You looked up to me as if I had some secret, but I didn't have any meaningful advice. I was trying to think of something, and saw the cup of coffee in my hand, so I told you that you should drink lots of black coffee. I figured it wouldn't hurt you, and I could tell you weren't going to leave me alone until I told you something." I'll admit I'd come to suspect that had been case, but I was glad, finally, to have it confirmed. We laughed about that for a long time, though, by that time, I had drunk a lot of black coffee (and still do today.)

After high school graduation, I enrolled at Trenton State College (now The College of New Jersey) in the music program. Back then, it was primarily a teachers' college, but I chose that school because my choir teacher, Mr. Wallace, had recommended it to me for its outstanding music program.

Trenton is across the river and not too far from the little town of Bristol, Pennsylvania. As was becoming a habit for me, I attended a show there, again promoted by The Couriers, at which I met three guys: Bob DiQuattro, his twelve-year old brother, Joey and a friend of theirs named Danny Sinacore. They sang, and wanted to put a group together, and most importantly, they needed a bass singer. In May of 1962, we decided to form a group—and since Pennsylvania is the Keystone State, we chose the name The Keystone Quartet.

I would go to class during the day, and then many nights, I would drive the twelve miles over to Bob's house where we would practice and rehearse. On weekends we would go out and sing in churches or at shows—really just anywhere we could, and for anyone who would let us.

In the earliest days of the group, in addition to my bass, Bob sang lead, Danny sang baritone and played piano, and Joey, whose voice had not yet changed, sang the high soprano part. We actually started having some success right away. Looking back, it was probably a combination of a pretty good group of singers coupled with the novelty of having a little kid singing with us. He really was an entertaining little singer, and we didn't hesitate to stick him out front. It was just another way to try to bring attention to the group so that we could get more shows.

Occasionally, along with some of the big names in Southern gospel music, The Couriers would hire us to work on some of the shows they promoted. Once, during this time, they unwittingly set the stage for something that would positively impact me for the rest of my life. And the funny thing was, I had no idea that it happened. We were one of the opening acts on their big show at the *Hershey Sports Arena*. As we were doing our set, it came my time to sing a solo: "Let The Lower Lights Be Burning." As fate would have it, at the same time, through the turnstiles walked a brash, young kid from Philly who loved gospel quartets. Though I wouldn't know about it for almost a year, when we actually met, that was the first day my eventual best friend and singing partner, Joe Bonsall, would ever hear me sing. And that was the day he decided that he, one day, wanted to sing with me.

Unfortunately, as is only natural, too soon little Joey DiQuattro's voice changed, and with it, so did the group dynamics. Bob had recently gotten married so his wife, Esther, joined us, and in the tradition of groups such as The Weatherford Quartet, she began singing the female tenor part and Joey moved to baritone, to replace Danny, who had departed. At the same time, Nick Bruno joined us, playing piano.

Things went well enough during that first year that we thought we might have something worth dedicating ourselves to, so we decided to try to become a full-time singing group. I remember one of the hardest things I'd ever had to do in my young life was to tell my parents that, after only one year of college, I was going to drop out to pursue a career singing gospel music. They were disappointed—perhaps even a little mad—and, of course, they tried to talk me out of it. Finally in an unusual show of certainty, rather than defiance, I simply told them that I wasn't going back. I honestly believed I was doing the right thing.

I wanted to make sure that I was truly following God's will as opposed to simply convincing myself that God must want for me what I wanted for myself. On campus, we had a brand new chapel called Alumni Meditation Chapel. It was situated in a grove of sycamore and oak trees across from the library. It was small, seating only about 50 people, and featured a very modern design with a sweeping A-frame roof framing a beautiful stained-glass window. On the day that I would tell my parents, before driving to their house, I walked to the chapel and spent a long time in prayer. When I emerged, I had a peace about my decision to leave college. Even though it was contrary to everything that seemed "normal" or expected of me, I knew that, not only did I want to sing, I truly felt I was being called to sing.

I've been asked if I might have just as easily gone into country music at that time or join one of the doowop vocal groups that were becoming the rage—especially in the northeast region of the country. The fact is, I couldn't have been happy doing that. I loved gospel music, and I wanted to sing it. Since my earliest years, it was the music I wanted to listen to, and that followed me right up to college. I can't recall what my roommate's musical preferences were but I can say that when I was in our dorm, and it was my turn to play records, we were listening to gospel quartets.

The feeling inside of me ever since I'd become a Christian also led me to believe that singing gospel was to be my life. And that experience in the chapel definitively drove that point home, and I knew I was destined to sing it. I came to understand that not everyone could be called to be a Billy Graham-type evangelist or a missionary, but a calling to sing, for me, was just as real, and just as sincere.

Finally, my parents accepted my resolve and my decision, and said they'd try to understand. (As evidence of their unconditional love and acceptance, for a while after I left college, I moved back into their house and commuted to Bristol to sing.) But leaving school was definitely a tough decision for a lot of reasons. Chief among them, I didn't want to disappoint my parents, but also I didn't want to be a dropout. I wanted to finish school, but I just didn't know if I'd ever get a chance like that one again. It was a struggle for sure, but once I made up my mind, there was no turning back.

It went pretty well for The Keystones for a time. Among the dates we worked was one at the First Assembly of God Church in Binghamton, New York. This was a large church that held its services in a historic building that was formerly a Masonic Temple. The church is still there and ironically its located right across the street from *The Forum Theater,* which is a regular tour stop, still today, for The Oak Ridge Boys. The pastor back then, a man named R. D. E. Smith, had a leadership role of some sort in the Assembly of God denomination. He took a liking to us and started helping us book dates at various churches in the area and around the country. Once we even drove all the way to Des Moines, Iowa to sing at one of their churches. That was a big deal for our little group, though it was a terribly long drive. So, Pastor Smith was helpful enough to us that, for a while, we relocated to Binghamton, and used that church as our home base. Looking back on it, it might have been an impulsive move. I'd just gotten married to my long-time girlfriend, Sandra, so moving away from our families wasn't the most convenient decision, but the fact that we did speaks to our dedication to my career, such as it was at that time.

Even though we weren't making enough money, for a while it went pretty well. We stayed fairly busy singing at churches and small auditoriums, first on the weekends and then throughout the week. While we'd had hopes that we could become and remain full-time singers, eventually Bob and Esther decided that they might not be quite suited for a life spent singing on the road. So, in early 1965, The Keystone Quartet ceased to exist.

Sandra and I packed up and moved back down the road to Camden and for a while I didn't sing but instead took several odd jobs to try and earn some money. The fact that I wasn't singing, however, did not mean I had lost interest; I still went to gospel sings. At one I attended, I became reacquainted with a man I had met singing at a show a few months earlier. J.R. Damiani was the leader of a "weekend group" called The Eastmen Quartet, and also owned a shoe store and repair shop in Lansdale, Pennsylvania. We became friends, and in summer of 1965, I joined J.R., Frank Sanchez and Ronnie Landis as a member of The Eastmen Quartet along with, Nick Bruno on piano, who had also played with The Keystones.

Frank Sanchez might have been the first "clothes hound" I'd ever known. He worked in a men's clothing store, and always dressed very sharp. I remember being impressed with how he looked all the time; even when he was casual, he looked well put together. I really liked fashion and even thought that I might like it for a career if singing didn't work out. Following Frank's lead, not too long after, I applied for—and got—a job selling men's clothes at a Gimbels Department Store in Northeast Philadelphia.

Again, unbeknownst to me, while doing a show with The East-men Quartet, Joe Bonsall heard me sing again. Then, a couple of weeks later, when I was pulling another shift at Gimbels—trying to improve the fashion sense of some of Northeast Philly's rising middle class—I met Joe for the first time. He had heard through the "gospel word-of mouth" that I was working there, so he came in to seek me out. I thought he was pretty cool, and we became pretty fast friends. Here was another kid about my age who loved to talk about gospel music—gospel quartets, in particular—and believe me, that was not an easy thing to find back in those days, and probably is even less so now. On one of his visits he might have actually bought a shirt or something but for the most part—and probably to my manager's dismay—we had purely social visits. We'd spend our time talking about gospel quartets. Over time, we continued to see each other, either at Gimbels or at gospel shows around the area. In fact, Joe even had a quartet of his own at the time called The Faith Four Quartet. Of course, there was no way that either of us could have ever known just how intertwined our lives would eventually become.

There was a big Assembly of God church in downtown Philadelphia, where I visited a few times, that had a choir that was unbelievably good. I used to love to sit in the congregation and listen to them sing. Betty McDowell sang in the choir and once after a service I talked with her. It turns out that she was a voice teacher. I told her that I was an aspiring singer and asked if she might have some time available to give me a lesson or two. She agreed, and I began taking lessons from the lady who I would come to call "Aunt Betty."

One time at Gimbels when I was talking music with Joe instead of selling someone something, he mentioned that he would like to take some voice lessons. I told him about Aunt Betty, and soon he, too, was working with her. I distinctly remember one day the two of us sitting in a small waiting room outside her studio (which was in her home) and waiting for our own lessons as we listened to her giving a lesson to one of the other members of Joe's Faith Four Quartet. As I look back on it, perhaps I should have asked for commission on the lessons I booked. As active as I kept Aunt Betty, I could probably have earned a better living than I did at Gimbels.

In order to be closer to the other members of The Eastmen Quartet, Sandra and I moved again—along with our new son, Rich—to Woxall, Pennsylvania, where I rented an apartment above a garage building next door to J.R.'s house. In fact, it was the same apartment that J.R. and his wife, Bev, had lived in when they first got married. Eventually I tired of driving the hour-long commute to Gimbels so I took a job running a press at a print shop owned by a friend of J.R.'s. The living and working arrangements were convenient for our rehearsals, as almost every night would find us in J.R.'s living room practicing our harmonies.

To show what a small but wonderful world those times were, I remember the first date I ever worked with The Eastmen Quartet was on a bill with The Couriers, and the second was with The Statesman Quartet. It was a great feeling. As much as I loved singing on stage, I enjoyed, even more, sharing a stage with some of my heroes.

Because J.R.'s shoe shop was so successful, in the beginning, The Eastmen could only work on weekends. By the early spring of '66, however, J.R. gave up his shop and we went fulltime – and it started out great. In April of that year, we worked somewhere, a show or service, every single night of that month. We maintained a similarly busy schedule for the next couple of years, but in the latter part of 1967, with several records to our credit and many miles logged, J.R. had tired of staying on the road all of the time, so Nick and I left The Eastmen Quartet and J.R. rehired Ozzie Myers, the bass singer I'd replaced, and the group went back to singing part time.

Without missing a beat, Nick and I set our sights on forming another group. I relocated my family to a suburb of Harrisburg, Pennsylvania called Camp Hill. As they had done so many times before, The Couriers continued to positively impact my life and career. Don Baldwin who was the leader of The Couriers had an office and a recording studio (for their own Hymntone Records label) in Harrisburg, and they allowed me to keep an office there. In their studio was where we auditioned singers for the new version of The Keystone Quartet, and later where we would rehearse the group. In addition to me singing bass and Nick singing baritone, Ron Kelly became our tenor singer, and David Enloe (brother of The Couriers' Neil Enloe) sang the lead.

The Couriers were still promoting shows in Pennsylvania and all over the region: Hershey, McCaskey High School in Lancaster, The Farm Show Arena in Harrisburg, and others, but the Hershey show became their big flagship show—sort of a regular event. In another display of friendship—maybe even Christian charity—they continued to help us out by throwing some work our way and hiring us to sing on some of their shows. Even though it might have paid only $100 or $200 per show—certainly not enough to survive— we were still very grateful for them giving us the opportunity to do that thing we loved so much.

Later still, on some of the package shows we were doing, we worked with Joe and his Faith Four Quartet, which at that time also featured his thirteen-year old sister, Nancy. On these dates is where Joe and I really began to forge a strong friendship. In the spring of 1968, when David Enloe decided to leave our group, I asked Joe if he would be interested in leaving his group and joining us to sing lead. In addition to singing on the weekends, by then, Joe had a really good job at Jack Frost Sugar Company, but thankfully, he, too, wanted to sing fulltime so he accepted my offer and thus began our life spent sharing a stage.

Around this time our little group really started grinding. We worked lots of places—some big, some tiny—really anyplace we could. We traveled in a car with a trailer, then a beat-up van (left over from Joe's old Faith Four days) then eventually we graduated to an old blue 4104-model bus. As history has recorded, J.D. Sumner is credited with coming up with the idea for gospel groups to use a bus to travel across the country. This occurred when he was with The Blackwood Brothers. It really was an idea whose time had come. While now it seems an obvious component of life on the road, prior to that, quartets had crammed into cars, or, if they were lucky, a station wagon. After the Blackwood Brothers had paved the way, all quartets aspired to travel in these homes on wheels. Many groups, including the Keystone Quartet, bought buses to use for travel—and many did so long before they could afford it. (A replica of that first Blackwood Brothers' bus is on display at the Southern Gospel Museum and Hall of Fame at Dollywood, in Pigeon Forge, Tennessee.)

Looking back, it seems we had trouble keeping tenor singers so sometimes the quartet was intact, but other times, it would be a trio traveling: just Joe, Nick and me. In these configurations, I would sing baritone. Paul Furrow joined and sang with us for a while and then, eventually, while performing in Minneapolis, we met David Will who was a seminary student at North Central Bible College. We sang with David informally and loved how his voice fit with ours. Soon after that, he joined us singing tenor, but pretty quickly we decided that he was better suited to sing lead, which allowed Joe to move back to tenor where he was meant to be. With those changes, that quartet was set for a while.

All quartets had one member who filled the role of the business manager for the group. At that time, I was that person for The Keystone Quartet. I would spend hours in the office on the telephone talking with promoters or preachers trying anything I could to find us some work. It was not exactly in my nature to take this kind of role but it was my group—I had the most tenure—and we wanted to eat, so I did what was necessary. Sometimes we would get hired—paid perhaps $100 or $200—and other times we would work for a love offering, a collection that the congregation would take up for us. It was definitely a hard way to make a living but we stuck with it. Eventually we began working for a couple of gospel promoters from Southern Ontario, Canada for whom we did a lot of shows—almost enough to keep from starving, but it was still tough.

Oddly, to go along with those Canadian dates, we began finding a quite a bit of work in Western New York—so much so that, soon, some promoter friends from the area began encouraging us to move up there. After some soul searching and praying about it, we, as a group, decided that it made a lot of sense. We were doing the majority of our dates in the area so it would be most convenient to live there. So, in early 1969 we each moved to Kenmore, New York, a picturesque suburb of Buffalo. By then, Sandra and I had two sons: Rich and Doug, and a third, Chris, would soon follow. We made our home in a quaint little house on Harding Drive.

As with most gospel quartets, new music was the way to survive. We could often make more money selling records off the table than we would earn for singing. As 1970 dawned, we went into the studio and cut a new album: *Keystones Shine in the 70's*. It was the eleventh record we had cut—the sixth since Joe had joined.

Once while living in Kenmore, we heard that Jimmy Dean was going to appear in North Tonawanda, New York—just a couple of miles from our homes—for a week of shows. We decided to go see them one night because some of our friends, The Imperials, were backing him. The show was great, and The Imperials invited us out to eat with them afterwards. We were excited when Jimmy showed up and joined us for dinner. It was the first time we'd had the opportunity to meet him. Though, at the time, we were only going to see friends and hear a famous star, both of the acts, and the venue itself, would later have a huge impact on both Joe and me.

I remember Terry Blackwood, their lead singer, saying something that night that would impact me for years to come. It was the first time I'd heard it suggested that a gospel group could also sing secular music. In fact, he made me see that secular success could allow entre into new and unusual venues in which gospel could then be performed. I would certainly live that later with The Oaks, but at that point in my life and career, that was a brand new concept to me and to Joe.

As the dinner was coming to an end and we were all preparing to leave, Joe Moscheo, with The Imperials pulled me aside. He said that while it was still premature, and not public, there was a chance that their bass singer, Armond Morales was going to leave the group. He asked if I would be interested in auditioning to be his replacement. The group was staying at the Howard Johnson Hotel, so I drove there the next afternoon to meet with them. I was really excited for this opportunity; to think that they would even consider hiring me to replace a great bass singer like Armond was almost unbelievable to me. The Imperials were on top of the world as far as I was concerned. Here they were traveling the country with Jimmy Dean, and they were singing on stage with Elvis in Las Vegas and also on tour. To have the chance to sing with them would be a dream come true—like a minor league kid getting called up to the Yankees.

When I arrived at the Howard Johnson, I went to Moscheo's room, where I found him sitting at a piano. Terry was there with him though Jim Murray, their tenor singer, had not yet arrived. The three of us sang some of the Imperials' songs and then I sang a couple of the songs that Armond was singing with them at the time—and I tried to sing them in the smooth style that Armond employed. Towards the end of the audition, Jim came in, and the four of us sang a couple of songs together. It was a great afternoon, and the audition went very well. Now, obviously, Armond didn't leave the group at that time and I never became the bass singer for The Imperials, but it was an exciting day for me, and just having the chance to sing with, and audition for, them was a nice little boost to my ego.

Despite my afternoon of flirting, ever so briefly, with the big time, The Keystone Quartet was still my job and still my priority. Following the lead of The Couriers and some other successful groups—and as we had done with The Eastmen Quartet—The Keystones began promoting some of our own shows throughout upstate New York and southern Canada. It created a riskier situation for us because we were no longer just looking to get paid to sing for an audience. As the promoter, it was our job to book the talent and advertise the shows that would attract a ticket-buying audience, and there was always the risk that we wouldn't make enough money to pay the other groups, let alone ourselves.

Once we promoted a three-day run in Corry, Pennsylvania, and Jamestown and Elmira, New York with The Oak Ridge Boys who were, at that time, one of the hottest and most sought after gospel quartets working. Herman Harper, then with the Don Light Agency, who was their booking agent, offered them to us for $1,000 per night. Since we were doing three nights in a row, I was able to negotiate the fee down to $900 per night. On those shows, The Keystones and The Oaks hung out together, and it was the first time we had what might be called real quality time together onstage and off. We got to know each other, and see and hear each other's shows, and I enjoyed getting to know their bass singer, Noel Fox, whom I had never met before. Though I couldn't have known at the time that Bill Golden and Duane Allen had taken notice of me and my singing at those shows, I can definitively say that I became a bigger fan of theirs over those three days. I wish I could say we made money on the dates but we didn't, though I can proudly say that we did pay The Oaks every penny we owed them.

Later, in July of 1970 they repaid us by inviting us to Nashville to perform in War Memorial Auditorium at the International Gospel Music Festival. This was the event where The Oaks were perceived as really changing their course and turning the gospel world on its ear. When they took the stage, on that day, for the first time, they had replaced their simple snare drum with a full drum kit and a full-fledged "rock-and-roll" drummer. It was a thoroughly modern sound, and one that definitely caused a stir. It was also here where it seemed that our relationship with The Oaks went to a higher level. It felt as if they began taking us under their wings. They would talk with us, listen to us, and offer career advice when we asked for it.

One of the things they had mentioned to us, just in passing, was that we should attend the National Quartet Convention sometime. Taking that simple suggestion to heart, in September of 1970 we decided we wanted to attend. By then, the Convention, which had been founded in 1957 by J.D. Sumner, and James and Cecil Blackwood, had become a huge three-day event attended by 15,000-20,000 people each year. Some of the best quartets from around the country came together to perform for the audience and for each other. In many ways, it was a competition as much as it was a concert.

That was the last year the convention would be held in Memphis. We piled in our old bus and set out on our 1,100-mile odyssey from Buffalo. The interstate system was still in its infancy so this trip was no small undertaking. It might have seemed less so had we actually been officially invited to attend and/or perform. Looking back, we barely knew how to get to Memphis let alone how to gain access to the Convention. We were setting out on equal parts faith and brash naïveté.

It was a very long trip. I remember the initial feeling of relief as we crossed from Virginia into Tennessee, but that was short-lived as we realized that we were little more than halfway to Memphis. It seemed like it took forever just to drive through Tennessee. Interstate 40 was not complete, so as we approached Nashville, we had to get off of the four-lane highway and pass right through downtown. (It was the first time I'd ever seen Music City.)

When we finally arrived in Memphis and found our way to Ellis Auditorium, the organizers weren't going to let us come inside without buying tickets. I tried to explain to them that we really weren't there as attendees but that we were a "well-known quartet" from upstate New York. The man at the door was unimpressed with my "don't you know who we are?" routine, but as luck would have it, as I was trying to make our case one last time, over his shoulder, I saw Duane Allen. I called to him and he walked over, warmly greeting us. After I explained our predicament, Duane went to bat for us, and because of his clout in the gospel world, he was able to convince the gatekeeper that we should be allowed to enter as a quartet rather than as part of the audience.

At that same convention, and in their continuing role as our de facto advisors, Duane and Golden spent a lot of time with us. Golden, who has always been a great visionary, talked with us about how to make our stage presentation more exciting. He explained how to pace the show, when to talk and when to sing; he advised us on how to "work the stage." He gave it to us straight, even telling us which of our members, because of their talent and personality, should be out front and which ones we should keep in the background. I always appreciated his vision and his willingness to share it with us to try to help us get better. As far as I was concerned, there was no one better on the subject.

Duane also set up a meeting between us and Herman Harper, The Oaks' booking agent. At that meeting, Herman agreed to do whatever he could to help us find some work. In reality there was probably little that he could do for us—we just weren't well known enough yet. Regardless, we were very grateful to all three of these professionals for taking the time to sit down and meet with us, treating us better than we probably deserved.

It was a thrilling experience for us to go to the convention. Despite the rocky start, it was the motivator that we needed to bear down even more on our music. We rededicated ourselves to continuing to improve so that one day we could be invited to perform on that stage. That trip was another step for us in our maturation process. It was also on that trip, we began talking with Duane Allen about the possibility of him producing the Keystone's next record. It was an agreement that would soon be reached, but by the time The Keystone Quartet would record that album, I would no longer be a member.

CHAPTER THREE: *This is Your Bunk*

O ne day in the fall of 1970, out of the blue, I received a phone call from Ed Enoch of The Stamps Quartet, who said that his father-in-law (J.D. Sumner) was looking to retire from the road. At that time J.D. had publishing companies as well as a talent agency that booked some of the top gospel acts of the time including The Stamps, The Imperials, The Blackwood Brothers and others, and he wanted to devote more of his time to running those businesses. To be able to do this, he wanted to hire a young bass singer to do the shows, thereby allowing J.D. to pick and choose the dates that he would do.

Though I wish the reality had been different, at that time, despite our renewed dedication to the group, we were still starving to death. I loved The Keystone Quartet but with a wife and kids at home, we were just not making enough money, so I was excited at the prospect of making good money. As a member of The Stamps, I would earn $225 per week—not a fortune by any means—but receiving a regular paycheck that I could count on would mean a lot to my family and me.

After talking it over with my wife, I decided it was the right move for me. Again, I felt at a crossroads, much as I had when I'd left Trenton State College nine years earlier. I knew I wanted to be a full-time singer but the time for doing it as a hobby had long since passed. I needed to make a living and we believed the best way to do that was for me to accept the Stamps' offer.

I went to Joe and delivered the news—not quite as hard as telling my parents when I left school, but difficult nonetheless. In addition to being in business together, Joe and I had become extremely close friends. Our lives had blended as well as our voices had over the last two years. We somehow felt it was the end of a good thing. We hoped that the good Lord might bring us back together sometime in the future, but for now we shook hands and parted ways. He took over the business of the group, and one of the first things he did—in a show of progressive thinking— was to add some additional band members and drop the word "Quartet" from the group, thereby becoming the leader of The Keystones.

I took my first airplane flight from the Greater Buffalo International Airport en route to Nashville. Despite the coach seat, it was an infinitely easier trip than our bus ride to Memphis had been earlier in the year. Upon landing, I went directly to a small theater on the campus of Vanderbilt University for a rehearsal. In addition to their regular shows, The Stamps were part of a package tour at the time, called *Gospel Fest U.S.A.* that also starred The Oak Ridge Boys and The Rambos. This was a show that was primarily sold to promoters for weekend dates, and it was an innovative approach in that it featured concert performances for the first half of the show, then after intermission—time to sell records, of course—the acts would stage a dramatic play titled "The Three Nails." The drama, created by Duane Allen, J.D. and Ed Enoch, and directed by a professor from Vanderbilt, was based on a song written in 1970 by former Louisiana Governor, Jimmie Davis. Members of the groups would play the roles of various characters in a dramatic retelling of the Crucifixion. I remember that Bill Golden and Ed Enoch both played Roman soldiers, Dottie Rambo played Jesus' mother, Mary, and J.D. had one of the lead roles. He portrayed the man who had sold to Pilate's soldiers the three nails that would be used to nail Christ to the cross. As the newest member I served as the narrator, moving the story along.

I remember one powerful scene towards the end of the play in which J.D.'s character has a life-changing moment and realizes not only what he had done, but also the ramifications of his actions. One of his most powerful and haunting lines was when, speaking of the nails, he asked the soldiers "Please, can I buy them back?" But, of course it was too late, Christ's fate was sealed. As my voiceover script described, it definitely was a "gripping sacred drama."

We staged that show nearly one hundred times during my first year with J.D. We had played to one sold-out house after another. The promoters were very successful, and the acts made good money (at least for that time and for the genre.) It was always well received, and while we hated for it to end, it had pretty much run its course after that year. Not only that, but as the old saying goes "familiarity breeds contempt." Some of the members of the cast didn't especially like each other, which sometimes lent an extra air of credibility to the fight scenes in the show. Despite what some might expect or hope, even in gospel music, feuds can exist—whatever the cause. Sometimes it was simple competitive zeal. The top of the gospel "world" was finite; there were only so many top promoters and venues, so the biggest gospel acts were always vying for the best slots. Sure you wanted to see other acts become successful, but, in some situations, success for one group took away success from another group. As a result, feuds existed.

In addition to these shows, The Stamps were also doing the usual collection of church services, special singings and small shows. While little rehearsal was necessary for the singing portion of The Stamps show, we did have a couple prior to my first show dates with them. I was very familiar with their songs, and the part I was to sing; however, I have to admit I was a little nervous at that first rehearsal. Even though I already had the job, it felt a little bit like an audition. We were on stage, and there was J.D.—basically a hero to me—the only person sitting in the audience listening to all of us, but judging only me. Or at least that's how it felt. But J.D. was very kind and complimentary. He liked what I was doing. In fact, he said my singing reminded him of the smooth style of Armond Morales the bass singer I'd auditioned to replace earlier but who was still singing with Elvis's back-up group, my old friends, The Imperials.

So The Stamps now consisted of Ed Enoch, Donnie Sumner, Gary Buck and myself—and, of course, J.D., when he traveled. We also carried Tony Brown on piano, Duke Dumas on guitar and Kenny Hicks (J.D.'s cousin) playing bass. Kenny was a great kid—and, by hiring him, J.D. was just taking care of a family member who needed a job—but he wasn't a terribly accomplished bass player. He could hold his own on our regular repertoire but could sometimes go off in the ditch on songs he didn't know.

One time we were doing some shows in Louisiana with Jimmie Davis, who was a friend of J.D.'s. Of course on these shows, the Governor would sing his hit "You Are My Sunshine" along with a few other standards. Occasionally though, he would "go off the set list" and do songs he didn't normally sing. This wasn't a problem for us as we could usually fall in pretty quickly and sing our parts. For Kenny, though, some of these unrehearsed songs caused problems as he wasn't entirely comfortable on the bass—especially on songs he didn't know. I'll never forget one night; the Governor was singing a song as he strolled around the stage with his handheld microphone. He walked over and stood beside Kenny. Apparently having taken all he could take, and without missing a sung note, the Governor reached his hand over and grasped the neck on Kenny's bass, preventing him from playing. He finished the song, never releasing his grip on Kenny's bass neck. I often wondered what he might have done if he didn't like the way one of us sang along with him. (Incidentally, not long after The Stamps started backing Elvis, Kenny ended up being hired by Elvis to work as a sort of assistant or valet. Elvis really took a liking to him and he ended up working closely with Elvis for years.)

Though he wasn't with us for long, and since we were both the new guys, during my first months with The Stamps, on the road I roomed with Gary Buck, and he and I became good friends. In fact, even today, Gary who went on to a very successful career singing with The Four Guys, will come out to see The Oaks anytime we're near his home on the space coast of Florida. We were only with The Stamps together for a couple of months before he left to be replaced by Bill Baize, but he had become a good friend.

After relocating to Nashville, J.D. put me up in a motel for a few nights and then later moved me over to a local YMCA, because they had weekly rates. After about a month, I was able to rent a place in Madison— at the Berkley Hills Apartments—ironically, just about a block from the home of Colonel Tom Parker who managed Elvis. I moved my wife and sons down from Buffalo to join me, though "join me" isn't exactly accurate because The Stamps toured almost constantly, so I was rarely home.

Riding in a bus with J.D. could be a lot of fun or it could be tense—just as it can be with any artist. People sometimes forget that by the time I joined The Stamps, J.D. had been on the road for almost twenty-five years, so while it was a new and exciting experience for me, for J.D. it had been his way of life for a long time.

I was quoted some years ago in a media interview for The Oaks in which I addressed life on the road. I said then, and I still believe now, that I don't get paid to sing on stage every night; I do that because I love it. Rather I get paid to be away from my family, to ride on airplanes and buses, and sleep in hotels, and eat meals away from my wife and kids. It's really how I feel. And I think it's how J.D. felt. While the road could still be a lot of fun for him, it could also be a grind.

When I first joined, I'd heard rumors that life on the road with The Stamps could be a little wild. I was still a young man without a lot of life experiences. I'll admit, in a way, I was apprehensive that it might be too wild for me, but at the same time I was kind of looking forward to having the chance to experience some new and different things. As it turns out, if I was expecting the wild life, initially anyway, I was to be somewhat disappointed.

It seems that one of the effects of the play, *The Three Nails,* was that it had convicted J.D. that the group might need to straighten out their lives and live a little more the way they knew they should. So when I arrived, the rules on the bus were pretty strict. While we were on the road, there was to be no drinking or cussing or womanizing. In fact, J.D. had placed a jar in the front of the bus. If there were any infractions of J.D.'s rules, then a fine would have to be paid by the offender, and the money placed in the jar.

After several weeks, as the jar continued to fill up, J.D. was in the back of the bus in his room while the rest of us sat in the front talking, as we watched one town after another pass by the bus windows. One of the guys complained saying that he couldn't wait till this phase passed and we could go back to having fun on the road. Almost as if on cue, J.D. came up front and announced that we were going to have a party when we got to the hotel. In another show of irony, we used the money from the "sin jar" to finance the party. Such was the roller coaster of life on the road. We were all Christians and gospel singers, but we were still human.

We all have struggles and weaknesses. For us, many of them occurred while we were on the road, since our jobs kept us traveling. But that wasn't an excuse. We could have just as easily been traveling salesmen or airplane pilots, schoolteachers or factory workers. I understand that temptations come in all shapes and sizes. The fact that we were gospel singers didn't make us immune to them but neither did it justify some of our behaviors. As the old adage says: "An idle mind is the devil's workshop," and life on the road, though hectic, is certainly filled with lots of idle time for idle minds.

The bus was configured with a lounge up front, bunks in the middle and then in the back, a private "suite" for J.D. One of the most vivid memories I have of those early days with The Stamps was the first time I walked on the bus. Tony Brown, who would later go on to produce more than one hundred Number One records for the likes of George Strait, Reba McEntire, Vince Gill and many others, was playing piano with The Stamps. He gave me my first tour of the bus, and I still remember how excited I was when he pointed to one of the bunks and said "Richard, this is your bunk." I couldn't believe it. After years of having to share in the driving, I couldn't get over the fact that now after a show, I could simply crawl into my own bunk and sleep while someone else would be responsible for getting us to the next town.

In an ironic turn of events, Tony, who had been a strong ally for me when J.D. was considering which bass singer to hire, would leave The Stamps soon after (being replaced by my old pal, Nick Bruno) to join The Oak Ridge Boys. A couple of years later, he would play a similar role in The Oaks hiring me. And, of course, upon leaving The Oaks, Tony would become a member of Elvis's TCB Band. He was a cheerleader for me even before we knew each other well, and he would become a close friend. We had many great times on the road through the years.

Tony was always a very funny guy, one of those "life of the party" kinds of people. He and J.D. had a little shtick, that they would do on stage every night, where they would joke back and forth. He could definitely keep the audience—and us—laughing. One of his routines, that he started with The Stamps and then resurrected with The Oaks, became sort of an annual occurrence. Each year, one of the biggest gospel festivals was held on the baseball field at the old Bush Stadium in Indianapolis, Indiana. During our show (whether when he was with The Stamps or The Oaks) he would, without warning, stand up at the piano, run to the edge of the stage, leap off, and proceed to run the bases. After touching home, he would jump back up on the stage, sit down at the piano and continue to play as if nothing unusual had occurred. That was Tony Brown.

On many of our trips, J.D. would stay in his room in the back of the bus. We would sometimes hardly see him except on stage. Other times, he would sit up front with us—or more often—invite us to join him in the back. He had a refrigerator in his room where he would keep soft drinks and cold beer. He wouldn't allow any alcohol to be kept in the front of the bus because he didn't want to be blatant in front of promoters or fans that some members of the group liked to have a drink.

When he was inclined, he could keep us entertained by regaling us with great stories from the road, dating back to his time with The Blackwood Brothers. He used to have a little friendly rivalry with Hovie Lister and The Statesman Quartet, and they loved to pull practical jokes on each other. Often, one of them would hide in the audience and heckle when the other was on stage singing. Then the challenge became how to top the other act. The audiences loved to see the back and forth between them.

He loved to tell a story from a show The Stamps did with The Imperials in southern California. They were scheduled to come back in just a few weeks and perform with The Statesmen. All through the evening, the emcee had been announcing the upcoming show by saying that the show would occur if Jesus didn't return first. After he had made that announcement several times, it was time for J.D. and The Stamps to sing. During their portion of the show, J.D. decided to have some fun with the audience at the expense of his old friend. He announced: "I know what the emcee has been saying, but I wanted you folks to know that knowing this area as I do, I feel pretty confident that even if Jesus does come back, there'll be plenty enough folks left to still have the show. And the good news is, I know Hovie well enough to know he'll probably still be here to sing!" He loved to get on "old Hovie." He'd laugh and laugh in that huge bass voice.

Practical jokes have long been a part of life on the road. I remember once The Keystones were doing a show with The Couriers. We were onstage when they decided to pull one on us. I forget the song we were singing, but it was one that featured one of those big "southern gospel endings" with the last note drawn out while each member harmonizes around each other in a show of vocal acrobatics. While we were working our way towards that climactic ending, unbeknownst to us, The Couriers were gathered around live microphones backstage. They began singing along with us on the last lines of the song. As we reached our crescendo, we four cut off the last note in perfect timing, but we—and the audience—were confused by the fact that once we were done, the vocal acrobatics continued for another several seconds. We soon realized that we had been the victims of a prank courtesy of our friends, The Couriers.

We pulled our share of pranks through the years, whether with The Keystones, The Stamps, or later with The Oaks. Some were elaborate while others were simple (but effective). The simplest of them might have been the time The Oaks were appearing at a festival with The Statler Brothers. During their show, we snuck up to the back of their bus and replaced their license plate with a souvenir Oak Ridge Boys plate. It was weeks before they noticed, and we heard that they weren't especially happy when they discovered it, but it was all good-natured fun.

Years before his tenure with The Blackwood Brothers, J.D. had sung with a quartet called The Sunshine Boys, in the late forties and early fifties. With that group he'd even had the opportunity to go to Hollywood and make some movies. He told us lots of stories about those early, exciting days. They were all westerns—very big at the box office at that time—starring the likes of Smiley Burnette and Charles Starrett, with the Sunshine Boys playing the roles of a posse or singing cowboys. It was pretty heady stuff for them at the time.

But, by the time he led The Stamps, the reality was that J.D. was the undisputed boss. There was a definite hierarchy on the bus, on stage and in the group. Everyone understood that it was J.D.'s group and that J.D. was the star. In fact, as I mentioned, his whole reason for hiring me in the first place was that he wanted to retire from regular dates. He would still travel and appear at our bigger concerts—when we were working for big promoters, and on "The Three Nails" dates—but if we were just playing small shows or church services, J.D. would not even leave Nashville. Occasionally, a buyer would refuse to buy a Stamps date unless J.D. would appear as well, so to keep from losing the date (and the money) J.D. would agree.

Even on the concerts on which he did appear, J.D. wouldn't do the whole show. The Stamps would perform the first half without him and then he would be introduced and make his "star entrance," and close the show by singing some of his hits that the people had paid to hear; songs like "Walk That Lonesome Road" and "The Farmer and the Lord."

J.D. could also be a very serious taskmaster. Because of the competitive nature of the business, the best groups were always fearful of being surpassed by another. Constantly working together in the 50's and early 60's was one of the reasons The Blackwood Brothers and the Statesmen Quartet had always been so good. The constant comparisons pushed each of them to try to outperform the other. In our case, it was

The Oak Ridge Boys that worried J.D. The touring we did on the *Gospel Fest U.S.A.* dates put us on stage with The Oaks for every one of those shows. The Oaks were a dynamic act full of excitement and youthful energy, and it nearly drove J.D. crazy. Like a boxer training for a championship fight, J.D. would constantly rehearse us. It's amazing that our voices survived the strain. It seemed if we weren't singing on stage at a show, we were practicing. It definitely made us better, but it almost killed us too. J.D. was serious about making sure his group was perceived as the top group in the country. I think that was the reason for some of his related business interests.

When J.D. bought the rights to use the group name "The Stamps" from Frank Stamps he agreed that he would also continue to run *The Stamps-Baxter School of Music,* which, at that time, was held each year at Southwestern Bible Institute in Waxahachie, Texas. (Eventually, Ben Speers purchased the Stamps-Baxter School, and it is now based at Middle Tennessee State University in Murfreesboro, Tennessee.) The school was actually more like an annual weeklong camp where aspiring singers would come to learn the ins and outs of singing gospel music. The "professors" at the school were none other than us, the members of The Stamps Quartet.

My job at the school was to teach a class for all of the bass singers. I tried to take my responsibility seriously, but, honestly, I felt unqualified. Sure, I could sing bass, but I certainly didn't know how to teach it. These people had paid to be there; I couldn't just tell them to drink black coffee (though I probably did tell them to); I felt I owed them more than that. I'd listen to them sing, and if I heard something obvious and specific that I thought I could help with, I would comment, but I'm still not confident I was able to impart to them anything that did them much good.

As if that weren't bad enough, since all gospel quartets would inevitably have to use (and set up) their own sound systems at performances, Donnie Sumner and I co-taught a class on how to do so properly. We would teach them the secrets of coiling microphone cables so that they wouldn't tangle, how to efficiently pack the system under the bus, how to equalize it to get the best sound, and other such nuggets of wisdom.

On the final night of the school, all of the kids would come together to perform a concert—to show off what they had learned at the feet of us "masters"—and then, The Stamps would close the week by giving a concert of our own. Maybe, that somehow helped the attendees to feel that the school was worth the price of tuition.

Actually, despite my less-than-proud memories, the students did, apparently, feel that they got their money's worth because, though I was only there two times, every year when the time rolled around again, students would come out by the hundreds. (Ironically, my grandson, Tyler, is preparing to attend college at Southwestern Assemblies of God University, which is now the name of Southwestern Bible Institute. I have a feeling that he'll acquit himself better on that campus than his grandfather did all those years ago.)

❧❧❧

We were, of course, aware of J.D.'s history with Elvis Presley. Occasionally he would tell us stories about when he and Elvis first met. Though they hadn't stayed in constant contact, he would have occasion to keep in touch with Elvis when he would attend the National Quartet

Conventions. Like the rest of the free world, we also knew that Elvis was touring again, and that The Imperials were serving as his background vocal group. I still thought it was cool that he used a quartet to back him up onstage but otherwise, it really wasn't of much consequence to us.

Late in the summer of 1971 we started hearing rumors that The Imperials were going to stop working with Elvis, and perhaps go with Jimmy Dean fulltime on his stage and television shows. When Elvis had first started working Las Vegas, in 1969, he'd tried to talk The Jordanaires into working with him just as they had back in the 50's, but because of their extensive studio work—they were often doing three or four sessions per day—they had to decline. The next thing we knew The Imperials were there. Now, two years later, we began hearing varying stories as to why The Imperials would be leaving. Similar to The Jordanaires, one story had them with too many competing bookings to be able to remain with Elvis. Yet another suggested that they were holding out for more money from Elvis's management. I've always felt that their commitment to tour with Jimmy Dean irked Elvis. In fact, they'd already bailed out on both of Elvis's tours in the fall of 1970, on which the Hugh Jarrett Singers had replaced them. As we would later learn, Elvis didn't like to be told "No." In any case it seemed clear that when Elvis toured again, The Imperials would not be on stage lending the harmonies.

Soon the rumors started to reach just a little bit closer to us. The word was that Elvis was considering one of two groups to replace The Imperials: The Oak Ridge Boys and J.D. Sumner and The Stamps. J.D.'s brother-in-law, John Matthews, who was helping J.D. run his Sumar Talent Agency—and who was largely responsible for keeping us so busy on the road—worked behind the scenes with the Elvis's manager, Colonel Tom, lobbying on behalf of The Stamps to get the Elvis gig. Additionally, unbeknownst to us until later, J.D. had undertaken his own campaign to position The Stamps to be the chosen group. In his role with the *Gospel Music Association,* as well as the *National Quartet Convention*, he often traveled, when not on the road doing shows with us. One such trip was to New Orleans where The Imperials happened to be performing. Though he might have had other business of which we were not aware, we later heard that at least part of his motivation was to lobby The Imperials for their recommendation to Elvis.

Whatever else might have been in play at the time, something indeed worked in our favor for in early October of 1971, J.D. informed us that beginning the following month, we would be the male voices on stage touring the country with The King of Rock. It was hard to believe that less than a year earlier, I had been working myself to death trying to eek out a living with our little Keystone Quartet. The last year had been huge in my progression as a bass singer, but somehow I suspected I hadn't seen anything yet!

CHAPTER FOUR: *The Suite Life*

L ate in the night on Thursday, November 4, 1971, our bus driver, Glen Tadlock, nicknamed "Nowdy," steered The Stamps' big Silver Eagle bus into the parking lot of The Marriott Hotel in Minneapolis, Minnesota. The next day would be a momentous day for us. We were scheduled to, not only rehearse with Elvis and his whole group for the first time, but also appear onstage with him, in concert. We had been listening to recordings and working on our parts ever since we'd learned we would be singing with him, but still, we needed to actually rehearse with him to make sure we were ready.

The rehearsal was scheduled to begin after lunch on Friday afternoon. As we entered the rehearsal hall, called the Decathalon Club, there was already a lot of activity. The TCB Band members were noodling on their respective instruments. There was James Burton with his pink paisley Fender Telecaster, John Wilkerson on rhythm guitar, Ronnie Tutt was sitting behind his kit with double bass drums, Jerry Scheff worked high on the neck of his Fender bass, and Glen D. Hardin was writing on a chart on his piano. Charlie Hodge, Elvis's friend since his Army days and his harmony singer, was sorting through music charts. The Sweet Inspirations (or the "Sweets" as everyone called them) were sitting, laughing and talking with Kathy Westmoreland, the classically trained soprano singer. The conductor and musical director, Joe Guercio, was off-site rehearsing the orchestra. We shook hands all around. We were officially part of the group.

The only member I hadn't yet met was Elvis himself. As I've said, I was certainly familiar with his music—and liked much of it—but I wasn't what would be considered a huge fan. When I met him, though, I immediately understood the attraction that fans had to him. I thought, "Wow, there's a reason this guy is the biggest star in the world." It sounds like a fantasy or a cliché, but I swear you could almost sense him before he walked into a room.

On this occasion, he was "fashionably late." Everyone was ready, even anxious to begin but, as we would learn, rehearsals—like recording sessions and sometimes concerts—would begin only when Elvis was ready for them to begin. Eventually, we heard footsteps coming down the hall and then, suddenly, the door to the ballroom opened and in walked "the guys." It seemed as if there were six or more guys who came in and then parted, like the Red Sea, to reveal Elvis strolling in behind them, looking every bit like the King of Rock. He was dressed exactly like one might expect to see him: a dark two-piece suit with his signature high, Napoleonic collar, a patterned high-collared shirt, and carrying a black cane with a gold ornament on top. He immediately came over to J.D. and grabbed him in a bear hug.

While it's been told many times, J.D. had been somewhat of a hero to Elvis when he was growing up. As the bass singer for The Blackwood Brothers, he had allowed Elvis to come in the back door of various Memphis all-night gospel sings—long before Elvis could afford to buy a ticket, let alone became famous himself. Also, when Elvis's mother died, J.D. and the rest of the Blackwoods sang at her funeral. Elvis never forgot J.D.'s kindness, and as he did with so many others, he seemed to make it part of his life's work to repay such kindnesses many times over.

Standing in that hotel ballroom, Elvis and J.D. quickly caught up, and soon J.D. began introducing each one of us to him. Elvis interrupted him to say he didn't need the introductions because he felt as if he already knew us. He hugged me and then we shook hands. I still remember looking into his eyes that first time. The magnetism was indescribable. I couldn't believe that he knew my name and knew that I was the bass singer. I don't know how we gathered ourselves well enough to sing at that rehearsal, but apparently we did. I just kept thinking over and over that there was Elvis Presley, and here we were singing with him. It was a feeling that would continue every night; it never got old to me.

After we'd gotten the gig, J.D. had told us that he still did not plan to tour with us all the time. I was really surprised by this because, after all, I always considered him to be the reason we'd been hired in the first place. It didn't take long, however, for it to become clear that Elvis had expected him to be involved, just like I had. J.D. agreed to back him (I'm not sure he had much choice) but told me that he planned to let me sing most of the parts, and he would just do some fill-ins and also give Elvis those "dive-bomb" endings he liked so much. I don't know if Elvis told him he wanted more or if the old entertainer in J.D. came to the forefront but, pretty soon, he was singing all the time, so Elvis always had two bass singers singing behind him—an arrangement that he always seemed to like.

My first time on stage with Elvis, later that night, was almost magical. Some 17,600 fans jammed into the Metropolitan Sports Center. We stood backstage and watched the Sweets who would open the shows. Next came a comedian, a veteran comic named Jackie Kahane, who had the unenviable task of filling time until, what the crowd considered to be the "real show," could start. Though in later years, after my departure, The Stamps would also be one of the opening acts, we were not during my time with the group.

Finally, after intermission and a wait that seemed as long for me as it must have for the audience, it was time for the main attraction. The lights dimmed, and the screams rose as the orchestra played the first strains of the theme from *2001 A Space Odyssey*. Ronnie Tutt's maniacal drumming kick-started the TCB Band's opening theme. Suddenly there was Elvis, dressed in his white pinwheel jumpsuit (also known as the Red Lion or the Matador suit) complete with red-lined white cape with matching studded design. As he strode past where we stood, he was immediately thrown into what the *Minneapolis Star's* reviewer, Jim Gillespie, later described as: "A blinding, stroboscopic sea of Instamatic flash cubes (that) turned his entrance into a stop-motion light show." It was like nothing I had ever seen. He walked, sidestepped and strutted back and forth across the stage soaking in the adulation, repaying it with smiles, winks and glances.

We stood there clapping in time with the band, trying to remember that this was now our job; we were not there, simply, to enjoy the show. He walked to Charlie Hodge, who stood beside the piano holding Elvis's black Gibson Dove guitar—the one with his name inlaid on the neck in a cool, cursive mother of pearl. Elvis draped the guitar over his shoulder and then purposefully walked to center stage. As was common, his microphone awaited him, positioned a good eight inches taller than he stood. He reached for it, tilted it back to him and towards his mouth, and he began. "Well, that's alright, Mama. That's alright with you. That's alright, Mama, just any way you do, well that's alright." The background singers at this point echoed with "that's alright," my first official words sung onstage with the King—an obvious understatement of the moment for us all.

Over the next hour, Elvis sacrificed himself to that audience. He sang his heart out on old songs like "I Got A Woman," "All Shook Up," "Love Me Tender," and "Hound Dog," along with new ones like "Bridge Over Troubled Water," "I'm Leavin'," and "You Don't Have to Say You Love Me." As had become his standard—and would remain so at every show—he closed with "Can't Help Falling in Love," a mid-tempo ballad from his movie "Blue Hawaii." He laid down the microphone, stretched out his arms, revealing the cape that had been placed again around his shoulders for the finale, and after rising from his knee, he again paced the edge of the stage, shaking hands and smiling while the band played the closing vamp. Soon he strode past us, gave J.D. a friendly wink as he passed, bound down the stairs and disappeared. As the crowd continued its frenzied screams, the announcer, Al Dvorin, delivered the shocking news: "Ladies and gentlemen, Elvis has left the building. Thank you and good night." And with that, it was over. Nothing could have prepared me for the spectacle that was an Elvis Presley concert in those years.

৵৵৵

We had to leave for the airport early the next morning to fly to Cleveland for two shows, an afternoon matinee and an evening show. I was so keyed up from the Minneapolis show I barely slept that night. I would have to get used to it because that became a typical travel schedule for us. More often than not, we would stay overnight in the town in which we'd just performed, and then rise the next morning, get on the chartered bus or vans, head to the airport and fly on to the next town on show day. The early bus calls were made all the more difficult because, on most nights, Ronnie Tutt or Glen Hardin would have arranged for a suite at the hotel where after-show parties would be held. These gatherings would never include Elvis—on tour, we almost never saw him except at the venues—but they were usually fun, nonetheless.

Upon landing in the next town, we'd usually be taken to the hotel where we'd clean up and perhaps relax for a while before eating and heading to the venue that night. Of course, on two-show days—usually a matinee around 2:30 and then an evening show at 8:30—there would be little time for relaxing. In fact, sometimes we'd travel, already dressed in our stage clothes, because there wouldn't be time to get dressed before the matinee. On those occasions it felt like we were a minor league baseball team having to arrive at the stadium already wearing our uniforms. It wasn't always glamorous, but it was often necessary to maintain the hectic pace.

While years later, Elvis would arrive at the auditoriums just minutes before his scheduled show time, during my time with him, he would often be backstage early, during the opening acts. On those occasions, I'd see in him a unique blend of tension and cool. He was always a little bit uptight in the moments before facing those screaming crowds, but at the same time, very often he'd come over to The Stamps' dressing room and, with no warning, start singing "He Touched Me" or "You'd Better Run" or "I, John" or one of many other old gospel songs. As we would come to understand, singing helped Elvis relax.

It was ironic for me—and also very endearing—when I learned, during some of these informal sessions, that Elvis loved many of the same groups that I had grown up listening to. He wasn't just a casual fan; he knew the songs and he knew the singers—especially the bass singers. It was one of our most frequent topics of conversation. Of course, he'd loved J.D. since his days with The Blackwood Brothers. Some of their songs that Elvis had recorded included "In My Father's House" and "Where No One Stands Alone." He loved The Statesman Quartet with Hovie Lister, and their bass singer, James "Big Chief" Wetherington, by whom he'd first heard songs like "His Hand in Mine," "It Is No Secret" and "Known Only to Him," all of which he'd recorded. He loved The Harmonizing Four and Jimmy Jones, whose version of "Only Believe" most influenced his own cut in 1970.

It was quite humanizing to be reminded that this man, idolized by millions, at his core, was just another fan of gospel music. Just like the millions of kids who would put on Elvis records and pretend to be him—and, just as I had done with those Blackwood Brothers and Courier records—Elvis had done the very same thing with his favorite gospel quartet records. Though I was—and remained—quite in awe of Elvis the entire time I knew him, this knowledge, this small but significant thread of commonality that we shared, helped draw us closer.

It often surprises people to learn that, though Elvis received fourteen nominations for Grammy Awards, the only three that he won were for gospel recordings: the 1967 album, *How Great Thou Art*, the 1971 album *He Touched Me* and the 1974 live performance of "How Great Thou Art."

I've never had a religious experience onstage like the one I had each night when Elvis sang "How Great Thou Art." While being in his presence—or on his stage—was mesmerizing, more than any other time, when he sang that song, I have to admit that I could really feel the Spirit move me—more so than it would at a traditional gospel show. When he'd look Heavenward and sing those words, I could almost see Jesus appearing in the clouds. It was so emotional when we sang it. It was clear that he believed, and loved, what he was singing.

The twelve nights of that first tour were a blur of movement and activity. We played Cleveland, Louisville, Philadelphia, Baltimore, Boston, Cincinnati, Houston, Dallas, Tuscaloosa, Kansas City, and the last stop of the tour, Salt Lake City. We experienced the same routine every day of the tour: wake, travel, sing, party, sleep, wake, travel, sing, party, sleep, and so on. The pace was exhausting and exciting, mind numbing and memorable. After the last show of the tour, the usual party would take on a different feeling. These parties, Elvis would usually attend—and when he did, it often turned into a night of us gathered around the piano with him, singing gospel songs. Sometimes he would just stand there beside us, or sit on the piano bench, and let us sing. Other times, he would request particular songs from each of us. We might do a few rollicking numbers to liven up the party, but invariably he would request a slow, old-time song, and just close his eyes and seemingly drift off to some place of peace in his mind. In addition to being the greatest performer, he was also a wonderful audience. At the end of every song, he would applaud, usually while laughing or appearing to shake off a chill. As we would learn, he could just never get enough of those great old gospel songs.

The long night would end with hugs all around and heartfelt thanks for a good tour. I don't know about him, but I knew that we couldn't wait until the next one would begin!

On this first tour, we had traveled more than seven thousand miles and performed fourteen shows for more than 185,000 people. Some of the cities had never experienced a clamor for tickets such as they had when Elvis's shows were announced. Every venue sold out within hours, and in the case of Cleveland and Dallas, additional shows were added in an attempt to satisfy the overwhelming demand. In Cleveland, the television news reported that on the day tickets went on sale, there was a line more than one mile long leading to the ticket office. Elvis was indeed on top of the music world.

శౄశౄశౄ

An Elvis tour utilized three planes. Elvis's manager, Colonel Tom Parker, was in a small jet going ahead to make sure the next city was prepared for Elvis's arrival; Elvis flew in his chartered jet and the rest of us—band, singers, Guercio, Al Dvorin, and others—were on another plane. We always had the same plane with the same crew. Over the course of the tour, we became friends with the flight attendants, and would hang out together—in fact, for a while some of the guys became "more than friends" with them. Sometimes we'd even do touristy things. Once, on a later tour, when we were in Milwaukee, a bunch of us, along with the flight attendants, toured the Miller Brewing Company. So over time, we would become a mostly tight knit group that enjoyed being together enjoying new experiences.

One such brand new experience—for The Stamps, anyway— came our way in the third week of January 1972 as we traveled to Las Vegas for our first of Elvis's semi-annual engagements at the gargantuan Las Vegas Hilton. As would become the norm, Elvis would be booked to play for four weeks, two shows per night, and we arrived a week early to rehearse the songs for that season. Because Elvis and The Colonel had recently signed a deal with MGM to film a documentary that would follow Elvis on his spring tour, our first week of rehearsals was pretty intense. We must have worked on thirty or forty new songs, some of which, as it turns out, we never performed on stage.

Las Vegas was a very different experience for us. The main reason, of course, was that we were used to arriving in a town, singing and then heading off to the next town. It was rare for us to stay in the same place more than one night. But here we sat, in one city for over a month, while nearly sixty new audiences would come to us. There was something very appealing about staying in one place so long, but I'll have to admit that there also became something very maddening about it. In retrospect, it was easy to see how a performer could get burned out. For us though, especially in the beginning, it was different and exciting.

One "different" thing I distinctly remember was something that was referred to as "the tree." I would learn that in the lobby of the Las Vegas Hilton—just outside the elevators—a tree that sat in the middle of a big, circular couch had long been a gathering place for dozens of beautiful young women. It seriously looked like the waiting room of a beauty pageant. I wondered what was going on the first few times I saw it. Every evening, an hour or two before the dinner show was to begin, the ladies would gather in all of their finery. As it turns out, they were there waiting, hoping, to be picked—like fruit from a tree—to accompany some high roller to the showroom to see Elvis. It was really something to see. As we would be in Vegas for a week or so before the engagement began, I can attest to the fact that I never witnessed "the tree" in action for any of the other artists who performed there. I guess it was just another part of the Elvis phenomenon.

There were certainly temptations. If we faced them as a gospel group traveling across the country singing at churches, then how many more must we have faced singing with the King of Rock? Once after a Stamps date, the promoter took the opportunity to corner J.D. to criticize Elvis—and The Stamps by association. The disdain just poured from this promoter's mouth. "How dare Elvis sing gospel music. How dare he claim to be a Christian while he lives the life he leads. He ought to be ashamed to profess himself a believer." On and on he went.

J.D. really stuck up for Elvis. "How dare you stand there professing to be a Christian and judge any man, let alone Elvis Presley. You have no idea what it's like to be Elvis. You have no idea the temptations he faces every day of his life. Look at you. It's easy for you. You have no concept of his struggles."

I was so impressed with the vigor with which J.D. defended his friend. He wasn't making excuses for him; it's just that we saw the strength and the faith that was required for Elvis to fight his temptations. Sometimes he was successful, and other times, not as much. To a lesser extent, we faced many of the same temptations ourselves. Virtually every day, I had to choose the road I was going to walk. Every day I was faced with the opportunity to live the way I knew I should, or live the way that, perhaps, I wanted to at that particular moment—whether the temptation was women other than my wife, or too much alcohol, or any other of the plethora of sins that could find us. J.D. was simply reminding this man of the Bible verse where Jesus cautioned against throwing the first stone. "Judge not lest ye be judged." And Lord knew, many were the times when I didn't want to be judged over a decision that I had made.

It was still a job, however, and one thing that wasn't different was the pay we received. The financial arrangements for The Stamps were between Elvis and J.D. I've heard various figures tossed around—that for The Stamps, Elvis paid $4,000 per week in Las Vegas and $700 per night on tour—but I really can't say for sure. Whatever the gig paid J.D., what I do know is that our individual paychecks never changed. Whether we were playing sold out shows at Madison Square Garden or two shows a night at the Hilton with Elvis, or small Southern churches on our own, as members of The Stamps, we were always paid the same: $225 per week. (After about a year with the group, I was given a raise to $275 per week.)

Of course, we were reminded, there were other benefits of being with Elvis. But one time, even one of those benefits didn't quite make it to us. After the first November tour, Elvis gave each of The Stamps a bonus of $1,000, however J.D. kept the money. We were all more than a little upset about it because that was a lot of money in those days, and it had been intended for each of us. After the next tour, when it came time for bonuses, Elvis gave each of us a check directly. In fact, he handed Donnie his check first and he said, "Now, Donnie, this money is for you… it's not for J.D." So apparently Elvis had heard what had happened last time, and wanted to make sure it didn't happen again.

Another benefit that did not always extend to us was the opportunity to stay in fine hotels. During our stands in Las Vegas, Elvis, of course, stayed where he performed. As has become legend, the Hilton maintained a luxurious suite for him in the penthouse overlooking the famed Las Vegas strip. Some of the band and background singers—including J.D.—also stayed at the Hilton, though in somewhat lesser accommodations. Since Elvis's deal was with J.D., however, and since our expenses came out of the money that J.D. was being paid, my fellow Stamps and I each called home the less-than-swanky Bali Hai Hotel. It was actually far from the worst hotel we ever stayed in, though it would never be featured in any travel brochures either; and after five weeks, the walls of our rooms could start to close in a little bit. A more convenient arrangement existed when Elvis was on tour, as the entire traveling party—including us Stamps—stayed at the same hotel. On tour we felt—and were treated—as part of the group. Our rooms were nice, and our luggage was handled for us. Being on tour definitely felt like the big time.

I don't want to give the impression that J.D. was a tight-fisted cheapskate. Though he could definitely squeeze a dollar, there were times when his generous heart would come to the forefront, and he would surprise us. One such time occurred after Elvis had given him a beautiful watch engraved with his name. We admired it, of course, but it never occurred to us that we should have received one. For some reason, though, J.D. felt bad that Elvis had only given one to him and not to the rest of us. Certainly he couldn't, and wouldn't, ask Elvis to give one to each of us, but he did do something that was very unexpected. He went to the jeweler from whom Elvis had bought the watch and he had an identical watch made for each of us, and presented them to us as a gift. I was blown away that he would do that; it was such a kind and giving act on his part. So, while he could faithfully follow the so-called "golden rule" of "he who has the gold made the rules," he could also, sometimes, not deny his own heart of gold.

With Elvis doing two shows a night in Vegas (except opening night), we didn't have a whole lot of time to spend in our rooms—or to do much of anything else—which I suppose was a blessing in disguise because I still didn't have a lot of money to spend. We would, however, get out occasionally and see some sites, hang out together and listen to music in the lounges, or have a drink at the bar. On several occasions, I remember going to see Bill Medley—then split from his Righteous Brothers partner, Bobby Hatfield—singing in the lounge. In the Hilton's heyday, playing the lounge, especially while Elvis was in the main show-room, was a pretty prestigious gig. There would almost always be over-flow crowds, and I remember Bill appearing there pretty regularly. It was a cheap place to sit and kill a few hours, plus Bill was a great singer.

Once rehearsals would end and the engagement begin, we would, pretty quickly, fall into a routine. Most nights I would eat in my room be-fore heading over for call time. For all that they lacked, the rooms at the Bali Hai did have kitchenettes. I would try to keep groceries on hand and eat in, though many nights, dinner was a peanut butter and jelly sandwich. The other guys and I would typically arrive at the Hilton around 7:00 p.m., and go to our dressing room to dress for the early show. That would typically end around 10:00 p.m. or a little after. Between shows, we would usually just hang out in the dressing room. There really wasn't time to do much else, and there was no reason to go to the bars because we all knew that we'd have the opportunity to get free drinks after the late show. The big gold curtain would go up at midnight for the opening acts and then we would be back on stage around 12:45 a.m. for another hour of singing to another sold-out showroom. By 2:15 a.m., we'd be cleaned up and changed back into street clothes, but while we might be tired and ready for bed, the night would seldom end for us then. As has become legend, however, more often than not, it wasn't the allure and bright lights of Sin City that kept us awake.

While they began as an occasional invitation, late-nights spent with Elvis in his suite soon became a regular thing while we were in Vegas. For us, it was a chance not only to hang out with the boss—a little "face-time," as it were—but also, the drinks were free and good-looking women were plentiful. For Elvis it provided several things. As would become more widely known later, Elvis fought insomnia and loneliness during his concert years. Simply stated, he didn't want to be alone after a show, so he'd surround himself with the people he knew and with whom he was comfortable.

Though we were on stage with him every night, all of that adulation from the audience was directed at him, not at us. For most people, it is impossible to understand what it was like for him to stand on that stage for an hour every night, and feel the love and adoration coming off of those standing-room-only audiences, and then, minutes later, be in a quiet hotel suite all alone. The sheer energy that was coursing through his body, the adrenaline, had to be overwhelming. (I would come to experience a little of that myself in the later years, but for Elvis, it had to be a numbing experience.)

In addition to companionship, it also provided another outlet for Elvis the entertainer. As was memorialized in the movie, *Elvis on Tour*, some nights it would manifest itself in all-night gospel sings. Invariably, Charlie Hodge or Nick Bruno would end up sitting down at the piano and Elvis would start singing. Of course, he'd expect us to join in. Some nights he would be the star in the suite, and other nights he would request one song after another, content to stand beside us and just soak it in. We'd take turns singing his requests, and sometimes, of course, he'd join in. And as has been documented in some informal recordings that have since become available, he loved to stand next to J.D. and me and add his voice to the bass chorus. He was definitely a frustrated bass singer.

On one of those recordings, later released by RCA, Elvis can be heard complaining that J.D.'s voice covered his up. He said that he could feel for me having to put up with that every night. We all laughed, though at some level, it was probably truer than not. Sure, we were on stage night after night in huge coliseums in Chicago or Charlotte, New York or Salt Lake City, but when you got right down to it, I was the second bass singer in a background vocal group. There were some nights when I even wondered if my microphone was on! That nagging feeling definitely played a role in the decision that I would eventually make.

Other times in the suite—especially when martial arts master Ed Parker would be in town—Elvis would have the guys push all of the furniture back in the huge living room, and create a big open space where he would proceed to do Karate demonstrations. He would spar with Ed or, bodyguard, Red West; he would do very detailed choreographed patterns, called *katas*, and explain to us what he was doing and what they meant. He would break boards—and sometimes furniture or fingers (his own or someone else's). Elvis had been a long-time student of martial arts, having begun studying during his Army years, and he often spoke publicly about how much he enjoyed the discipline. In these cases, while I think it was a way for him to burn up some of that after-show energy, as much as anything, I always thought it was also a way for him to show off in front of the women that were gathered in the suite.

One night up in the suite after the midnight show, we were all sitting around having a drink—everyone except Elvis, that is. Though I can't speak for all the time, I can honestly say, in all the times I was in Elvis's presence, only once did I see him drink alcohol. Anyway, we were sitting around and Elvis started talking about the time just after his famous "comeback" in 1968. He was, at that time, still obligated to make films—or as he described it, "stuck in the movie contracts"—which he hated, and was really starting to feel that he wanted to return to the stage and live performances. At some point in his discussions with Colonel Tom, he could see that the Colonel's "vision" was straying from the one Elvis had, so he decided he had to lay it all out on the line. There were times when he'd let the Colonel steamroll him on decisions, but this was one time when he felt that he could not. Elvis said he told him exactly what his terms would be. He said he desperately wanted to get back on stage but that if he was going to do it, he had to be allowed to put together the rhythm section that he wanted. Additionally, he made it clear that he wanted an orchestra, and not one, but two sets of back-up singers. He wanted a black female group and a male quartet, and on top of that, he wanted a female soprano singer.

Elvis would walk over to the piano and play chords illustrating how he liked to have the voices stack up on stage. He would have J.D. and me singing two notes below him, Ed just below him, Donnie right with him and Bill singing the note above him. On top of all of that would be the Sweets and then Kathy at least two notes above. Mix all of that together—not to mention some of the brass instruments that would fill above and below him—and you had one heck of a chorus. There were virtually no notes left uncovered. And that's exactly how Elvis wanted it.

To hear Elvis tell it, the Colonel blew his top and started ranting about how expensive that type of show would be and how there was no way they could afford that; he simply had to scale it down, and so on. Elvis just smiled as he recalled telling the Colonel that was just the way it was going to be: end of discussion. Obviously, the Colonel eventually relented, and Elvis got to put together exactly the kind of show he wanted. Looking back, perhaps it would have been better for Elvis had he chosen to take more stands against the Colonel.

ॐ ॐ ॐ

We spent a lot of time laughing. One night in Las Vegas, Elvis threw J.D. a curve by asking him to step out front and sing "Walk That Lonesome Road." While J.D. had sung it many times on stage at Stamps shows, and even a few times onstage with Elvis, this night was one of the few times in my tenure with The Stamps that I can remember hearing J.D. really struggle with a song on stage. He just was not hitting those low notes on this night. He was having to fake it out there—something that all bass singers, including myself, are very familiar with. Later that night between shows in the dressing room, Donnie even brought it up. "Uncle J," he said, "man, what was wrong tonight?" "Well," J.D. said between puffs on a cigarette, "Son, I didn't know Elvis was gonna call on me to sing that one tonight; I messed up, and went out there sober." We fell on the floor laughing.

During that first engagement, one of the most memorable (and funniest) things that would ever happen during my time with Elvis occurred. The story has been told elsewhere, but I have to include it here, just as I remember it. We were down in our dressing room after one of the dinner shows. Everything seemed normal. We were changing our clothes, and getting ready to go do whatever we were going to do that night between shows. All of the sudden, with no knock, the door opens and in comes Elvis followed by his guys. He had changed from his stage clothes, but still was dressed to the nines. In other words, he still "looked like Elvis." So, he kind of just wandered into the dressing room. It didn't really seem like he wanted to talk, he just kind of stood there. Finally he said that they had received a phone call from someone who said he was going to come "get Elvis." He wasn't sure if it was from an irate husband or just some crazy guy, but he said he was coming after him, and he was going to do it on that night's midnight show. He said that while this sort of thing had happened before, this one seemed credible and had them worried. There was going to be a meeting in his suite in a few minutes with his security team and the security guards from the hotel, and he wanted us to come up and sit in on the meeting.

This news seemed to have shaken Elvis—and I can guarantee you that it took away any appetite any of us had for a between-show meal. We sat in the dressing room for a few minutes after Elvis left, just kind of looking at each other, lost in our own thoughts and then finally, as a group, we headed up the elevator to Elvis's suite. As has become known in subsequent years, the suite Elvis used while at the Hilton was an amazing piece of Las Vegas lore. Situated on the 30th floor, it occupied the entire rooftop penthouse, five- thousand square feet in all.

Sonny West, another of Elvis's bodyguards, met us as we came off the elevator in the large vestibule that led to the door of the suite. As we approached the door, there was a commotion behind us, some-one coming from around the other side of the vestibule. Sonny quickly moved towards him and pushed him back through the door telling him, in no uncertain terms that he did not belong there. Sonny then led us into the suite. As we walked in, Elvis was standing, plinking the keys of the grand piano, which sat right in the middle of the suite. He nervously thanked us for coming and said that as we were the last ones to arrive, we could get the meeting started.

Again, he told us what had transpired, and without explaining why they felt so strongly about it, simply repeated that they thought this guy might just be the real deal and would try to make his move to "get" Elvis tonight. In addition to a bunch of hotel security guards, Sonny and Red were there, and Elvis instructed Red to brief us on what we were to do at the show. Red then took over, very seriously explaining that he would be positioned on our side of the stage and that Sonny would be stage right. He said that we were to all constantly keep our eyes on the audience and signal to them if we saw anything at all out of the ordi-nary. Again, though there had been threats before, this one was real and needed to be taken seriously.

At that moment, the door to the suite burst open and we hear this unfamiliar, brutish voice growl "I warned you, Presley, and now you're dead" (or something similar to that.) The next sound that met our confused yet terrified ears was the sound of gunshots. Immediately, Red and Sonny drew their pistols, as did the Hilton security guards. Bullets and curses were flying as bodies dove for cover. We knew we were going to die. Nick Bruno dove behind one of the couches. I dove under a table, banging my head on one of the legs as I did. The flash of pain blinded me as I hit the floor. I was praying to God asking him to forgive me for every bad thing I had ever done. I looked over and saw that J.D. and Elvis were behind another couch. In a testament to J.D.'s true friendship to Elvis, he had crawled on top of Elvis so as to shield him from this mad gunman.

Donnie Sumner, who had dove behind the bar, in his own show of bravery to stop the assailants, started throwing cans of orange and pineapple juice and bottles of tomato juice that were stacked behind the bar to be used as mixers. Seeing this, Sonny screamed at him to stop throwing cans and to put down the juice. He said that it was all a joke— and apparently not one worth staining the light carpet with a shattered bottle of tomato juice.

J.D. later said that before Sonny's words could sink in, he had become aware that Elvis was shaking—almost violently—beneath him. As sanity finally prevailed, J.D. realized that Elvis wasn't shaking but rather was laughing hysterically. It had all been a very elaborate and very well executed practical joke. We were the only ones not in on the joke. Elvis, his guys, the security guards—everyone with guns, basically—was in on it. And, of course, they were all firing blanks but in our state of heightened anxiety, we thought we could actually hear and see bullets whizzing by. He had gotten us good.

When it was over, we were physically drained. I don't know how we even got through the midnight show. It had seemed so real; our lives had passed before our eyes. On stage that night, Elvis never mentioned it, but several times through the night, he'd look over at us, and just laugh. He loved to pull practical jokes on people and that may have been his finest moment. He was very proud of himself.

We learned a somber footnote to this story sometime later, over which we felt extremely blessed. As it turns out, behind the cans of juice on the bar was a loaded pistol that Elvis kept there. If Sonny hadn't stopped Donnie from throwing those cans at the would-be assailants, he would have undoubtedly, eventually, reached that pistol and then there's no telling how this joke might have turned out. Donnie was a brave guy who loved Elvis. There's no doubt in my mind, he would have done anything in his power to protect him.

☙☙☙

The suite was the site of many memorable experiences. Countless celebrities who would attend Elvis's show would often visit afterwards—stars as diverse as Red Skelton and Redd Foxx. I remember, once, the great actor Richard Harris visited after a show. In addition to his career on the dramatic stage and in movies, Richard had enjoyed some success as a recording artist, with songs like "McArthur Park" and one called "My Boy." When he visited Elvis, the latter was high on the charts. Elvis loved the song, and really seemed to like Harris as well. He greeted him with a big hug, and then visited with him a long time. After he left, I remember Elvis saying, "Can you believe that guy thinks he isn't a singer? Man, I love that record!" And, he obviously did, because, a year or so later, Elvis cut it, and it was a big record for him, becoming a hit on the pop, country and adult contemporary charts. He also performed it in concert. In fact, I remember he sang it the last time I ever saw him perform live.

Elvis also like Harris' version of "McArthur Park" but I remember how he laughed at the line that said "someone left the cake out in the rain." He'd start to talk about it and just collapse in a fit of laughter. He'd try to catch his breath and then say something like "serves the son of a _____ right. Why'd he take it outside in the first place?" And then he would start laughing again. He had one of the most infectious laughs of anyone I've ever known.

There was another time when a post-show visit didn't go quite as smoothly. We were up in the suite singing after the second show when word reached Elvis that the nightclub performer, Bobby Darin, who had attended the show, wanted to come up and introduce some of his friends to Elvis. Now I had seen photos taken in the sixties showing Bobby and Elvis together smiling and relaxing, so I assumed they had a cordial relationship, but for some reason on this night Elvis wasn't thrilled that Bobby was on his way up.

Upon entering Elvis's suite, there was a raised foyer of sorts and then a couple of steps down into the sunken living room area. After a few minutes the doorbell rang and one of the guys opened it to reveal Bobby and his own little entourage of people. Despite his earlier grumblings, Elvis met them at the bottom of those two steps and greeted Bobby and his guests. After a few moments, he called us over and introduced us. We all shook hands and briefly chatted; it was my first time to meet Darin. We began wandering back towards the piano leaving Elvis and Bobby with his group still standing at the entrance. I must admit that I don't know exactly what happened or what was said, but clearly I missed something because the next thing I knew, Elvis had pulled his gun and stuck it in Bobby's face. "You sorry son of a _____," Elvis growled, "Get your ___ out of here now." With that, Elvis backed Darin and his group up those two steps, and backed him out of the suite and slammed the door. Elvis never told us what had happened that set him off so badly, and after another twenty minutes or so things were pretty much back to normal and we were gathered around the piano singing as if nothing had happened.

Another time I witnessed a variation of something that has become legendary in Elvis lore. Again, it occurred in his suite. It was during our week of pre-engagement rehearsals. We were sitting around relaxing with the television on, watching one of the late night talk shows—most likely Johnny Carson, though I don't distinctly remember that. We were talking and not really paying attention to the show when suddenly, we heard the unmistakable voice of Robert Goulet coming over the airwaves. Of course, Elvis's hatred of Robert Goulet is as well known as it is unexplained. Some have said it was left over from some affront Goulet committed in the '50s regarding one of Elvis's girlfriends. No one seems to know, beyond a doubt, why he didn't like him, but he sure didn't.

The television in Elvis's suite was a big console model with a built-in stereo and speakers flanking the large screen. As soon as Goulet's voice came through those speakers, Elvis stopped talking and stood up, staring at the set. While since those years, I have heard the tales of Elvis shooting out television screens, I never witnessed that happening, though I don't doubt it. On this night, Elvis wore a double holster that crisscrossed his back and ended with one holster under each armpit. But instead of housing pistols, these holsters each held a shiny silver martial arts throwing knife—sometimes referred to as "assassin's knives." In a split second, Elvis drew the knives, and with pinpoint accuracy, he threw them across the living room, sinking one in the left speaker and the other in the right speaker of that television. It didn't exactly silence the offending voice of Goulet, but it seemed to make Elvis feel better. He walked over and dislodged the blades, re-holstered them and looked at us sitting around on the couches with an unapologetic shrug and said simply, "I hate that son of a ____." He walked towards the bedroom of his suite and announced to everyone and to no one: "Tell 'em to send me the bill for the stereo."

Everything in his suite—including that television—was the best of the best, simply the highest quality of craftsmanship for the time. For that reason, we were shocked one night to enter and find buckets scattered across the floor, especially around the dining room table. While it almost never rains in Las Vegas, there had been strong storms on this evening and some very heavy rainfall. Even still, we would have never expected to find this opulent suite to have a leaky roof, but indeed water was dripping into each of the buckets that had been placed around. After a few minutes of wondering on our part, Elvis came in from his bedroom. We asked about the buckets; how could we not? He smiled and then broke in to a little chuckle. "It's nothing really," he said as he walked to a light switch on the wall, and turned on the big chandeliers. At that point we saw that only some of the light bulbs in the chandeliers were burning; in fact many were missing altogether. He continued, "I was just taking a little target practice. I wanted to see how many of those bulbs I could hit." From the number of buckets that were present, it was clear that even the bulbs he hit carried with them the price of the bullets that had to land somewhere. I guess it's like that line from the old Mel Brooks' movie: "It's good to be the king."

I suppose I must address a topic that, over the last thirty years, seems to enter any conversation about Elvis, and that is the issue of drugs. With the presumed benefit of hindsight, some automatically assume that any of his erratic behavior can be explained by his reported habitual intake of prescription drugs. The reality is, I can't speak to this. Just as I rarely saw him drink alcohol, I can honestly say that in all the nights we spent in the suite or on the road, I never once saw him take even a single pill.

Sure I saw unusual behavior, but, after all, his nickname was "Crazy." Elvis was the greatest entertainer in the world, but at the same time, he was a funny and fun-loving boy from Mississippi. He could, one minute, display a temper that would terrify a room full of people, and the next, charm them with a shy graciousness. He could be profane, and he could pray like a preacher. Elvis was an enigma, and I don't think that was always a result of a drug habit.

I never saw him when I thought he was high or stoned. That could be the result of my naiveté; of a carefully controlled maintenance of his image, even around us; or of a habit that didn't yet rule his life. The stories that have surfaced since his death first surprised me, and still make me sad, because the picture that they paint are not of the man I was blessed to know. I'm not in denial; I'm not unwilling to accept what is apparently the sad truth about the last several years of his life, but I can only talk about the things that I witnessed with my own eyes. And, thankfully, most of those were good.

There were so many once-in–a-lifetime experiences that occurred in that suite, and while I could never rank them in terms of memories, there was one that was very special. It also occurred during our first Vegas engagement in 1972. We were in the suite singing, and after finishing a number, Elvis turned and headed towards the bedroom, saying over his shoulder that he'd be right back. When he returned, he was carrying five small boxes in his hand. He told us to line up side by side. He set the boxes down and then opened the hinged top on one, revealing one of the gold TCB necklaces like he wore. Though they weren't as well known at that time, the TCB—and the motto "Taking Care of Business"—has almost become synonymous with Elvis, an iconic representation of his life in the 70s.

He conducted a little ceremony, presenting one to each of The Stamps one by one. J.D was first and then I was next. As I bent at the waist and leaned towards Elvis, he placed the necklace over my head and around my neck. He looked me in the eye, shook my hand and with that famous grin, said simply, "Welcome to the mafia, Rich." I have to admit it was another one of the most amazing moments of my life.

I no longer have my TCB. I still want to kick myself about it, but it's been gone for many years now. They were solid gold and, as a result, "soft" with quality. Over the years I had noticed that the chain, where it connected to both sides of the pendant, was wearing, becoming thinner, with time. I knew I needed to get it repaired, but, frankly, I didn't want to take it off. One day it was around my neck as it had been for years, and the next it was gone. I still regret having lost it, but cherish the memories of the night I received it.

ॐॐॐ

During that same '72 Vegas engagement, RCA Records continued its practice of recording songs live on stage to later be released on record. This was due, in part, to Elvis's waning interest of going into the studio to record new material. We appeared on record on far more live recordings—both from Las Vegas and later Madison Square Garden—than on studio cuts, but I also had the opportunity to do one studio session with Elvis. I can attest that recording with him in the studio was unlike any other session I had ever done before or since.

We all arrived at RCA's Studio C in Hollywood on March 27, 1972, having no idea what songs were going to be recorded. All of the session players—in this case, the TCB Band and the Stamps—were in place and ready to go. After Elvis arrived, and when he was ready, he instructed Lamar Fike to play a demo of a song. Lamar had been a long-time friend and employee to Elvis and a member of the famed Memphis Mafia. One of his duties was to gather demos from which Elvis would choose songs to record.

Elvis would tell him to start playing songs. We might listen to the entire demo, or after a minute or so Elvis might say, "No, I don't like that. Play something else." This would go on until Elvis heard something he liked and he would, then and there, decide to cut it. Sometimes Lamar might try to convince Elvis to reconsider and give a song another listen—and sometimes Elvis would consent. With other songs, though, Elvis stuck with his first inclination and refused to record it.

When a song was chosen, Ronnie Tutt, Elvis's drummer, who served as the de facto session leader, would write out a chord chart for the band. Then we would listen to the demo another few times; the players working out breaks and fills, and the vocalists listening for our parts. The process actually came together pretty quickly, and we would begin putting the song down on tape.

As has been proven with the recent release of studio sessions and outtakes from Elvis's time in the studio, though there was an engineer and a producer in the booth, when he was engaged and interested in the session, Elvis, essentially, was his own producer. He would direct the band, telling Glen to lay back on a certain section, or perhaps telling Jerry to walk the bass line during the chorus—a "chug-a-lug" as Elvis called it. And the vocalists were not excluded from his direction. Sometimes he would immediately like something that we did—some stacking of harmonies or something—while other times he would stop us and completely change our arrangements. In the studio or in rehearsals, Elvis often had the exact sound in his head that he wanted to achieve.

Of course, that doesn't always mean that it was easy to capture his performances on tape. In the studio, Elvis was an engineer's nightmare. He preferred to record in the studio like he performed on stage. He would not stand with headphones at a stationary microphone in a vocal booth like the artists do today—and as most did even then. In our session, Elvis recorded with a handheld microphone walking around as a live band accompanied him. One minute he'd be over beside Ronnie, then the next, he'd walk over and get right beside J.D. and me. He just seemed to go wherever the music and his spirit took him.

While he had a certain sound and arrangement in his head that he wanted to capture, still, there was a limit to how many times he was going to sing a song. Sometimes he would stick with a particular song, singing it for several takes, until he was satisfied. Other times, after just a few takes, he would seem to lose interest, and want to move on to another song—or even end the session.

The session I did with him ran for three days though part of that was really just for the benefit of the *Elvis On Tour* cameras. Overall we cut six songs: "Burning Love," "Separate Ways," "Always On My Mind," "For the Good Times," "Fool," "It's a Matter of Time" and "Where Do I Go From Here." Looking back on it, in my opinion, this was one of the last recording sessions where Elvis recorded some really great material. Of course, there were some gems over the next four years, but I just think that this represented some really strong work on his part.

I remember at the time there were whisperings of whether Elvis could still "cut it" with rock-and-roll songs. His affinity for ballads and sad songs is well documented, but if only for a little while, with the release of "Burning Love," he dispelled any rumors of his inability to rock. That was, unquestionably, the highlight of the session for us. We believed we had just sung on a hit record, a fact that would be born out when it peaked at Number Two on the Billboard charts, his best showing in three years.

☙☙☙

I always found it difficult to believe, when I heard years later, that Elvis didn't like performing "Burning Love." Though, when it was new, he sometimes had trouble remembering the words—often reading them on stage—during my time with him, he always seemed to enjoy singing it. And he definitely lit up in the studio when he heard the demo. It really seemed to be a song that he liked, but even if he didn't, I suppose the good news was that the fans loved it.

Ironically, around this time Elvis, who had always been the top record seller on RCA, was eclipsed in sales by the country singer, Charley Pride. Though some people like to claim that Elvis didn't care about the business, I can attest that he was aware of his standing, and when he learned that he was being outsold, he did not shy away from showing his displeasure. One night in the suite, he went on and on about it. After venting for a while, in a moment of acceptance—or perhaps resignation—he commented on the irony of the situation. He reflected on his early days, and how he was described as a white boy who sounded black. And now, all these years later, he was being unseated in sales by a black man who sounded white.

After one of those recording sessions in Hollywood, we finished in the very early morning hours. It was still fairly warm outside—especially for March—and as we exited the building, we were amazed at how many fans were still waiting outside. His bodyguards got Elvis out of the building and safely into the waiting limo. It pulled away from the curb to the dismay of the fans, but then, suddenly, it stopped. The next thing I knew, Elvis popped up through the sunroof in the back of the limo. He waved to the fans—even signed some autographs—before finally departing for the night. I took note of the way that Elvis tried to accommodate his fans. Here he was, arguably the biggest act of the last twenty years—maybe ever—and he could always make time for his fans. It was a high bar that, in later years, The Oak Ridge Boys would always try to reach.

As mentioned, this same session marked the beginning of our involvement with the documentary project that would become *Elvis On Tour*. It would follow Elvis through nineteen shows in fifteen cities and fifteen days. Additionally it would capture some rehearsals and recording sessions as well as some of the most extensive and insightful monologues that Elvis would ever give. It offered a unique perspective, and gave the viewer at least a glimpse of what it was like to be Elvis Presley. It offered a dizzying look at the whirlwind that was created when a force like an Elvis Presley tour moved across the country. The film was well received, and won a *Golden Globe Award* for "Best Documentary of 1972."

The film followed Elvis as we started in Hollywood for rehearsals, and then on the tour, which opened in Buffalo, then moved on to

Detroit, Dayton, Knoxville, Hampton Roads, Richmond, Roanoke, Indianapolis, Charlotte, Greensboro, Macon, Jacksonville, Little Rock, San Antonio and finally Albuquerque. The cameras weren't there for every show, but they sure seemed to be there a lot. Though much unseen footage has surfaced in recent years, there is no doubt in my mind that hours of footage still remain unseen. Hopefully it'll turn up sometime soon. I'd sure like to see it!

I remember one of the rehearsals for the movie that was not captured on film. We were all on stage, and Elvis was singing. They weren't yet filming, but part of the crew was already there setting up. Some stagehands were adjusting the stage lights during the rehearsal. At the same time, part of the band was fumbling whatever song Elvis was singing. This combination soon irritated Elvis. Suddenly, he stopped singing and threw his microphone across the stage. He growled at the band that they were the highest paid musicians in the world, and as such, they should be able to follow him on these songs. Then he stormed off stage, and, for the next few minutes, we could hear him in a side room. It sounded as if he was stomping around, or perhaps breaking boards. I'm still not sure what was happening in there. He would loudly complain about the band and the rehearsal, and then we'd hear a karate yell followed by a crash.

All of us—the band and singers—just stood there, unsure of what to do. After several minutes of this, the noises ceased, and then after a few more minutes, Elvis walked back into the rehearsal room, and we picked up right where we'd left off. I wish I could say that things improved from that point on but, unfortunately, they did not. After a few more attempts at the same song, Elvis simply dropped the microphone where he stood, he turned to face the band and said two words: "Rehearsal's over." With that, he left, and we were done until the next day.

Some rehearsals were filmed: the one at RCA in Hollywood, and the one before the show in Buffalo, New York (a snippet of which is seen in the movie with us singing "I, John.") Others were recorded on audio but not filmed.

One nice, personal diversion occurred while we were appearing in Buffalo. I was able to see my old partner Joe Bonsall. As usual, we'd arrived in town the day before the tour so we could rehearse. The night before the first show, Joe invited me to his house for dinner. It was fun to catch up, to hear how things were going with The Keystones, and to share some stories of life with Elvis. I invited Joe and his sister, Nancy, to come see the concert the next night. I have to admit to feeling pretty proud standing on stage with Elvis and knowing that my friend was out there watching. After the show, we were able to visit some more backstage. It had only been about a year since we'd seen each other but so much was happening in our lives that it was a welcome opportunity to reconnect.

࿎࿎࿎

After the spring tour ended, for the next six weeks, The Stamps went back to our comparatively mundane lives of singing gospel music in churches. Once again, to capitalize on the connection to Elvis, this included a return visit to Buffalo where The Stamps headlined a show at Kleinhans Music Hall, that was promoted by Joe and The Keystones.

The most memorable thing that happened for me during that time was the first, and only, time during Elvis's lifetime that I visited Graceland. We had a few days off, and Elvis invited all of us Stamps to Memphis so he could show us "the house" as he called it. With Elvis, it was never "the mansion" or "the estate" or any other grand description;

it was always and only "the house." So, we hopped on J.D.'s bus, and rode the three hours between Nashville and Memphis.

We arrived late in the afternoon and pulled the big bus through those famous music gates. (I've always found it ironic that even though the gates of Graceland, featuring a likeness of Elvis playing a guitar, were designed and installed in the 1950s, that if you look closely at his legs, it looks as if he's wearing the bell-bottomed pants he made famous fifteen years later. The gates were conceived long before the bell-bottom fashion trend even existed, and yet in some prescient example of irony, he appears to be wearing them on the gates.)

After we arrived and parked the big Eagle on the driveway beside Graceland, Elvis came outside and greeted us. He led us inside and gave us the grand tour of the house. It was clear that he was extremely proud of it. He wasn't exactly boastful about it, but he definitely enjoyed showing us some of the material results of his achievements. I remember the multiple television sets that he had, not only downstairs in the TV room but also upstairs in his bedroom. As most fans know, he loved to watch multiple channels at once—especially during football season.

After he'd walked us through all of the rooms upstairs and downstairs, we went into the dining room and gathered around the table for a big southern meal. It was just us, along with Elvis, Charlie Hodge and one of Elvis's girlfriends. I have to admit I don't remember her name. It wasn't Linda or one of the others who we would see regularly. I do recall that her car was sitting in front of Graceland and that one of the tires had gone flat since it had been parked. As he was showing us through the house, I remember Elvis griping that now he'd have to "take care of that." Though I'm sure he wasn't going to go out and change the tire himself, clearly it was a nuisance that he didn't want to have to deal with.

With supper finished we went into the living room and sat around and talked, just like friends would do. Then, as invariably would happen, we ended up in the adjacent music room singing gospel songs late into the night. At around 4:30 in the morning, he announced that he wanted to go outside and show us the property. So, even though it was still dark, we followed him out, and he showed us some of his cars in the carport, and the stables out back where his horses were kept. He took us in and showed us his horses, "Rising Sun," a beautiful golden palomino, seeming to be the one of which he was most proud.

After he'd shown us the property, he decided we should see it again, this time in golf carts. He led us back to the carport, and each of us got on our own golf cart. He led us on a site-seeing parade across his property that soon turned into a race. He was laughing, trying to leave us behind. There were many paths that had been worn in the back field— and not just by horses—so this was clearly not the first time he'd enjoyed golf cart races. As we raced around the far end of the house, we eventually made our way back onto the asphalt driveway, but instead of circling back around the front of the house over to the carport again, he swerved and headed down the hill towards the front gates.

Still standing on the gas pedal, he suddenly yelled to an unseen (by us) guard in the small guard shack beside the gate, "Open the gates!" Though it surprised all of us, this clearly did not shock the guard because almost immediately the big music gates swing inward, and without slowing down in the least, Elvis rocketed his cart through the gates and turned right onto Highway 51, more famously named *Elvis Presley Boulevard*. My cart was next—thankfully I also made the turn without wiping out—and then the rest of The Stamps followed, and what had been some harmless fun in the pre-dawn darkness around Graceland became a tour of the Whitehaven section of Memphis.

The joyride lasted several minutes—and probably two or three miles—before we steered back towards the relative safety of Graceland. By this time, though the sun wasn't quite up yet, Memphis was starting to wake up. The streets, which had been all but deserted when our ride began, were now dotted with early morning commuters likely heading to start the day shift at their jobs. At one point, we got passed by a couple of city buses spewing smoke and diesel fumes. Cars would honk as they passed us. I think they were honks of anger at the carts and drivers at the back of the pack because members of The Stamps weren't recognizable to them. But, by the time they got to the lead cart and saw that it was Elvis, the honks seemed more friendly and excited, as if after seeing him, this spectacle suddenly made sense.

After we got back to the house, we parked the golf carts and returned inside. We sat around for another little while, mostly laughing about the adventure we'd just taken, but soon, after the sun had risen, it was time for Elvis to retire to his bedroom so he could get his "good day's rest." After saying our goodbyes, we went back out to our bus and crawled in our own bunks to catch up on our sleep while Nowdy drove us back home to Nashville. It had been quite a twenty-four hours for us. It certainly was an unforgettable and welcome diversion from what would have otherwise been just another month and a half of Stamps touring.

But we knew that, in just a few short weeks, our low-key existence would, again, come to an end and that June would find us embarking on another Elvis tour. This one, however, was even more special because it would kick-off with Elvis's first ever concert appearances in

New York City. Eighty thousand tickets were sold in two days making El-vis the first artist ever to sell out Madison Square Garden for four shows. In addition to the fans, many celebrities—including Simon and Garfun-kel, George Harrison, Bob Dylan, and a young Bruce Springsteen—would attend the shows.

Because these shows were so important to Elvis—even he wasn't immune to the axiom of not truly making it until you "make it there"—we, again, arrived a day early to rehearse. On Friday, June 9 we gathered in a ballroom at the New York Hilton and ran through the possible songs for the next four nights, interrupted for about an hour so that Elvis could charm the media in, perhaps, his most famous press conference ever. His handling of the press that day was masterful as he answered their ques-tions and charmed them with his smile and his personality. It was all the more impressive to me when I saw it because I remember when he ar-rived in the ballroom for rehearsal, wearing that two-tone blue suit with the cape and the gold belt, he was none too happy about the fact that he was going to have to interrupt rehearsal to face the press. Though, relatively speaking, he hadn't done many press conferences since his comeback, I always thought he handled them very well. For some reason, though, he got uncomfortable anytime he knew he was going to have to face the press.

RCA would record both of the Saturday shows and release the evening show on a record titled simply enough: *Elvis As Recorded at Madison Square Garden*. For whatever reason, that show really cooked that night: Elvis was great, the band was hot, and the singers were re-ally on. Even at the time, we knew we had nailed it; it was a great show. I was always glad that RCA was there to record that night. Amazingly even before the tour ended in Tulsa eleven days later, the live album would be released and on it's way to selling several million copies. Elvis had proven to anyone who still doubted that he was, indeed, still the King. (In 1997, RCA would release the recording from the afternoon show, titled *An Afternoon in the Garden.*)

కళళళ

July found us back on J.D.'s tour bus performing around the country again on Stamps shows. In some cases we would revisit towns, like Tulsa, where we'd just performed with Elvis—to attempt to capitalize on residual interest—but otherwise we were working where promoters and the people wanted us. We played quite a bit on the Gulf coast of Texas and the Carolinas, and also lots of churches in pretty close proximity to Nashville; towns like Murfreesboro and Clarksville.

We would also appear on television quite a bit around this time. Jake Hess, formerly of The Statesman Quartet and The Imperials, had a show called *The Noon Show* that taped in Nashville, in the studios of the local CBS affiliate. Much like some of the country music shows of the day, such as *The Porter Wagoner Show* and *The Wilburn Brothers Show,* Jake's show featured a live studio audience watching gospel groups perform. One way in which it was different, though, is that the groups would come in and sing several songs that Jake would catalogue for later use. The Stamps would arrive with a couple of changes of stage clothes. We would go out and sing two or three songs for the audience, and then we'd change into another outfit, come back and sing some more songs. Jake would then edit the shows to feature a song or two per episode. It really was an efficient way for Jake to produce a series of shows featuring gospel stars of the day, and to promote the music in general, and various bands in specific. J.D. would never perform on these shows with us because he saw these appearances as a way to show the ticket-buying public, as well as the gospel promoters, that The Stamps—with me sing-ing bass—was a good show, and it wasn't necessary for him to travel and do the dates. I don't remember how long *The Noon Show* stayed on the air, but I do remember that I would also appear on it with The Oaks several times in later years.

かかか

The end of July meant another five-week residency in Las Vegas. The rehearsals found us learning several new songs including "My Way" and "What Now My Love" that would be added to the repertoire. Elvis was frequently rehearsing songs, some of which became regulars, some he would perform occasionally, and some, we never sang on stage. Though the audiences expected some of his hits—especially the early ones—at every show, Elvis's setlist truly was a reflection of songs he liked.

One such song that Elvis had added earlier in the year, which we occasionally sang, was a medley of "I Got A Woman" and "Amen." At the end of "Amen," Elvis would have J.D. do a little dive bomb routine to showcase his low range. The more we did it, the more drawn-out was the dive bomb portion. In the years after I left, it became a regular part of the show. He would open with "See See Rider" and then immediately move into this medley, with the dive bomb extending the song a good thirty or forty-five seconds. For the repeat fans, it became sort of a throwaway song, simply to be tolerated in anticipation of the rest of the show. But when he first started performing it, the fans enjoyed it—and it was very obvious that Elvis enjoyed it. As the frustrated bass singer he always claimed to be, he loved to showcase J.D and that voice of his. That's the reason he would occasionally call J.D. out to sing songs like "Walk This Lonesome Road" and later, "Why Me Lord?" More than it being something the crowd would enjoy, it was something that Elvis wanted to hear.

One group who didn't like it at all, even from the beginning, was some of the members of the band, and they didn't mind being vocal in their disapproval. They would grumble about "this crap," and referred to it as a "freak show." But the fact is, Elvis didn't care what they thought. It was his show, and he determined very early on that he would run it the way he wanted to, and include the set list he wanted to sing. It was much like the conversation he'd had with the Colonel prior to his comeback. There were certain elements he demanded, and there were certain songs he wanted to sing and to hear.

I remember when we first rehearsed the Three Dog Night cover "Never Been to Spain." Elvis just loved it. He sang it over and over, and quickly added it to the stage show. I think he hoped the people would like it because he liked it.

While, in many ways, this was just another typical Vegas engagement, in another way it was very different. In retrospect, many believe that this represented the time period when things forever changed for Elvis.

The very first time we ever did one of those all-night sings in Elvis's suite, I met his wife, Priscilla. She was, of course, very pretty, and always extremely nice to us. But then shortly after that, we didn't see her around much anymore. Of course, we soon heard the rumors that would fly, the ones that in this case turned out to be true. Since our last engagement, the separation between Elvis and Priscilla became official and final. Of course, we'd see Elvis with different girlfriends at various times, but overall, I remember that being an especially sad time for Elvis. While I would never claim to know what Elvis was feeling at that time, having gone through divorce myself some years later, looking back, I know he must have been hurt and sad, perhaps a little embarrassed or ashamed.

It's not a good feeling, of course, and even less so when it happens publicly. During that time, he sort of withdrew. There were fewer after-show
parties, and no all-night sings, He didn't joke around on stage as much.
He would snap out of it somewhat by the next tour, but I'd have to say
that things were never exactly the same with him after that.

After the last show of the engagement, Elvis did a press conference to announce to the world that he would perform a satellite show
in January that would be broadcast around the world. The news of this
show, which, became known as the *Aloha from Hawaii* concert, was as exciting to us as it was to the media and fans around the world. We had only
to survive two months of standard Stamps fare and then we'd meet Elvis
in Texas, head to the west coast and finally to Hawaii for three shows to
tune up for the live worldwide telecast in January. Things couldn't have
been going better for us as a group and for me personally. Our lives were
scheduled; well in advance, we knew exactly where we would be almost
every day of the year. There was little chance for deviation. Shows were
booked and tickets were sold. But what's that old saying about the best-
laid plans?

CHAPTER FIVE: *Potential and Perseverance*

The Stamps were off the road one day—a very rare occurrence—and I happened to be home, at the little house we were renting on Anderson Lane in Madison, Tennessee. The phone rang, and it was Bill Golden, with The Oak Ridge Boys. After a little small talk, he told me that Noel Fox (their current bass singer) was going to leave the group, and that they'd like for me to replace him. In fact, he said that there was no one else they wanted to consider. He then went on to talk about the plans they had for the group and that even though they had still only recorded southern gospel music, their short and long-term plans were to branch out musically. He was proud of the fact that they were not just singers but strove to be consummate entertainers.

I was immediately interested in taking the job but told Golden that I wanted to discuss it with my family. So I waited a day before I called him back and told him that I accepted. And waiting even a day was difficult; I wanted to jump through the phone and accept as soon as he called.

I was excited with the prospects. I had always liked The Oaks and believed that we would have great potential. My family supported my decision. For them, as much as they might have hoped we would do great things, they were also hopeful that I would return to a more traditional gospel quartet lifestyle. They had never loved the fact that touring with Elvis took me to what they considered "worldly places," such as Las Vegas. Of course, I knew "the world" could be found anywhere and while I, obviously, loved gospel music, I had no interest in being confined in the music that we sang. I always had dreams of something more. The immediate attraction was that it might provide the opportunity to earn a little more money. Ironically, as it turned out, I was hired for the exact same salary that I was earning after my raise with The Stamps: $275 per week.

I distinctly remember being a little nervous to tell J.D. that I was leaving. I put it off as long as I could; I didn't even give him a full two-weeks notice. We were in Texas doing a series of shows; it was October of 1972. We were working in Beaumont, and had checked into a hotel so that we could watch the World Series between the Cincinnati Reds and Oakland A's. I finally got the nerve to tell him that Golden had called and offered me a job, and that The Oaks needed me right away. I told him I had accepted. J.D. was both disappointed and a little angry that I was leaving. As much as anything, it was because I was going to a group that he saw as a competitor. To his credit, though, after he stewed about it for a few minutes, he did admit that he could see the same potential for The Oaks that I saw.

The A's ended up beating the Big Red Machine in seven games, bringing an end to an exciting Fall Classic. The Stamps worked a few more shows in Texas, winding up at East Orange Junior High School, in Orange, Texas, for a show on an October Sunday evening. We performed to a sold-out house—not typical of a Sunday night show. After we'd packed up the record table, I got on the bus with the rest of the Stamps for the long ride back to Nashville. I can't remember where the next Stamps show was, but I knew for sure that my next shows would be in Illinois, then Michigan, and then on to a Canadian tour beginning in Calgary and Alberta. As soon as we rolled in to Nashville, for the last time, I took my stuff off The Stamps' bus. I was officially an Oak Ridge Boy.

Though it may sound cliché, my time spent with the Stamps had truly felt like earning an advanced degree. I had achieved one of the first goals I'd set for myself: to be a full-time singer. And I had achieved that one in a big way, for it had seemed we'd worked seven days a week. I know that wasn't the case, but we definitely spent more time on the road that we had spent at home. I can't begin to remember how many dates The Stamps played over those two years—it had to be several hundred. I do know that with Elvis, we'd worked three tours consisting of forty-six shows and two Las Vegas engagements of 121 more shows for a total of 167 times on stage with the greatest act of all time. With him, we had performed for almost 900,000 ticket buyers. Trust me, that was an amazing two years that served not only to fully submerge me in the world of full-time singing, but also prepared me well for the future that would soon become mine.

Just prior to my arrival to the group, The Oaks had completed a new studio album called *Street Gospel*. It wasn't out yet so I went into the studio and re-sang some of the bass vocal parts, so that my voice would appear on the record. The record was released with Noel singing much of the harmony parts; I just re-cut his solo parts and some of the lines where it would be obvious that it was him, and not me, singing. We also shot a new photo for the album cover. So, that was the first Oaks record I appeared on—along with Duane, Golden and "Little" Willie Wynn, our tenor singer.

FROM ELVIS TO ELVIRA: *My Life On Stage*

Much like that first record, my first shows with The Oaks featured both Noel and me singing. The four of them would come out onstage and do part of their show, and then they would introduce me, and I would join them. It was a generous way to "ease" me into the shows, and into the acceptance of their fans.

In addition to singing his parts, eventually, I also wore Noel's stage suits. By then, another way The Oaks were shaking things up in the gospel world was that they no longer wore the traditional matching suits and ties, having replaced them with color-coordinated suits and fancy, open collared shirts. Noel was a little bit bigger than I was so we stacked his suits in my car, and I drove over to a tailor near my little house in Madison to have them cut down to fit me. In a huge note of musical irony, as I drove in my car that day listening to the radio, I heard myself singing with Elvis on his latest single, "Burning Love," which was sitting at Number Two on the Billboard Top 100. Though we couldn't know it at the time, it was the last time during his life that one of his songs would chart that high. Of course, since his passing he has topped the charts again, which in itself is an unbelievable feat.

Even before we made the move towards country, The Oaks were never just southern gospel in the strictest sense. In his heart, Willie Wynn really tended more towards the traditional gospel so, by the fall of 1973, he came to us to say he thought it best if he left to form his own group, one that could pursue a more pure gospel-only path.

When it came time to hire another tenor singer, there was only one person I wanted to see fill out our group. I really lobbied for The Oaks to hire Joe away from The Keystones. Both Golden and Duane liked Joe and his singing. In fact, by that time, Duane was producing Joe and

The Keystones. It is a revealing testament to Duane's dedication to The Oaks that he wanted to hire Joe because doing so would, in essence, cost him a client for his studio. His priority, though, was with his group. Like Golden and myself, Duane knew that the best thing for The Oak Ridge Boys would be to add Joe. So with that, by October '73, The Oak Ridge Boys were ready to take on the world!

Around this same time, we thought our ship had arrived in the form of a CBS/Columbia Records deal. We were still "straddling the fence," trying to do country in addition to gospel, and in Columbia, for a while, at least, we thought we'd found a label that would support this approach. Our first release on Columbia was titled simply enough *The Oak Ridge Boys*. George Richey was producing us at that time, and he wanted us to get a country hit almost as much as we wanted one, but it wouldn't come easy. (Ironically, our first record for CBS was already recorded before Joe joined us, so just like we did when I replaced Noel, Joe went into the studio and re-sung Willie's leads. So on that record, Willie's voice can still be heard on the group harmony parts.)

The first single that would be shipped to country radio was the Johnny Russell-penned "The Baptism of Jesse Taylor." While it was a great mid-tempo song that suited our sound and our style—a straight country sounding song with a gospel message—on the country charts we, unfortunately, couldn't compete with Johnny's own version of it. On the gospel side, however, we did win a Grammy for Best Gospel Performance (The Oaks' second such award.) The album itself gave us a little glimmer of hope for the future country success as it peaked at Number Thirty-Eight on the charts.

The next two releases, *Sky High,* in '75, and the inauspiciously titled, *The Oak Ridge Boys Old Fashioned, Down Home, Hand Clappin', Foot Stompin', Southern Style, Gospel Quartet Music,* in '76 saw little chart action and neither featured the type of music we really wanted to be doing. Our distribution was extremely sparse, and, from these albums, the label only released singles to gospel radio, Some of these included "Rhythm Guitar," and "Where The Soul Never Dies," (which incidentally featured a young slide-guitarist named Charlie Daniels.) The irony was, signing a major record deal had actually taken us a little backwards, in that we were not really recording the type of country songs that we'd planned and we were making less money on record sales with the gospel stuff we were now recording. Eventually, we approached label head, Billy Sherrill about producing us, but because of his other commitments to George Jones, Tammy Wynette, and others, he could not, so he did the next best thing for us: he worked hard to help get us released from his own label—a move we greatly appreciated.

It was around that time that things were so bad for us that Duane and Golden considered selling off the Oaks' publishing company just to create some cash flow. It mostly consisted of gospel publishing, which had been more valuable to the group when the gospel dates were going well. But now that we were falling somewhat into disfavor, it wasn't generating the money that it had been. Joe and I were not yet partners in the group so we weren't involved that deeply in the day-to-day business decisions, but we knew that after much soul-searching, Duane and Golden had approached Johnny Cash to try to make this deal.

Seeing the desperate straits we were in, Johnny refused to buy the only thing The Oaks had of value at the time, instead offering us a loan and some dates. It was an obvious demonstration of the kind of man Johnny Cash was. Even though we would have been more than willing to sell, he knew that he would have been taking advantage of us. Instead, he booked us to open some dates for him, so, about a month after Joe joined us, there we were, in Lake Tahoe, opening for the "Man in Black." Then, February of 1974 found The Oaks in a brand new spot—and me in a very familiar one—as we spent ten days at the Las Vegas Hilton opening for one of the top draws in country music. It was a portend of things to come, as it would be the first of many times I found myself on stage with The Oaks at venues I had played earlier with Elvis.

On those shows, we had ten minutes in which to sing three songs. After our short set, we would then move to the side of the stage to watch the show, as well as provide background vocals on some of his songs. While Elvis's shows were spectacles of sight and sound—with the orchestra and band and all of the vocalists, Cash's show was very different but just as powerful in its own way. The house would go dark, and with no fanfare, no introduction, no accompaniment, Cash would stroll out in the dark and take his place at the center microphone, with his back facing the audience. With no warning, he would appear in a spotlight, spin around and say, "Hello...I'm Johnny Cash." And for the next seventy-five minutes he would charm and entertain that audience as if his life depended on it.

I've talked about the charisma that Elvis possessed, but Cash was also a force of nature. Both onstage and off, when you were in his presence, you knew that he was something special. Perhaps one of the most common stories among artists in the '70s was the influence that Johnny Cash had on them. Those who had any personal involvement will, undoubtedly, attest to the kindness that he and his beloved wife, June Carter Cash, lavished on them. The Oak Ridge Boys are certainly no different, for they were uncommonly good to us. He allowed us to open shows for him on several different engagements in either Lake Tahoe or Las Vegas. He hired us when no one else would; he paid us more money than we were worth, and at the end of each engagement, he would bonus us by paying us more that we'd agreed on. I've often said if it weren't for John R. Cash, there would not be an Oak Ridge Boys today.

But as significant as the financial rewards were to us when working with him, that doesn't compare to the words of encouragement that he constantly offered. He could see the desperation in our eyes; he knew that we were a struggling act. After our last engagement in Las Vegas, we were looking at an immediate future with no dates booked. We wondered if we were going to be able to keep the group together.

One afternoon before a show he asked us if we would come up to his suite to meet with him—that very same suite where I'd spent so many hours singing with Elvis. When we arrived, John invited us in, and June greeted us all with hugs. We sat down on the couches, and as we began to talk, June's iconic mom, Mother Maybelle Carter came in from another room, and told Cash that she wanted to go downstairs to gamble. He reached into his pocket and pulled out a roll of bills, peeled off a few and handed them to her telling her to behave and be careful. I don't know if he'd given her a couple of hundred dollars or a couple of thousand but whatever it was seemed to satisfy her. She said her goodbyes and was out the door.

Cash returned to our conversation, and, after a few minutes, it began to turn a little more serious. June rose and excused herself, and John continued: "I can tell you guys are struggling because your heads are hanging, but I also can tell that there is something special about this group. I know it, and you all know it. If you give up, it'll never go any further than here, and nobody else will ever know what we know. You've got to find a way to stick it out. I'll help you every way I can, but you've got to stay together. If you do that then other people are going to find out about this magic that you have. If you guys will just persevere, I guarantee that it's going to happen for you. I can feel it."

Well, when we left that suite to head down to our own rooms, we all four were walking straighter and taller than when we had arrived. We felt an energy we hadn't felt in a long time. We truly believed that if Johnny Cash thought we could make it, then we definitely could make it!

In 1978, Johnny was hosting the *Country Music Association Awards Show* when we were nominated, for the first time, for Best Vocal Group. We were up against The Statler Brothers, who had won it for the six previous years, The Kendalls, The Original Texas Playboys and Dave & Sugar. When our name was announced as the winner, we jumped up and ran on stage, but instead of running to where the presenters, Johnny Paycheck and Eddie Rabbitt, were standing and where we were to receive our award, we—without having previously discussed or planned it—ran to where Cash was standing on the other side of the stage. We all hugged, and in the midst of the applause, what we heard more than anything else was Johnny saying, "I told you guys this would happen. I knew you could do it!"

Physically and spiritually, Johnny Cash was a giant of a man. He remained a part of our world and our lives for another twenty-five years.

While he would often say that his life was as much about showing others what not to do, the truth is he taught us all so much more than he could have ever realized.

June Carter Cash dedicated the last years of her life to caring for her husband, As his health began to fail him, she served as his caregiver. Though she had always been pretty healthy, in April of 2003, she went into the hospital for serious, but fairly routine, heart surgery. At this time—when the caregiver needed to be cared for—Johnny, though weak and in a wheel chair, took care of his beloved wife. While in the hospital, she suddenly passed away. Though she'd been sick, her death was very unexpected.

Something that did not come as a surprise to anyone who knew her was that, in preparation for her death, she had made all of the arrangements for her own funeral. After her passing, we were informed that among others, including Larry Gatlin, Sheryl Crow and Emmylou Harris, June wanted her "babies" to sing. (She always referred to us as her babies). That performance on Sunday, May 18, 2003, in the overflowing First Baptist Church of Hendersonville, Tennessee, was one of the toughest things I've ever had to do. We sang "Loving God, Loving Each Other."

I can remember being on the stage, and immediately in front of us was June in her light blue coffin, and directly in front of that, was Johnny, the once mountain-of-a-man, now frail and broken, confined to a wheelchair. As we began to sing, John reached for a box of tissues and began sobbing. Each of us desperately sought some source of strength or solace amidst all of the sadness. I've never asked my partners how they got through it, but I distinctly remember how I did. As we sang, I searched the crowd—looking for something and nothing in particular. At one point, I saw Ricky Skaggs. Though I've known Ricky for years— he opened for us a few times in the early eighties, and even bought our offices and studio some years back—we have never been especially close. But on this day, as our eyes met, he smiled and nodded, and that simple act gave me the strength that I needed to get through that song. Not long ago, I shared with Ricky just how helpful he was to me that day. His gentle act of kindness had meant so much to me; I wanted to make sure he knew.

Another side of Cash, the man, is reflected in a story that came from this sad day in his life. After the service, Kris Kristofferson was sitting beside John's wheelchair attempting to comfort him. In the midst of their conversation, a woman walked up to them and said, "Excuse me, Mr. Kristofferson, I know this isn't the appropriate time or place, but I may never have the chance to tell you this again, so I wanted to say that I'm a huge fan of yours, and I just really love your singing." After she walked off, Cash turned to Kris and said, "Well, that's one."

Four months after June Carter Cash's funeral, we found ourselves right back in that same church for the funeral of The Man in Black. As many had predicted and worried since June's passing, we feared that John would soon follow, having lost his reason to live. Whether that's exactly what happened or not, it was indeed how it appeared. Johnny Cash had been such an awesome presence in our professional and personal lives; there was no way we could have ever repaid him. On this day, we did the only thing we knew how to do: we sang. Our contribution to the service was "Farther Along." It was one of the toughest performances we ever had to give. I was never so relieved that I had only to sing in four-part harmony with my partners; Duane had to sing a verse of the song solo. I can remember the awe I felt for him, for his ability to get through that alone. I've never asked him how he did it. Perhaps, just like I had done with Ricky a few months earlier, Duane found strength in the unspoken support of someone in the congregation.

I was reminded that I was in that same church, on another extremely difficult day, some ten years earlier, when we sang "Amazing Grace" for the funeral of another icon—my friend and baseball buddy, Conway Twitty. I remember Steve Sanders, who was, at that time, a member of The Oaks, being especially heartbroken as he sat in the pew in front of me. Like me, he was also very close to "the best friend a song ever had," as Conway was known. Conway and I had been friends and neighbors for many years, not to mention partners in the minor league baseball team, the Nashville Sounds. He had died on the road, which was fitting, I suppose, for a touring entertainer. After the funeral, I tried to sneak out the back of the church so I wouldn't have to see or speak to anyone. Before I could get to my car, one of the Nashville news stations cornered me. I tried to respond to the reporter's questions, but I broke down in tears.

Remembering that experience at Conway's funeral, after John's service, I didn't want it repeated, so I made a beeline out the backdoor and to my car. This time I did not stop for the reporters who tried to block my way. Public figure or not, sometimes one simply has to be alone with his thoughts and memories.

Following Cash's funeral, there was to be a small, private graveside service. While my partners didn't attend, at the last minute, as I was heading for home, I decided that I should go. Here was my final opportunity to pay my respects to this man who had been so important to me personally and professionally. I'll never forget the site that greeted us on the drive from the church to the cemetery. The road that runs through that part of Hendersonville is officially named The Johnny Cash Parkway. On the mile-long drive, both sides of the street were lined with fans and mourners, many crying, many holding signs of support or condolence. Though I didn't attend Elvis's funeral, the scene reminded me of some of the pictures that came out of Memphis on that hot August afternoon. It was a last-minute reminder of the impact that Cash had had on the world.

After the service, some of us were just standing around the grave, not even talking, seemingly reluctant to leave, as if staying could somehow maintain our connection to him. From the midst of our silent sadness, Larry Gatlin, in his sweet vibrato tenor, began singing the first lines to a song made famous by Cash's in-laws, The Carter Family. He sang: "Will The Circle Be Unbroken, by and by, Lord, by and by." By the time he got to the next line, we had all joined in and were holding hands. The impromptu choir was comprised of Ronnie Dunn, of the mega duo, Brooks & Dunn; Cash's daughter, Roseanne; Sharon White and her husband Ricky Skaggs; Marty Stuart and his wife, Connie Smith; and myself. "There's a better home awaiting, in the sky, Lord, in the sky."

Johnny Cash's life was well documented. His trials and tribulations, his demons, his wrestling matches with sin were all part of his legacy. He'd often said that he knew he would go to Heaven when he died because he'd suffered his hell here on earth. In the end his faith won out.

It had enabled him to get through those times in darkness, and make it through to the other side. Those trials, his demons, might have been different from mine or anyone else's, but the fact is, we all have them; we all have to face them in our own way. I often reflect on him and his struggles. He showed us that even when we're weak, God is still in charge and just waiting for us to remember to call on Him. There certainly have been times in my life when I forgot God for a little while, but I can attest to the fact that He never forgot me.

As a footnote to the Johnny Cash legacy, in 2006, his heirs sold his lakefront estate to Barry Gibb, of Bee Gees fame. Barry, who is a talented singer and a nice man, was in the process of renovating the house in preparation of moving into it. In April of 2007, the house burned to the ground. The site is just down the street from my home. Because of our friendship, as well as the proximity of our homes, I was contacted by several news agencies for my thoughts. The comment that seemed to resonate the most around the country was when I stated that perhaps this was just God's way of saying that that was Johnny Cash's house and would forever belong to only him. I meant no offense to Barry; it was simply how I felt.

જીજીજી

For Labor Day 1974, we had been invited to appear on the *American Song Festival* at Saratoga Springs Amphitheatre in upstate New York. The festival was a weekend of shows in which the acts, in addition to doing a normal show, were to perform a contest-winning song that had been submitted by an amateur songwriter. We shared the bill with acts as varied as The Pointer Sisters, Jose Feliciano, The Eagles, Helen Reddy, Ray Charles and Roger Miller. It was a pretty prestigious thing for us to be involved in, and we got a great song ("Plant a Seed") that became a regular addition to our show for a long time.

It was an odd time, to say the least. We were appearing on television shows as varied as *The Mike Douglas Show,* and *The Porter Wagoner Show*; we played shows like Saratoga and the Wembley Festival in England; we won another Grammy for Best Gospel Song (for "Where the Soul Never Dies"); and yet, we were broke. Those were our hungriest of years.

Without a doubt, the best thing that would come about, as a result of the Columbia Records association, was that it would lead us to meet the man who would become "Godfather" to us, Jim Halsey. In November of 1974, we were doing a label showcase at the Ryman Auditorium. At those types of functions, the group was always approached by various people who would tell us the things we would want to hear—lots of empty promises and vague offers—but there was something believable about Jim Halsey. Of course we knew his reputation; he owned a very large and successful booking agency in Tulsa. That night at the Ryman, he didn't make us any promises; he just told us that he liked what we did, and that he would keep an eye on us. We'd heard things like that before, but for some reason, in the backs of our minds and our hearts, we believed what he said. Somehow we felt that wasn't the last we'd see of Jim Halsey.

Over the next few months, we continued to work—and starve—ourselves to death. It just seemed like the harder we tried, the worse things became. The traditional gospel audiences seemed to be turning more against us every day, and we hadn't even begun to move into the country-music direction.

We tried to modernize the stage production values of our shows—nothing too elaborate, because, Lord knows, we couldn't afford it—but we were carrying some stage lights. For even that we were ridiculed, not only by supposed fans but also by other gospel acts. We would hear cries of "turn off those lights. This isn't a nightclub. You're supposed to be singing about Jesus." It's fair to say, at first, it troubled us, then hurt our feelings, but, eventually, just helped steel our resolve. We just didn't want to be like every other group, standing stiff onstage in three-piece suits and ties. I'll admit, we wanted to appeal to the younger crowd; we wanted to loosen things up, but we didn't want to change the world. We knew our own hearts. We knew we believed in the words we were singing. But we also knew that music could be modern and fresh and contemporary, and still be good.

When things were at their worst, the vast majority of the mail that we were receiving at our office and fan club was negative. The letters from dissatisfied fans (or former fans) far outnumbered letters of support. It was a challenging time for us. While I would never be so bold as to compare ourselves to such iconic men of God, I have to admit that we felt a little like Paul and Silas, and the story in Acts 16 when they were jailed. They were doing what they thought was right in God's eyes, and were banished because of it. While, of course, we were never physically imprisoned, much like them, all we could do was keep on singing until we found our way out of our situation.

On shows where we were the only act, or the headliner, we didn't have as much of a problem with protests, since those in attendance were coming because they liked what we were doing. And we were still getting a few church dates. At those, we were pretty popular with the young people; they thought we were trendy and cool, with our flashy clothes and long hair.

Most of the demonstrations were occurring on package shows. It got to the point where segments of the audience were planning their "spontaneous" exit-in-protest at a particular point in the show. We would be introduced, and would sing a couple, or a few, songs, and then a group from a particular church would rise and leave the building. I remember once at the Fairgrounds Arena in Richmond, Virginia, it occurred after someone requested that we sing "Green, Green Grass of Home." We did it—for the first and, as far as I remember, only time ever—and, in response, a group of people got up and left.

We were working a series of shows up in New England. The Sego Brothers and Naomi opened the shows to great applause, and then we came out, and a group of the audience stood up, turned their backs and stomped out. Duane, who was doing most of the talking on stage in those days, would never even acknowledge the situation. It was uncomfortable for us, of course, but all we could do was continue on with our show.

Wayne Newton once said to a reporter that artists couldn't worry about the people who didn't come to their shows, but only those who did. That is true for us—and was especially so in those days. We could do nothing to try to entertain the people who didn't like us and who wanted to demonstrate their dislike by leaving the show. What should we have done? Chase after them down the aisles and beg them to come back? Of course not. All we could do was what we knew how to do: Oak Ridge Boys music.

Salem, Virginia was the site of the last gospel show we did. We were on the bill with The Kingsmen and a couple of other groups. The way that the audience treated us—not to mention the other acts on the show—we knew that it was over; we would never do another gospel show like this. After that show, we were on our way to perform in Las Vegas with Johnny Cash, and I remember thinking that he—and that casino audience for which we would perform—would, no doubt, treat us more Christian-like than did this group of gospel performers and fans. We still had Christ in our hearts, and we were willing to continue to sing our style of gospel music, but that door just seemed to be closing for us.

For us, it wasn't only the music that we sang that mattered as much as the music—the belief—that was in our hearts. Later, when country music success replaced the gospel music success, we didn't cease to be Christians. Our beliefs didn't suddenly change. In fact, our country music success has given us the platform to perform in many diverse places—casinos, state fairs, television shows, political forums and others—where gospel music might have never been performed. We always put gospel songs into our shows and part of the reason was to attempt to spread the Word and minister to folks who might need it.

As gospel singers, I'll have to admit that oftentimes it felt like we were only singing to the choir. Of course, I know that wasn't true; there were probably unsaved people in any congregation or audience, but with the country success that came later, we truly felt privileged to be able to sing gospel to an audience that, perhaps, hadn't expected to hear it. We're not booked to preach, so our primary goal is still to entertain the people with the best show possible, but we recognized that one of our shows might be the only time in someone's life when they would ever hear "Amazing Grace." It was a responsibility that we treasured, and one that we took very seriously as part of our mission.

I often wonder what would have become of The Oak Ridge Boys had gospel music fans not rejected us back then. I honestly can't say we would have continued doing only gospel music. The move to country music was gradual—and not completely of our own design—but, at a certain point, we recognized that we had no future in gospel music, and if we didn't change our focus, we would probably end up disbanding. In our minds, it wasn't so much that we'd left the gospel field but that the gospel field had left us. There's no denying that our aspirations probably extended farther than gospel music could take us. We did not fall into country music by accident; it definitely evolved. We had a style of music that we wanted to perform. We'd set out to do it in the gospel world but certain doors closed and other doors opened, and we had to follow our instincts and our hearts, not to mention finding a way to feed our families.

Sometime in the spring of '75, we received a call at our offices from Jim Halsey asking if we were available to open a few country shows for him in the Northeast later that summer. Of course, we jumped at the chance, even though the dates wouldn't mean much money. The reality was, we had almost no dates on the books anyway; gospel promoters had all but stopped using us. The first couple of nights would be opening for Mel Tillis and Tommy Overstreet in Warwick, Rhode Island. The next shows, we would be 475 miles away in North Tonawanda, New York opening for Roy Clark and Tommy Overstreet (ironically in the same building where Joe and I had met Jimmy Dean and The Imperials while we were singing with The Keystone Quartet.)

We rehearsed and prepared like crazy for these two shows. We really saw them as a possibility to break through, so we packed as much of our brand of gospel/country fusion as we could muster into our allotted twenty minutes. And the crowd's response was, to us, overwhelming.

We hit it off great with Mel Tillis, as well. For those who may not know, there was a time when Mel Tillis and his band, The Statesiders, were infamous for being some of the hardest partiers in country music. Though they took their jobs—of performing onstage—very seriously, when they were off stage, they liked to play hard. After that first show, Mel came on our bus and told us that while his band could party with the best, they had never partied with a gospel group. Further, he said that our reputation as partiers preceded us, so, after the show that night, he intended to put us to the test. While I can't say that The Oaks, at that time, really did have a reputation—or whether we deserved one—I can say that those first shows with Mel were memorable, not only for the opportunity they offered us onstage but for the experience of seeing Mel and his band in action off stage. While Mel has settled down—and is a strong Christian now—back in those days, I believe they could have given any rock band a run for their money. Party like a rockstar? That's for amateurs. Show me someone who could party like a Statesider!

Unbeknownst to us at the time, after those Rhode Island shows, word made it back to Halsey in Tulsa just how well The Oaks had done. As a result, he hopped on a plane and flew to Buffalo so he could see exactly what this rocking, quasi-gospel group was doing.

It was after the Saturday night show when he approached us with what has become known in Oaks circles and history as the "three-minute speech." He told us that he felt we were only three minutes from superstardom. By that, he meant that we were only one song—one hit record—from "making it" and he wanted to help us find it. That night, five men shook hands on a deal that has lasted thirty-seven years (and counting!)

Earlier that year (in February of '75) before our association with him, Halsey had begun producing a show called *Country Music U.S.A.* at Howard Hughes' Landmark Hotel and Casino in Las Vegas. Twice a night, the show featured four acts, usually including a headliner, a band, a comic and another singer. The lineup would change every three or four weeks. It was credited with being the first series featuring country music at a major strip hotel. Headliners consisted of Halsey-managed acts including Tommy Overstreet and Hank Thompson, as well as Barbara Fairchild, Lee Roy Van Dyke and Johnny Paycheck. The concept was simple, yet brilliant. While other strip hotels featured major country headliners such as Roy Clark, Freddy Fender and Mel Tillis (all also managed by Halsey, and alums of the Landmark show), Charlie Rich, Buck Owens and Marty Robbins, Halsey could place newer, lesser-known acts in the Landmark's smaller "Jubilee Showroom" for a less-expensive ticket price—about half of what other showrooms charged for headliners. The success of this series was a tribute to Halsey's reputation as a finder-of-talent, as well as his strong relationship with Hughes' Summa Corp, which owned four other Las Vegas properties.

For The Oak Ridge Boys, it meant the opportunity to headline in Vegas for the first time, and probably before we deserved to. Though we had worked in Vegas three times opening for Cash, now we were headlining *Country Music U.S.A* at the Landmark for the then-staggering sum of $5,000 per week. In addition, our rooms and food were paid for! It really helped us survive some of those hard months.

It also marked the first time when, not only would it be acceptable for us to sing some country songs in addition to gospel, it would be expected. In fact, as the story has been told, Jim went to Walter Kane, who worked for the Summa Corp, to ask if it would be okay for The Oaks to sprinkle some gospel into the shows at the Landmark, to which Kane replied, "Absolutely. We have Christians in our casinos too."

Before the engagement began, Halsey had told us that we needed to learn some non-gospel hits by other people until he could get us a record deal and get us some hits of our own. So, we learned some covers to work into our show. These included "Faded Love," which I took the lead on; The Eagles' "Take it Easy;" James Taylor's "How Sweet It Is to Be Loved By You;" Merle Haggard's "Silver Wings," Waylon Jennings' "Good Hearted Woman;" and the Olivia Newton-John song "Let Me Be There."

While The Oaks, as a group, had spent years honing their stagecraft, it had up until recently mostly been on "friendly stages." When we would perform at churches or auditoriums, the audiences were most often there to see us. While we still knew we had to work to give them a great show, we were often starting from a position of familiarity. Las Vegas, on the other hand, provided us with a big stage—figuratively and literally—with our names on the huge marquee out front. With this came a pressure that helped push us to reach that elusive "next level." While there were support acts on the show—great singers like Linda Hart, and comedians like Hank Penny and Pat Buttram—we really felt like it was totally on us to satisfy those ticket-buyers. We knew that many of them were not even familiar with us, but rather just looking to be entertained in a city famous for its entertainers.

It was actually during this period that I had the opportunity to re-connect with my recent past. Elvis was back at the Hilton while we were at the Landmark. I had called Elvis's road manager, Joe Esposito, to see if I could bring my singing partners to see a show and meet Elvis. Though his engagement was cancelled after only five shows, we were, indeed, able to catch one of the shows. All these years later, I can still vividly remember walking across the street from the Landmark to the Hilton. We experienced the same excitement that the other fans felt, walking into that showroom, which, by Vegas standards, was huge.

Sure, he had gained some weight, and he seemed a little tired—sitting on a stool for part of the show—but he still owned any stage he worked on. For this show, he had placed a box in the lobby, into which fans could place song requests. He'd never done anything like that before. As I had already learned during my time with the Stamps, and as I would experience again with The Oaks, long engagements in Las Vegas—or Reno, Tahoe, and later, Branson—could be grueling and a little boring. We would look for ways to break the monotony. No doubt, taking these requests was another way for Elvis to "mix it up" and try to fight the Vegas boredom.

As I sat in the audience and watched this legend do his thing, naturally, my eyes wandered over towards J.D. and the Stamps. I had loved my time with them on that stage, but I didn't regret joining the three guys who now sat beside me in this booth.

After the big gold curtain dropped and the lights came back up, we were led backstage. After a few minutes, Elvis came out from his private dressing room, having freshened up after the show. I was very proud to introduce my partners to him, and he was very gracious making small talk with us, asking how things were going and encouraging us in pursuing our dreams. Later, as the gathering was coming to a close, Elvis motioned for me to follow him towards a quiet corner. He placed his hand on my arm and asked if I'd consider rejoining the group. "What would it take to get you back, Rich?" he asked with that famous Presley charm. I was really floored when he said that. Here he was, surrounded by great musicians and singers, and yet he missed me and my voice. I would be less than honest if I said it didn't make me feel really good. But I also have to say that I never considered it. He was the king and it had been an honor to stand on his stage, but I knew, without the slightest hesitation, that I was now an Oak Ridge Boy and that was what I would remain. He understood my feelings and wished us well. That was the last time I was ever with him, though, in many ways, he remains with me still today.

On a side note, I did "rejoin the group" for one night, in August of 2007, on the thirtieth anniversary of Elvis's death. My schedule with The Oaks had never allowed it, but for this special occasion, I was able to perform with The Stamps at *Elvis—The Concert*, which is a multimedia extravaganza that features the TCB Band, Joe Guercio and his orchestra, the Sweets, and the Stamps and Imperials performing live on stage while Elvis's image appears on gigantic video screens. Engineers have isolated Elvis's voice, recorded in concert, so he "sings" while the other musicians and singers back him up, just like when he was alive. With the proliferation of the video elements of large arena shows—where the audience spends much of their time watching the show onscreen—the effect with this Elvis show is that he's back again and performing onstage. In fact, the show, which has toured all over the world, gained an entry in the *Guinness Book of World Records* as the "first concert tour to be headlined by a performer no longer living." Once again, just as it always was with Elvis, this show is quite a phenomenon.

As I stood on stage, with so many of the same people I'd sung with thirty five-years before, and looked up on those screens and saw Elvis shaking and sweating and singing just like the old days, I was caught up in the moment. That is probably understandable; in fact, I'd expected it. He still had the same effect on me as always. What I didn't expect, however, was the emotion I would experience when J.D. (who had passed away in 1998) appeared onscreen, and The Stamps sang "Sweet, Sweet Spirit" along with him. I have to admit that I had tears in my eyes as I sang along with my old friend and musical hero. It was quite a night. I hope I'm able to experience it again at a future show.

৯৯৯

Not long after our dates at the Landmark, Jim booked us in the lounge at Harrah's in Reno and Lake Tahoe. We would do three forty-five-minute shows, each night, for ten nights in each location. Now, to most Las Vegas entertainers, playing the lounges was considered a downgrade from playing the showrooms, but at this point in our careers, The Oaks were less concerned about "appearances" and more concerned with surviving. In fact, in this instance, playing the lounges was, in no way, a come down because Jim was able to book us in at a mind-blowing salary of $10,000 per week. At that point, we really thought we had made it. We just couldn't see how things could get any better than that.

Of course, it did get better. As America's bicentennial year dawned, we were appearing with Roy Clark at The Frontier in Las Vegas. From there, we were off to conquer new worlds and foreign lands. On January 17, 1976, we flew from Tulsa (where the Jim Halsey Agency was based) to New York's JFK Airport, en route to the Soviet Union to tour with Roy Clark, on what would become the first country music tour ever behind the Iron Curtain. We would play eighteen shows in twenty-one days.

Weeks before we would depart, we attended briefings by the U.S. State Department. They advised us on what we could expect on our trip; the things we would be allowed to do as well as the things that would be prohibited. They told us to never become comfortable, to never leave our group or our hotel and wander off alone because, as they said, "This is a Communist country and the bottom line is, they don't like us." They kept saying that the worst thing we could do was to underestimate the severity of the situation. (One thing I specifically remember them cautioning us against was the dangers of associating with any Soviet women. Needless to say, the diplomatic officials got our attention.)

We were also required to submit the lyrics to each of the songs on our set lists. This was non-negotiable, as they wanted to ensure that we would not sing any songs with a message that might threaten their way of life. The one song that they found troubling was our recent Grammy-winner "Where the Soul of Man Never Dies." They had a problem with the opening line: "To Canaan Land I'm on my way, where the soul of man never dies." Ironically, they did not have a problem with the fact that it was a gospel song—in fact, we would do "Have a Little Talk With Jesus," every night, which they seemed to have no problem with. Instead, apparently the problem was that there was no Russian word to translate "Canaan Land." They either didn't know that it was another word for Heaven, or they didn't care. Their solution to the "problem" was to replace the words "Canaan Land" with the word "Disneyland" because even in the Soviet Union, they understood what Disneyland was. Our counter-proposal to their idea was to change "Canaan Land" to "that fair land," which they approved, thereby averting an international incident!

When we landed in Moscow, it was twenty-five degrees below zero. The frigid temperature matched the warmth of the relations between the Soviet Union and America at the time. There was so much suspicion and distrust in the eyes of the people we'd see, but we knew that deep inside, they were humans with the same wants and needs that we had. We were there on what was, officially, termed a "goodwill tour" and we intended to bring them some good old-fashioned American goodwill.

Twenty-one days later, we looked back on what had been a successful trip in every sense of the word. We were able to deliver the goodwill we intended for them, and we were proven right in that they had plenty to give us in return. There were many memorable, even life-changing, moments for us: the roaring adulation from huge crowds seemingly starved for entertainment; the hunger and poverty of a people living in a bland, monochromatic and oppressive world; the ever-present soldiers with their machine guns in-hand. I think more than anything else, what this trip did for me was make me a better American. Prior to the trip, I had never thought much about politics. I'm ashamed to say, I had never even voted. I would occasionally watch the news but just had never been that interested in current events. Like so many others, I just moved through life more concerned about my own little piece of the world, and ignorant to the fact that what happened in our country, and around the world, could impact me.

After we got over there and I actually got to see first hand how oppressive their society was—to see people who lived their lives day after day without the ability to make the simplest of choices for themselves—it really affected me. Though I'd always been proud to be an American, and thankful for my Christian foundation, I felt like I was finally getting some teeth to my feelings. People in this part of the world were risking their lives to attend prayer services. They were smuggling Bibles so that others could learn of God's love. It made me realize the ease with which we could become "lukewarm" in our worship. Sure, I knew exactly where my Bible was at home but not because I had spent time studying it the way I should. I'll admit I felt a little shame—some conviction. Attending church wasn't always possible because of our touring schedule—I'd long since come to accept that—but nothing prevented me from spending more time in the Word. I promised myself (and God) that I would try and do better in that area of my life.

Some of the differences we experienced over there were absolutely shocking. We were not allowed to lock our hotel rooms. Joe and I roomed together, and many were the nights when, without warning, the door to the room would open, and in would walk what we always assumed were members of the KGB. Without even speaking, they would search our rooms. One of the men always held something that looked like a Geiger counter. He would wave it over our bags and along the walls. The State Department had warned us that we would face these sorts of indignities, but it was a helpless and infuriating feeling.

We were assigned a "Government Minder" (whom we jokingly referred to as our tour guide.) It was his job to stay with us and observe us to ensure none of us wandered away, or otherwise did anything that might be perceived as a threat. As we would move from one city to the next, he would point out landmarks, and, according to him, each was "the biggest in the world" or "the finest anywhere" or "the nicest in all of Europe." As we entered one city—St. Petersburg, I believe—we passed a huge, vacant building clearly showing the decaying signs that accompany abandonment. He proudly proclaimed, "This used to be the stock exchange, but as you know, we no longer have the need for a stock exchange, so we closed it." While he tried to pass off this propaganda to us, I knew that what he meant was that the stock exchange had been rendered obsolete because there was no free enterprise, and that hit me like a ton of bricks.

Often, as we passed through towns in which we'd performed, locals would come to the bus and knock on the windows. They would tell us how much they'd enjoyed the show and how much they loved us. Then, as quickly as they appeared, they would look over their shoulders, duck their heads and skulk away, afraid of getting caught being friendly—or even worse, somehow praising something from the evil western world.

Upon our return to the states, for the first time in my life I understood why people might kiss the ground of their homeland when they return. While I didn't literally do that, the first thing I did do was go to the county registrars office and register to vote. And ever since then, I've done everything in my power never to miss the opportunity to cast my vote, not only in the "important" national elections but in local and state races and in the primaries as well as the general elections. I had learned my lesson and learned it well. They were all important, and America was a country worth protecting!

సౌసౌసౌ

Life for us, back home in America, started to get busier. Halsey kept us working, appearing with some of his great artists, including Mel Tillis, Freddy Fender, and Tommy Overstreet (in addition to Roy). Some shows from our January Las Vegas engagement with Roy had been taped and made into a TV show that began airing. For a little act that was barely making it, we sure felt good about our lives and career.

Paul Simon, the singer-songwriter who, at that time, was best known as half of the former duo Simon & Garfunkel, had gained some solo success with hits such as "Mother and Child Reunion," and "Kodachrome." His latest record, "Loves Me Like a Rock" which included a black gospel group, The Dixie Hummingbirds, singing back up, had been his first Number One. When he wrote, "Slip Slidin' Away," in 1976, he decided he wanted to feature a southern gospel group singing back up. He called the *Gospel Music Association* to ask them for some recommendations. They suggested a few groups including The Oaks. We had actually met Paul once at the Grammy telecast the year we won for "Where the Soul of Man Never Dies," so after reviewing the tapes, he decided that we had the sound he was looking for, and he contacted us. He flew us up to New York first class (the first time for me) and put us up in a fine hotel. The thing I remember most about the session was how much he wore us down. Before they ever even rolled taped, he had us sing the song repeatedly. I really worried that we were going to wear out our voices before we could lay down the track. But it turns out, that was exactly what he was trying to do: make us lose the edge in our voice.

On one of the countless passes, he suddenly stopped us and said, "That's the sound I want." He walked over and unlocked a cabinet standing in the corner; he removed a bottle of Jack Daniels, poured himself a shot and said, "Let's cut this song." Once he'd worn us down, the session went pretty well.

I remember that the Boston Red Sox were in town to play the Yankees. Joe and I wanted to go if we could finish the session in time. Finally, I just asked Paul straight out how long he thought we might be and if he thought there was a chance we'd be done in time to see the game. He smiled and said, "Richard, I can guarantee it. I'm a season ticket holder, and I can promise you, I'm gonna be at that game too!" All three of us made it to the game, but not before we cut what would become a top five pop hit for Paul. It was a good day all around.

My most vivid memory related to the song after we'd recorded it is the day I was driving in Hendersonville between my house and The Oaks' office. While stopped at a red light, the song came on the radio. As I reached for the volume knob, another car pulled alongside me, and through my open window I could hear the song also playing on their radio. It was all I could do to keep from calling over to the other driver to inform him that I was one of the voices singing on his radio. It probably wouldn't have mattered much to him, but I would have sure liked to have been able to tell him.

❧❧❧

After our third and final release for Columbia, and the completion of our contract with them, Halsey was able to get us a record deal with

Jim Fogelsong, on his ABC/DOT label (which would later become MCA.) Next, we would need to find a producer. One of the producers in the ABC stable was label vice president, Ron Chancey, who had signed Jimmy Buffett, and produced, among others, Billy Crash Craddock. Fogelsong asked Ron if he would travel to Oklahoma City (where we were performing with Jimmy Dean) to check out our show and see if he wanted to produce us. He was hesitant at first because we were known primarily as a gospel act. He wasn't sure he would know how to produce us. Additionally, Ron had a very lucrative contract doing commercials for Anheuser Busch, and he didn't want to jeopardize that in any way.

As much out of company duty as legitimate interest, Ron agreed to come see us perform. We met with him before the show, which went well, and, apparently he liked what he saw from us that night because the next thing we knew, he had signed on to produce us. Later we heard that he'd told Fogelsong, "I don't know how we could ever capture their excitement on a record, but if we ever can, we are going to make some hit records!" Of course, there was no way for us to know if the association was going to work; only time would tell.

In August of 1976, we started searching for songs to record. As he had done so well in the past, Duane found some great material, but for the first time, he had someone, in Ron, who could help him. Two of the first songs that came, almost immediately, was a mid-tempo song called "Y'all Come Back Saloon" and an upbeat cover, originally recorded by Glen Campbell, titled "You're the One in a Million." We knew immediately we wanted to record them. These were followed quickly by a heartbreaking ballad, "I'll Be True to You," a couple of bluegrass numbers, and a song called "Freckles," (which years later would serve as proof that the Vice President of the United States was a real fan!)

The songs were chosen, and the studio time was booked for just after New Years, 1977. Suddenly, we felt like a rocket ship that was sitting on the launch pad.

CHAPTER SIX: *Silver Jingle, Gold Records*

S ome think that we made our move to country with a reckless disregard for our gospel audience, but nothing could be further from the truth. We always appreciated those who had been fans of The Oak Ridge Boys. As I've said, our fans were never the ones who'd protested us; it was fans of others who never particularly liked us anyway. In fact, we knew that if we had any chance of making in-roads in country music, it would happen, in no small measure, because of our fans—and that's exactly what happened.

We wanted a country hit for sure, and we thought we just might have found one in "Y'all Come Back Saloon." We first heard the demo sung by the writer, Sharon Vaughn, who would later write such hits as "My Heroes Have Always Been Cowboys." We loved the song, though we were a little leery of some of the lyrics. First, of course, we were a little worried about singing a song with the word "saloon" in the title, as if that might be perceived as thumbing our nose at our past. But it was such a great song—we actually thought that Sharon could have had a hit with her demo; it was just that good—that we decided not to discount it just because of the title.

We were also a little concerned with the line "late night benediction." We worried over whether that would be perceived as sacrilegious, but ultimately we decided to keep it. The line was so integral to the meaning of the song, and the dictionary did provide some similar, non-religious meanings, so we felt we could sing it and still maintain our morals.

We did, however, go to Sharon and ask her to rewrite one line that we thought just went a little farther than we were comfortable with. The line spoke of "lifting his glass as a tithe and offering," and that just didn't seem right to us. Sharon graciously agreed to change the lines and it became "lifting high his glass in honor of the lady and the song." With that, we began recording our first strictly country album.

This wasn't the first time we'd had an experience with lyrics we weren't comfortable with, but it was the first time we felt like we could do something about it. A couple of years earlier, we'd received a call asking us if we would sing backup on a recording session with Jimmy Buffett, who, at that time, recorded for ABC Records. He was in Nashville working on his *Havana Daydreamin'* release featuring his own brand of "gulf and western" music. While this was about two years before "Margaritaville" would change the trajectory of his career, by this time he was already making waves with soon-to-be-classics like "Come Monday" and "Trying to Reason with the Hurricane Season." We jumped at the chance to record with Buffett, so we immediately committed to doing so.

Our excitement was tempered almost immediately after we arrived at the studio. I can still remember the sinking feeling in my stomach as I approached the music stand that held the lyrics. It was a song titled "My Head Hurts, My Feet Stink and I Don't Love Jesus." What in the world had we gotten ourselves into? We were still doing gospel almost exclusively. We weren't sure that our status in the gospel world could survive this; it was already on tenuous standing. In addition, the title of the song just seemed so counter to our personal beliefs and feelings. True, if you actually pay attention to the lyrics, the song isn't overtly anti-

Christian, it's just intended to be a funny way of describing the exaggerated morning remnants of a night spent carousing. But at that moment, we didn't have much faith that we'd get a pass because of the semantics of the lyrics. All we could imagine were headlines confirming what many of our detractors already seemed to believe: "Oak Ridge Boys don't love Jesus!"

It really bothered me a lot to have to sing this song. I knew it would disappoint many of our fans and my family. I knew that God knew my heart, but the fact was, I also knew my heart and I knew this song wasn't the kind of music I wanted to sing. We had committed to sing on the session, and I knew we would have trouble getting out of it. We followed through on our commitment to Jimmy and the record company, and we sang our hearts out in the session. While we were there, we added our voices to another song on the record: the fun and tame-by-comparison, Steve Goodman romp "This Hotel Room." Though we couldn't believe we were hoping against a song on which we sang to be a hit record for Jimmy—or anyone, for that matter—thankfully, for us, the song wasn't released as a single and didn't become one of Jimmy's classics (and thankfully for him, many others did!) We certainly didn't want to have anything to do with hurting Jimmy's career but we really didn't want to kill our own!

The main takeaway for me personally—and for the group—was that we agreed to never again commit to singing a song without first knowing that we would be comfortable, professionally and personally, with the lyrics and the message. Admittedly, that's very different than saying we would never record a song that might offend any one person; that's a standard I never felt compelled to follow. I understood that I had to be true to the dictates of the relationship that I shared with God—not to some other standard established by someone else. And looking back over all of the songs that we have recorded, I can say we remained true to that commitment.

Coming back to June of 1977, "Y'all Come Back Saloon" was released as our first country single, and it would become a hit. I can remember the bus pulling into a truck stop just outside of Houston, Texas. I went in to get something to eat, and I couldn't believe it when I heard "Y'all Come Back Saloon" playing in the restaurant. It was coming from the jukebox. I went over to look and, sure enough, for the first time ever, I saw our little forty-five spinning. I was in shock; we hadn't known—or even considered—that MCA might service our record to jukebox operators. I ran back to the bus to get my partners. We ran back inside, and began plugging quarters into that jukebox. We were like little kids with a brand new toy. (Of course, thankfully, it became more commonplace to see that record, and others, on jukeboxes around the country. But I can assure you; we never took it for granted.)

"Y'all Come Back Saloon" shot all the way to Number Three on the *Billboard* charts, and went gold. This happened, in part, because of the phone calls that radio stations received to play the song. Certainly, as more stations began to play it, it gained some fans on its own—just because it was a great song—but those stations around the country might not have given it the chance to become a hit had it not been for those first phones calls that came pouring in. And we know—and knew then—that those callers were fans who had begun following The Oak Ridge Boys during our gospel years. So, not only did changing those lyrics ease our personal concerns, I think it had the added benefit of not alienating our fans.

The album, also titled *Y'all Come Back Saloon,* was released in September of 1977 and also included one subtle visual change. Through the sixties and early seventies, The Oaks had always included their band members in the pictures on album covers. It was a conscious decision to try and foster camaraderie with the band—to let them know that they were vital to the group. Though that sentiment remained, with this release, Halsey convinced us that it wasn't the best course for us to follow. While he appreciated our sensitivity to including the band in all of our cover shots, he convinced us that the time for that was past. He said only the four singers should be pictured on the covers; we needed to sell ourselves. We compromised for the *Y'all Come Back Saloon cover*—a photo that was taken at the Bucket of Blood Saloon in Virginia City, Nevada— keeping the band in the shot but grouping the four of us together, and closest to the camera. On every cover from that point on, though, only the four singing members would appear in the cover shot.

కికికి

Photo sessions are a tiring but vital aspect of the music business. Whether for promotional use, for album (now CD) covers or for some other commercial need, we constantly seem to be standing in front of a camera, singularly or as a group. I'm not complaining; in fact, I'm thrilled that, even today, we still have the need for new photos—a lot of artists don't. But while, on the surface it may seem as if it would be a no-stress day spent simply posing for pictures, it really is much more involved. It requires artistic direction, fashion design, make up, and travel time to the location, just to get ready for the shoot. Then, the actual photo shoots take several hours, during which we'll each change clothes numerous times. They are almost always very long days, but again, my partners and I recognize that we are extremely blessed to still have a career that requires this of us.

Sometimes the artistic direction puts us in unique situations. When we were shooting the album cover for *Step On Out* in 1995, some-one had the idea to photograph us, in the lobby of Nashville's Vanderbilt Plaza Hotel, walking a cougar on a leash. It was a tame cat, but as the day wore on, his purring became much more growl-like. We just knew that any minute he was going to snap, and chew one of our faces off! Thankfully, it might have been more our own trepidation and imagination at play than anything else, but we were not sorry when that shoot wrapped.

There was another time when we faced an aggressive animal—and this one wasn't our imagination. We were doing promotional shots on the grounds of Wayne Newton's *Casa de Shenandoah* ranch in Las Vegas. The ranch is a forty-two acre idyllic setting of beautiful gardens, the main house, stables, and several additional buildings. On the property, Wayne also keeps a veritable menagerie featuring many prize Arabian horses, several peacocks, penguins, ducks and other animals. At the time of our shoot, he also had a kangaroo, and while it wasn't scheduled to be part of our photo session, it definitely made its presence felt while we were there. The caretaker said we were doing the shoot in the kanga-roo's "spot" and he was pretty protective of it. In other words, we were invading his territory, and he was willing to fight to protect it.

It made perfect sense to us, simply, to move to another spot; per-haps the territory of a nice golden retriever puppy or some other cuddly pet. But, the photographer had a different vision and it involved us re-maining where we were, regardless of the kangaroo. The mad marsupial would bounce towards us, almost shadow boxing—just like in those old Bugs Bunny cartoons—dart and duck, bob and weave, and then move back away before taking another hopping run at us. I'm sure that if the rolls of film from that day could be reviewed, they would show each of us—or all of us—watching out of the corner of our eyes, ready to get out the kangaroo's charging path. Thankfully, we all survived the shoot, and, I hope the kangaroo was finally, again, able to relax as the reigning king of his spot.

☙☙☙

By the time of *Y'all Come Back,* all four members were actually partners in the group. Prior to that Joe and I had been employees on salary. But, as commercial success began to seem a real possibility instead of an empty dream, Duane and Golden, to their credit, wanted to ensure that Joe and I not only felt like partners in our progress, but, in fact, were partners and, as such, could share in the success that we hoped lay on our horizon. It was a gracious act, and one that I greatly appreciated.

In fact, in an unusual, if not unprecedented, show of magnanimity—and to show just how serious Duane and Golden were about making the entire group feel a part of the success—they offered everyone in the band the opportunity to buy in. As it turns out, none of the band members took them up on the offer, but, at that time, Joe and I did each buy in, to the tune of ten-percent, which was all we could afford. As hit records started to come, Joe and I continued to buy-in, to increase our percentage of ownership—a total of three separate times, in fact—until we became equal partners in the group.

With our new partnership, we also shared responsibilities in the group. Golden continued to serve as our manager, overseeing the business decisions. Duane remained involved with publishing, but also, he and Joe managed our merchandise. Back then we referred to it as "the record table." They made sure we had plenty of our records, tapes and sheet music in stock, and also manned the table at our shows. Though I also began doing our media interviews back then, my job was, primarily, to take care of the bus. When we toured, we would share in the driving of the bus; we would take shifts. But when we were off the road, it was my job to keep the bus clean, and to make sure that the tires were good, and the service kept up to date.

One hot afternoon in August of 1977, I took the bus to the General Tire dealership up in Gallatin, Tennessee, a few miles north of our offices. While I was there, with the bus up on the rack getting new tires, the manager working behind the desk said, "Mr. Sterban you have a phone call." Obviously, this was highly unusual. The office knew where I was, but there would be no reason for them to need to call me here. I went to the phone, and it was Norah Lee Allen, Duane's wife. She said, "Richard, have you heard? There's terrible news. Elvis has died." I couldn't believe it. It hit me like a ton of bricks. It just didn't seem possible that Elvis could have passed away. I was filled with so many thoughts and emotions, I don't even remember driving the bus back to the office. It was a sad few days—for me personally, but also for the country, and even the world. As our old friends The Statler Brothers later wrote and sung in their song "Child of the Fifties," "when Elvis died, we all knew that we could too."

As mentioned earlier, around this time, we were booked to do some shows with Jimmy Dean, the legend that Joe and I had met years before in North Tonawanda. They went very well and we ended up working with him fairly regularly. We would open the show, then come back out in the middle of Jimmy's shows and perform with him. He included a song from the Broadway show *Mame* that we would sing with him, just like we'd seen The Imperials do. He would always bring a woman up from the crowd to play the role of Auntie Mame, and we would dance around her, singing to her. It was a funny bit that the audience always enjoyed.

One of the highlights, of course, that he'd save for when we were back out there with him, was his smash hit "Big Bad John." Even though he sung the low notes on the record, when he performed it live on stage, he'd always time it so he was walking past my microphone as he got to the line "Big Jo--hn," and then he'd move his mic to my mouth, and I would sing "Big Bad John." The crowd ate it up.

As "Y'all Come Back Saloon" was winding up its run on the charts, our appearances with Jimmy were beginning to change pretty significantly. When we would finish our opening slot, the crowd would scream for more. When he'd bring us back out to sing with him, they would scream even louder. Jimmy could tell our star was beginning to rise, and so could we. To his credit, never once did Jimmy get upset with us or accuse us of trying to steal the spotlight. Instead, one night he called us to the dressing room and said, "Fellas, I love ya, but I think it's time for you to go out on your own. I can see it coming; you're gonna be big stars. I just don't think y'all need me anymore." I'm sure it wasn't an easy thing for him to say, but not only did we appreciate him saying it, I sincerely believe that he was proud of us and meant what he said. Jimmy Dean was a big star back in the day; he had hit records and hit television shows, and he was an accomplished actor. Of course, in

1969, he started a sausage company that grew into a mega-million dollar worldwide brand. Even eight years later when we were working with him, he was still working on recipes. Many were the nights that he would cook for us on a stove in his hotel suite, and the menu always included sausage. He was good to us professionally and personally. His friendship meant a lot to us.

As 1977 drew to a close, the second single from *Y'all Come Back Saloon*, "You're the One in a Million" reached Number Two on the charts and we were nominated for two Grammys: Best Country Album for *Y'all Come Back Saloon,* and Best Gospel Performance for "Just a Little Talk With Jesus." We won our fourth Grammy for the gospel song and were thrilled to have been nominated in a country category, as well. Even as we found ourselves back in the studio to record the second album with Chancey, we achieved our elusive first Number One record, when "I'll Be True To You" found its way to the top of the charts. It was an unbelievable feeling of achievement.

It did create an interesting dilemma for us, however. In our role of opening shows for other artists, we would often have only twenty minutes to perform. We'd always pace our show so that we'd open with a rousing song to really grab the attention of the audience. Around this time, most often that would be "You're the One in a Million," but then we'd need to keep them up. Joe would have to welcome them and tell them who we were and introduce the next song. By this time, we would already be seven or eight minutes into our allotted twenty. Of course, the crowd would expect us to perform our current Number One record— and, of course, we wanted to—but it was an almost-four-minute-long song about a woman who drinks herself to death over an unrequited love. It was a gut-wrenching song that also took a huge chunk of the time we had. We did it, though—every night—and, in retrospect, I believe it helped us understand the importance of pacing a show.

The next three years were a whirlwind. We released three more albums: *Room Service, Oak Ridge Boys Have Arrived,* and *Together* plus a greatest hits package, and sold over three million records. Every single we released was a hit. We won thirteen major, national awards, the most prestigious of which included "Best Vocal Group" from the *Academy of Country Music* ('77 and '79) and the *Country Music Association* ('78) as well as awards from *Music City News, Billboard, Cashbox* and *Radio & Records.* Chancey even got into the act winning "Producer of the Year" from the *ACM.*

In late 1979, we were part of another historical occurrence. Kenny Rogers, riding a crest of smash hit records, was the first country artist to do an arena tour. The bill for what was named "The Full House Tour" consisted of Kenny, The Oak Ridge Boys, and Dottie West. Of course, now, some country artists are doing stadium tours but back then it was a huge deal when Kenny took the major step to move out of theaters and auditoriums and do an entire tour of the newer, larger arenas, averaging 12,000–15,000 seats. We would do ninety shows, and, by the time it was over, that tour was the highest grossing tour in country music history. Each night, we would work "in the round" meaning that the circular stage would be situated in the center of the arena floor, and the audience would be seated 360 degrees around it. The band would be on the floor so that the audience had a clear view of the artist. In theaters in the round—places like the old Valley Forge Music Fair just outside of Philadelphia, Westbury Music Fair on Long Island, and the Circle Star Theatre in San Francisco—the stages were constructed to rotate slowly, thus allowing the audience all the way around the room to see the performers, but, in these coliseums, the stage would be fixed.

An arena configuration, with a stationary stage, is easier for a solo performer; for a quartet, it created some challenges. Rather than standing side by side the way we had done for years, the four of us had to learn to work different sides of the stage so that those seated on every side would feel a part of the show. While it was hard at first, we finally found our comfort level. Apparently, however, we learned it a little too well because, eventually, we began to get complaints from the audience that they never saw us standing together. With that, we had to concentrate, once again, on not only working to every corner of the room individually, but also to consciously come together as a group on all sides of the stage throughout the show so that everyone would see us and get the photographs they wanted. Though, we rarely ever worked in the round when we started headlining the major arenas on our own, we still employed many of the lessons we learned from our time with *The Gambler*. We'd long known that our musical journey would be a never-ending education process.

One of the most important lessons that an act has to learn when moving to arenas and larger venues is to make every attendee, in every row, feel and know that they are part of the show. In the small auditoriums and, even, churches, that we had played for years, this was easier to do. During the lean times, there were some shows with so few people, I almost felt as if we could have learned everyone's names. As the venues got bigger and the crowds larger, we had to learn to increase our awareness, as well. Any artist who has been blessed with this opportunity and challenge could attest to the fact that it's not as easy as it might sound. The stage lights and spotlights make it difficult to see past the first couple of rows, so you have to rely on a deeper connection. Over the course of one of our shows, the audience will notice each of us working every corner of the room. As Duane has always said, the energy of an audience builds from the last row in the balcony while a standing ovation begins in the front and works its way back.

Most every artist, who achieves any level of success, started in small rooms with small crowds. If they are blessed to grow into an act that can fill an arena, they would benefit from remembering those early days. The Oak Ridge Boys definitely do remember. All through the years—whether we were opening for Roy or Kenny or Cash, or whether we were headlining—we got excited with the crowds that came to our shows, and we still do! We'll give our all to make sure every person in that audience understands that we came to entertain them.

Of course, "entertainment" can come in many forms. A couple of years after the Kenny tour, when we were headlining big arenas on our own, we were playing at Roberts Stadium in Evansville, Indiana. This was a rare arena show where we headlined and played in the round. As we had learned to do with Kenny, we were working the stage with each of us playing to a different side of the audience. During the opening song, ("You're the One in a Million"), it became obvious that Joe was getting a much bigger response than the rest of us. He would run to the left side of the stage, and the crowd would go crazy. He would run to the right, and Duane would move to the left, and the right side would go crazy. I have to admit it was so noticeable that we couldn't help but wonder what was happening. As the song ended, Joe slowed down and began his welcoming remarks to the crowd. During this, a young woman came to the edge of the stage trying to get Joe's attention. While, especially during those days, it wasn't uncommon for girls to want to talk or shake hands or ask for a kiss or something, this girl was different. It was pretty clear she had a message for Joe. She was so insistent that Joe stopped talking and leaned down to see what she wanted. We couldn't hear what she said, but like he had been shot from a cannon, Joe jumped up and spun around and zipped the zipper on his pants. It seems that while getting ready for the show, Joe had failed to "close the barn door" and as he jumped around on the stage, his neon red underwear was making itself very visible. We tore the house down in Evansville that night, but I have to admit that we got no bigger ovation from the crowd than when Joe zipped up.

We went into the Christmas holidays of 1980 tired from touring almost non-stop, but energized from the success that had come our way. We were riding higher than ever, and we'd loved every minute of it. We knew that we had only just started our journey; there was so much more to accomplish. We were ready to see what the new decade would bring. All we had to do was stay the course, stay together, and stay focused. We could have never known the highs we would see, or the lows we would feel. And we could have never known that it would all begin with a gal named Elvira.

CHAPTER SEVEN: *Oom Poppa Mau Mau*

I t's been said that it's difficult, if not impossible, to fully appreciate or understand the magnitude of something as it's happening. While that might be true in some circumstances, I can honestly say that I— and we—could not have been any more aware of what was happening to us, as we rode the crest of the "Elvira" wave. We had struggled for so long, and then, enjoyed success, but, somehow, we knew we had not yet peaked. We knew that bigger things awaited us, and while I must admit we didn't exactly know that it would be "Elvira," it definitely didn't take long for us to realize it.

We'd had ten Number One records when we went back into the studio for what would become our *Fancy Free* project. All of the songs were selected, and the session was set for the first two weeks of January 1981, since the month after Christmas was, typically, a "down time" for The Oak Ridge Boys. Meanwhile, a song-plugger named Ronnie Gant, who worked for Tree Publishing, was in his home state of Texas for the Christmas holidays. One night, he was in a club, and heard the house band sing "Elvira" which was a song that had been recorded several times by then. When Ronnie got back to his office, he pulled out the original demo by Dallas Frazier, who had written it. He sent it to Ron Chancey, and the following week, at our final pre-session meeting, Chancey played it for us, and, immediately, we got excited. There was just something about it that we loved. We didn't care if it had been cut before; we didn't care that it was basically a novelty song. We just knew it was for us. It was a similar reaction to the one we'd had when Ron first played us Sharon Vaughn's version of "Y'all Come Back Saloon." Something about it just seemed special.

Recording sessions, though sometimes stressful and certainly hard work, can also be a lot of fun. You're in a room with no windows to the outside world, surrounded by some of the best musicians in the world; you're singing new songs—each one perhaps the next hit record. When things are right, the studio can be a very cool place. Looking back on the "Elvira" session, it seemed even the session players knew that some magic was being created. There were smiles all around as we laid down the tracks, and as we heard the song beginning to come together. I specifically remember the great guitarist, Jimmy Capps, who has played on hundreds of hit records (and is now known as the "Sheriff" on RFD-TV's *Larry's Country Diner*), just smiling and laughing as we worked on that song. The excitement and energy was just infectious.

Immediately after the session, we were back out on the road doing concerts through the Pacific Northwest. One night in Spokane, Washington, we decided to try "Elvira" out onstage for the first time. We dropped it in the middle of the show, with no introduction or explanation; we just sang it. The place went absolutely crazy; they loved it. We looked at each other and just smiled; we knew we possessed something big. They wouldn't stop cheering until we sang it again...and again... and again. Right there, in the middle of the show, we encored it. None of us remember exactly how many times we encored it—it was either three or five—but no matter how many times it was, it wasn't enough because we sang it once more at the end of the show, and the crowd, again, went crazy.

To make sure it wasn't just some strange anomaly, we sang it the next night in Portland, Oregon, and we got the same reaction. After the show, we called Ron to tell him what had happened and to tell him that "Elvira" needed to be the first single off of the album. Thankfully, Ron made MCA believe it, and it was the first single. Suffice it to say that ever since that night in January of 1981, in Spokane, Washington, The Oak Ridge Boys have never once performed a concert in which we did not sing "Elvira."

Before it finished its tremendous run, "Elvira" had sold more than two million copies as a single—almost unheard of, even in those days—and another three million for the album. It topped the country chart, and then crossed over to top the pop charts. It won us our first Grammy for a country record; won "Single of the Year" for the *ACMs, CMAs* and *Music City News* awards; and it was the most played song on radio for the year. It even won Chancey another "Producer of the Year" award, this one from the *CMA*. It absolutely carried us to another stratosphere. The song, especially the lines I sang, was seemingly on everybody's lips. It was unbelievable.

In a demonstration of how good "Elvira" was for all involved, as it was taking over the music world, MCA showed its gratitude to us by presenting us each with the biggest, heaviest Rolex watch I'd ever seen. It was like wearing an alarm clock on my wrist, but it was a very generous gesture, and I still have it. It was a reminder that our hard work was not only paying off for us, but also for others involved with us.

In addition to such tangible benefits, however, there were also less beneficial results. With our success came an unprecedented opportunity for excess. Looking back, I think it's true that God won't give us more than we can handle. The Stamps were in a "tame period" when I'd first joined. This allowed me to mature some before the wilder times presented themselves. Likewise, though temptations abounded for us during the Elvis years, the opportunity to see how much more difficult his road was allowed me to gain some perspective. During these go-go years with The Oaks, it took all of the discipline we could muster—and all the grace that we could find—to escape some of the traps of excess.

Every possible version of sin presented itself to us. Virtually any woman we could have wanted, any drug that existed, any situation that we could imagine (and many that we could have never imagined) were all there for the taking. In part, it had to do with the times—the free-wheeling, get rich, greedy, excess 1980s—and, in part, it was the result of the wild success we were experiencing. That we survived to live to tell about it is more a testament to God's grace than anything else. We found it sufficient to cover any appetites that could have destroyed us.

It would be disingenuous of me to claim that I always lived the life that reflected what I knew, in my heart, to be right. It's difficult to stay grounded in the midst of the hectic pace and the seemingly endless success. No matter how far I strayed though, I always understood that I was failing God; He wasn't failing me. As I Kings 19:11-13 tells us, God rarely hits us over the head with His love or with His judgment. He doesn't come in the storm or the earthquake, but rather in that "still small voice." Even when the idea of listening was far from my mind, I was still aware of that still small voice. It always brought me back to where I was supposed to be living. And for that, I am grateful.

ক্ষ ক্ষ ক্ষ

In all humility, we really had it going for a while. For about ten years, it seems like every thing we did with Ron Chancey turned into gold (records.) There's a reason we call him the fifth Oak Ridge Boy. That was a special time for us, and nobody was hotter during those years than the five of us.

As Bonsall has long said: "It's all about the song." You have to have good material in order to have any chance at all to make hit records. With a group, there's obviously a different dynamic than with a solo artist, in that the decision has to be made who will sing lead on the song. When gathering songs for a project, it always amazed me how frequently we all thought the same thing. It was as if the songs spoke to us, and we immediately knew, without even saying anything, which one of us should sing the lead.

One of Chancey's strengths was finding songs with a specific idea in mind of who should sing lead on it. Sometimes they were new songs, or, sometimes, covers. The most obvious example of a cover that still became a hit was "Elvira," and it was Chancey's idea that Joe should sing lead, and that I should do the "Oom poppa mau mau" lines alone. A couple of years earlier, Chancey had put out a call to the publishers and songwriters in town that he was looking for a song that would be good for a bass singer to sing the lead on. At the same time, Diane Petty, who ran ABC/Dunhill, the publishing arm at ABC/DOT Records, told Ron that her immediate wish was to get an Oak Ridge Boys cut. Ron challenged her to find something for me to sing the lead on. In the less than a week, she brought him a song that the Righteous Brothers had recorded, called "Dream On." As soon as we heard it, we knew that it could be a great song for me. I was pleased with the record we cut. I was really happy when I heard "Dream On" would be a single. And, of course, we were all ecstatic when it became a Number One record for us.

Other times, Chancey found songs on which we would share the leads. "Dig A Little Deeper (In the Well)," which was never a single but always a fan favorite, was one such song. Perhaps the best example was "American Made," from 1983, on which we each sang a line of the verses, and then harmonized on the chorus. That was a big hit for us that almost never happened. Chips Moman, the great producer at Memphis' American Sound Studios who had produced hits for Aretha Franklin, Waylon Jennings, B.J. Thomas, and several for Elvis (including "In the Ghetto," "Kentucky Rain," and "Suspicious Minds") had already cut the song on Tony Orlando. Bob Beckham, of Combine Publishing, which controlled the song, didn't feel like it could be a hit with Tony, so he gave us the go-ahead to record it, saying he could work everything out later. After we cut it and Bob heard it, he loved it. He called Chips to find out if he planned to release it as an "A-side" (meaning as a single), but Chips, who liked to hold his cards close to his vest, told him it would "either be an A-side or a "B-side." This struck Beckham as a disingenuous answer, which ticked him off a little, so the next day, Bob called Chancey back and said, "If The Oaks want to release 'American Made' as a single, please do it. I'll deal with the fall-out from Chips." So we released it, and as he expected, Chips got more than a little upset that ours came out first. He shelved the version that Tony cut, and for Bob's trouble, we gave him a Number One record on the song!

Our relationship with Ron was one of those beautiful, and all too rare, collaborative partnerships where we each knew the other so well, we could almost know what the other was thinking. Ron often likened it to the five of us being brothers: each unique but tied together in an, almost, cosmic way. Trying to record records that people would love and buy is a very difficult task, and very serious business, but that doesn't mean it can't be fun; I can promise you we enjoyed those sessions.

Ron has a distinctive accent and a certain high-pitched tone to his voice that allows him to say just about anything, in the way of criticism, while still making it sound friendly, even pleasant. Once we were trying to create some magic, where none existed, on a song called "Kamikaze Heart." It was an unusual song—sort of a novelty tune—and we were struggling to make something happen with it. We listened to the play-back a few times and weren't very happy with what we'd done. In a last move of desperation, we decided that perhaps what it needed was some additional background vocals. So, we went back in together and tried adding some high-register "ooooohs." After, apparently, having heard enough, Ron pushed the talkback button (which allowed us to hear him talking from the control booth while we were inside the studio) and in his distinctive voice said, "Now boys, I don't wanna tick nobody off, but I swear y'all sound a lot like a pack of dogs howling." We collapsed in laughter, and decided that this might be one song that couldn't be saved by The Oak Ridge Boys.

Sometimes, however, hard work and constant effort can really pay off. One of my favorite songs we ever recorded was a mid-tempo ballad called "I Guess it Never Hurts to Hurt Sometime," written by the late, great Randy Van Warmer. Joe was to sing the lead on this one, but after several attempts, he just couldn't get a vocal performance that satisfied him. He tried different phrasing, he tried various approaches in style but it just wasn't clicking. Finally, Ron called for a break to allow Joe to rest his voice, and, also, so each of us could clear his head. After a few minutes, Joe and Ron ran into each other in the men's room, and Joe was chastising himself for not being able to sing the song. In a moment of frustration, he said "Why don't you just get the Bee Gees in here to sing it?" He sang the first two lines in a small, falsetto-like, voice, and Ron, who was drying his hands at the sink, shouted "THAT'S IT! Use your little voice. Remember what your doing!" They ran back to the studio, and Joe jumped in the vocal booth and immediately captured the song in only a couple of takes. And, it was another little piece of Oak Ridge Boys magic that went to Number One.

A similar situation happened twenty-five years later when we were cutting Ray LaMontagne's "Hold You In My Arms" for *The Boys Are Back* project with producer, David Cobb. The vocals were slow to fall into the pocket but finally we had what we thought was a finished track. But, it turns out Joe wasn't satisfied. He kept thinking about it and as soon as the sessions were complete, Joe asked David if he could take one more pass at it. I'm not sure why he felt so strongly, but somehow, he just hadn't given the performance that he thought he could. So, he went into the vocal booth, and from somewhere down inside himself, at the end of a very long day of recording, Joe found the groove he had been looking for, in the form of a beautiful, tender vocal, and The Oak Ridge Boys got a very cool cut on a very cool song.

๑๑๑

The Oaks have recorded in just about every way possible: all together, individually, and in pairs. When Chancey came along, we did a combination, in that we would all four record together, and then go back in individually and re-sing, or fix our parts, as necessary. For the tracking sessions (when the music tracks are being recorded) usually only one of us would be there to sing the lead (called scratch vocals) for the band to follow, so they would know where the words would go and where there would be space for instrumental fills. Sometimes this vocalist would be the one who was to sing the lead on the finished track, but, most often, it would be Duane. Then after the tracking was complete, whoever had the lead on the song—let's say, Duane, for example—would come in and put down his lead vocals. Then Joe would sing the tenor, then Golden the baritone and then, finally, I would come in and lay down the bass.

One big exception to this pattern was, ironically, "Y'all Come Back Saloon," on which we recorded the master on all four vocals during the tracking session. In my memory, that was the only song—certainly the only hit—on which that happened. It's true that, later, we would get the "Elvira" vocals in one take, but even that magic didn't occur while the session band was tracking.

Chancey liked to have us all in the studio together when we recorded. He would set up baffles (portable, thick foam walls) between us (to provide as much vocal separation as possible) but he just found

153

that making magic was easier when we were doing it together. This was because it was the best and closest way to replicate our singing onstage, which had always been Ron's goal since that first night he'd seen us in Oklahoma City. Then, to complete that "Oaks' sound," he would have us go back in and gather around one microphone and stack the four-part background vocals.

When recording *The Boys Are Back*, in 2009, we tried a variation of this, but to an extent we'd never done before. David Cobb, had us sing all of our parts—even the leads—around one microphone, something that is almost unheard of, in order to get a more earthy, raw sound. When we're singing onstage, or individually in a studio, each of our voices requires very different volume levels on our respective microphones. Of course, you can't have that if we're all singing on one microphone, so as we sang, we each had to compensate to keep our levels balanced. If you were to see a photo from those sessions it would look like I was eating the microphone because I had to be so close to it, while Bonsall stood way back because of his power and volume, and Duane and Golden would be somewhere between.

We tried recording so many different ways for many different reasons. Part of it had to do with the technology that existed at the time, but mostly it had to do with the feel, or the vibe, we were trying to get on that specific project. We moved away from the group sessions as our regular approach out of self-preservation. Despite our long history together, the reality is, some songs are harder for one or the other of us to sing than they are for the others. If all four of us were in the studio having to sing our parts every time one of us missed a note, we could wear out our voices. That can sometimes cause stress—both physical and emotional—which usually only serves to worsen any vocal problems we might be having. So for us, in general, we've found that we're better served recording our parts individually. Having said that, though, for our recent session with Ben Isaacs, we recorded more as a group because the material called for it. As in so many other aspects of the business, versatility is crucial.

෨෨෨

I'll share a couple of little pieces of Oaks recording trivia, both of which involve Ron. First, if you'll listen closely to "Ready to Take My Chances" from the *Together* album, the last time before the song fades out, instead of singing, "ready to take my chances" we sang: "ready to take Ron Chancey." Listen to it. It's there. I promise. The next one pertains to the song "Sail Away" from our third strictly country release *The Oak Ridge Boys Have Arrived*. We were really actively touring at the time of the studio session when we recorded that one. As soon as the session was done, we were off on tour again performing for more sold-out houses. Back in Nashville, as Ron was mixing the various tracks, he noticed a mistake on "Sail Away." The opening lines of the last verse are: "Then a smile comes upon me as I look across the bow..." but during the mixdown, Ron noticed that Duane had sung, "But a smile..." instead of, "Then a smile..." After considering it, he decided that that one word changed the meaning of the song more than he was comfortable with. He called and said we had to fix it. We definitely trusted and believed in Ron's producing but we had a problem. He was on a deadline to get the tracks turned over to the record label, and we were doing a series of one-nighters and would not be back in Nashville in time for Duane to re-sing the line. We considered finding a studio on the road and shipping the tapes out but that wasn't feasible, and certainly would have been cost-prohibitive. After a little bit of conversation and deliberation, we decided that the only option was for Ron to sing the line. He did, and the song went on to be a big hit for us. So, the next time you listen to it, pay close attention to the two quick words: "Then a," and you'll hear the one time that Ron Chancey sang on an Oak Ridge Boys hit record.

In 1984, Jimmy Bowen replaced Jim Fogelsong as the head of the country music division at *MCA Records*. After much discussion and soul-searching, we decided that we would like to have Jimmy Bowen produce us. At that time, Bowen was one of the hottest producers in the business, at the forefront of the modernization and digitalization of the Nashville recording industry. His success had taken him to the "one-name status" meaning that when someone spoke of "Bowen," there was no mistaking who they meant. Having worked at several labels before coming to MCA, he, eventually, produced many artists who required only one name for identification: Strait, Waylon, Garth, and Reba, among others. In the midst of his successes, we hoped to add "Oaks" to that list.

When we first approached him, he was very hesitant, citing the headaches that can come with group dynamics. After some attempts to persuade him, he agreed to consider working with us, but only after he had the opportunity to meet with each one of us privately. So, we each went to his house to sit down and talk. I don't know how his discussion went with my partners, but my conversation with him was certainly not what I was expecting, and had the potential to have been devastating.

I'll admit to having been somewhat nervous as I drove to the meeting. Despite the record success that The Oaks had enjoyed over the previous decade, we were in a position of needing a boost to rediscover some of our old magic. Bowen and I sat in the living room of his Music City mansion. After very little small talk, he began explaining his vision of group vocals. While he didn't exactly say that bass singers weren't real singers, that was the essence of his monologue. He said that if he agreed to produce us, I should understand that I would be only a "role player," providing only bass harmony vocals; I would not—and should not—ever have the lead on a record. He believed that a bass singer was an artist whose specialty was only to provide the foundation to a group's sound. "If you're okay with that," he offered, "then I can produce The Oak Ridge Boys."

Though I've always considered myself a team player, I'd be lying if I said that didn't hurt my pride a little. Part of me wanted to remind him about the hits we'd had with all of our voices contributing, to ask him if he'd ever heard of a Number One record called "Dream On." I wanted to remind him that The Oak Ridge Boys and The Beatles were the only groups in music to have had Number One records featuring each of its members singing lead; no one else, not The Beach Boys, not Alabama, not The Supremes, not The Eagles, not The Statler Brothers, not The Jackson 5. I was blind-sided by his audacity, but as we used to say in the gospel business, I knew how to be a good quartet man. Despite my offense at what he said, I didn't want to do anything to hurt the group's chances for success that might come as a result of working with him, so I agreed to his terms.

Beginning with the first release in February 1987, Bowen produced four albums on us: *Where the Fast Lane Ends*, *Heartbeat*, and *Monongahela* and *American Dreams*. We made some good music in those years; we made some hit records: "Gonna Take a Lot of River," "Beyond Those Years," "True Heart" and others. He was there to produce the last record before William Lee Golden's departure, and he produced the first three albums that featured Steve Sanders. True to his word, I didn't sing any leads on those records. In fact, I think it's safe to say that in all of those sessions, Bowen never once heard me sing live in the studio.

When starting a new session, Bowen would be there for the tracking session—when the lead singer would be there to lay down his vocals—and then he would move on to track his next project, leaving his engineer, Bob Bullock, to oversee the vocal sessions. Since I didn't have any leads, Bowen was never there when I sang.

I always had the feeling that Bowen didn't even like country music that much, which was amazing to me in light of all of the tremendous success that he'd had. Though he was a Texas boy, he definitely had New York sensibilities and pop tastes. He had his own singing career doing rockabilly, and then his initial producing career was made with Frank Sinatra, Dean Martin and Sammy Davis, Jr. In country music, he always opted towards the more lush arrangements, all but eschewing country instrumentation. In fact, when working with us, if a song called for a fiddle, mandolin or banjo—what he called a "twangy" instrument—Bowen would overdub it (bring it in later to be recorded separately) and have Bob oversee it. It was if he didn't even want to be in the studio when that kind of instrument was being used.

I don't mean to suggest that Bowen was completely hands-off. As far as I know, he always came back for the final mixing—or at least signed off on the project after completion. And having said all of this, I'd have to say, despite his apparent initial distaste for me and other bass singers, there was something about Bowen that I liked. Eventually, I think he came to like me as well; we got along fine, and, in time, we found a pretty comfortable relationship. It certainly wasn't my most productive years as a singer, but I'm still proud of the music that we, as a group, made. The circumstances we faced when Steve Sanders stepped in to replace Golden were daunting, and could easily have proven overwhelming. The fact that we were able to face that dark period after losing a fourth of our soul and come through it on the other side with hit records—even a Number One—was an amazing feat.

After all of the success we had at MCA, the time came when we had to change labels, in an effort to inject some excitement into our marketing. Though the years at MCA had been our biggest, as so often happens, a "malaise" of sorts sets in where the marketing department isn't as excited about you as they once were—you become "old hat" to them. It's really just a normal part of the business that anyone who is blessed with longevity will likely have to face. In our case, we moved over to RCA because the label head, Joe Galante, seemed to believe in us very strongly. I still remember the day we signed; we were very excited. We each received a statue of "Nipper," the gramophone-listening dog in RCA's logo, and I remember gushing with Bonsall about the fact that we were now on the same label where Elvis had recorded—and we were there because they had sought us out; they wanted us. We felt like pinching ourselves.

As it turned out, that excitement would be shorter-lived than we'd expected. Shortly after our arrival, Galante was promoted to run the label in New York, and replaced in Nashville by Jack Weston. With that personnel change at the label, the focus moved away from us; they seemed no longer interested in our records. We soon found that RCA wasn't big enough for both The Oaks and Alabama.

Upon signing with RCA, though, we worked with a producer named Richard Landis. The good news for me, at least, was that Richard liked me and my singing! He'd had great success with Eddie Rabbitt, Juice Newton, Lorrie Morgan and others. As much as any producer we'd ever worked with, I thought Richard was actually a fan of my singing. He would encourage me, and he would get so excited over things I did in the studio. It was a welcome change for me after the Bowen years. I always thought if I'd ever recorded a solo album, I would have wanted Richard to produce it. I just really liked his style. We became personal friends as well as professional colleagues. We could sit for hours and talk about wine and Key West—two loves that we shared. He was good for The Oaks, too, producing, among others, for us, "Lucky Moon" and "(You're My) Soul and Inspiration."

The middle nineties was a period of great change in country radio. Fewer and fewer people were making the decisions on the music that was being played on major radio across the country. That's not to say that there wasn't a lot of great music being made. Some of the exciting acts filling the airwaves included: George Strait, Garth Brooks, Reba McEntire, Brooks & Dunn, Tim McGraw, Patty Loveless and many others. What the compressed radio playlists meant for The Oaks was that, while we were still actively recording and touring as much as ever, hit records were harder to come by.

Another change was in order and, unfortunately, we found ourselves in another uncomfortable situation involving a label executive. Capitol Records had wooed us, and our meetings seemed positive enough that we signed. When we met with the president and CEO, Scott Hendricks, it became clear that he had no idea who we were. I think it's safe to say that he had never heard any of our records, and maybe had never even heard of us. He may have been the one person in the world who could not sing along with "Elvira." It was really disappointing. In the end, they didn't know what to do with us, so we recorded a Christmas record, *Country Christmas Eve*. By that time, our Christmas recordings were becoming big sellers; I guess they thought that was a sure way to get a record released on us. The highlight of that project, for me anyway, was the return of Richard Landis as producer. It was a good release for us, and fifteen years later, some of the songs still find their way into our annual Christmas tour.

After Golden returned, we wanted to try, once again, to recapture some of that old Oaks magic in the studio. In 1999, we signed a record deal with Platinum Records, a young and aggressive independent label with major distribution. Not only were we thrilled to be back in the studio to record *Voices,* we had our fifth member, Ron Chancey producing. Once again, moving forward had taken us right back where we started! Duane and Chancey found some great songs for us to record. "Baby When Your Heart Breaks Down" became our first single sent to radio in almost seven years, followed by "Ain't No Short Way Home." For the first time in a long time, we felt great about recording. We were getting great songs, and we were getting great sounds in the studio.

There was a song from *Voices* project that Golden sang lead on called "Old Hearts." The chorus said: "Old hearts still fall just as hard. Old dreams still go just as far. It's true that time diminishes what your chances are. But there's still a lot of love left in old hearts." For us, that describes our situation with major country radio. Though the limited playlists and other current trends that had impacted radio might have diminished our chances of having another hit record, our dreams—and the work we were willing to put behind them—were still strong. But for us, it wasn't just about the hit records anymore. With the run of success we had enjoyed, we were afforded the luxury of continuing to tour and see the fans as much as ever, and to continue making some of that Oak Ridge Boys magic. After the reunion, Duane, Joe, Golden and I had been given a wonderful second chance; we were determined to redouble our efforts to make the most of our opportunity.

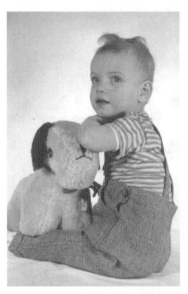

Believe it or not, I still have this stuffed
animal. It was indestructible!

I'm, obviously, excited and happy,
running to my Dad. That's mom in the
background.

A man used to come through town with a pony
and cowboy outfit, and take pictures. Like most
kids, I could not resist. Fortunately, this shoot
went better than later ones with animals!

From one of my grade school yearbooks;
already interested in fashion, I was just
finding my voice.

A high school shot. This was around the time of my first road
trip with a singing group.

The record album that set me on my course.
Photo Credit: Jimmy Blackwood

The Eastmen Quartet, with me behind the wheel of our first bus. L-R: Frank Sanchez, Nick Bruno, J.R. Damiani, Ron Landis.

The Keystone Quartet, my first group with Joe Bonsall (but not my last!) L-R: Paul Furrow, Bonsall, me, and David Will.
Photo Credit: Joe Bonsall

Another shot of the Keystones. L-R: David Will, me, Bonsall, David Holcroft and Garland Craft.
Photo Credit: Joe Bonsall

Flashbulbs illuminate my first minute on stage with Elvis, Minneapolis, November 5, 1971.
Photo Credit: Star Tribune/Minneapolis-St. Paul, 2012

The Stamps, The Sweets and Charlie Hodge with Elvis in Baltimore, 1971.
Photo Credit: Kieran Davis

Elvis listens as we sing our verse on "American Trilogy," in Macon, GA, April 15, 1972.
Photo Credit: Don Robinson

The Stamps backstage with Elvis, Las Vegas, 1972.
Photo Credit: Donnie Sumner

J.D. Sumner and me in the studio with Elvis during the filming of Elvis on Tour.
Photo Licensed By: Warner Bros. Entertainment Inc.

The watch that J.D. gave me in 1972.

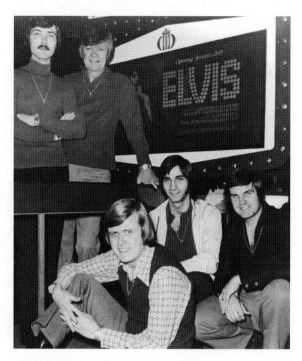

The Stamps in Las Vegas shortly after Elvis presented us our TCBs.
Photo Credit: Donnie Sumner

The start of yet another spectacle. I can promise you, it never got old.
Photo Credit: Ed Enoch

One of our first big breaks. A pretty impressive lineup.
Collection of Jon Mir

Onstage at Grand Place, Brussels, Belgium in 1981.
Photo Credit: Kathy Gangwisch

A heck of a lineup: The Oaks with Johnny Bench, Mario Soto, Gary Carter, Dale Murphy and Whitey Herzog, All Star Game, 1983 at Chicago's Comiskey Park.
Photo Credit: Kathy Gangwisch

Is this Heaven? Close. It's Yankee Stadium.
Photo Credit: Kathy Gangwisch

Sporting a Yankees tie with "The Boss,"
George Steinbrenner. Notice his Oaks button.
Photo Credit: Kathy Gangwisch

Giving a lift to Barbara Mandrell.
Photo Credit: Kathy Gangwisch

The day we learned George Bush was a fan, October 1983.
Photo Credit: Kathy Gangwisch

Donna and me with "41" in Kennebunkport.
Photo Credit: Donna Sterban

Performing during 43's Inauguration, 2005.
Photo Credit: David Balfour

Soviet President, Mikhail Gorbachev pounding my chest,
College Station, Texas, 2004.
Photo Credit: Steven Robinson

With my brother, Joseph; sister, Susan; and
mother, Victoria.

With my oldest son, Rich.

My son Doug at his 2006 graduation.
Photo Credit: Jackie Ayers

A picture of my daughters
Tori(Victoria) and Lauren.
Photo Credit: Donna Sterban

With my son, Chris.

With my wife and best friend Donna.

With the fifth Oak Ridge Boy, Ron Chancey celebrating Elvira.
Photo Credit: Kathy Gangwisch

In the studio recording Elvira for the "It's Only Natural" project for Cracker Barrel, April 2011.
Photo Credit: Steven Robinson

In the studio the night we re-recorded "Elvira." (L-R) Golden, Jim Halsey, Ron Chancey, me, Duane, Toni and Jim Fogelsong, Michael Sykes, Raymond Hicks, Julie Craig (from Cracker Barrel), Bonsall, and Kirt Webster.

Reception after our induction at the Grand Ole Opry, July 8, 2011.
Photo Credit: Jon Mir

All for the Hall, April 2012. Note Keith Urban and Vince Gill in the band.
Photo Credit: Jon Mir

My partners and me.
Photo Credit: Jarrett Gaza

My partners and me.
Photo Credit: Jon Mir

Where I always wanted to be.
Photo Credit: Jon Mir

ELVIS TO ELVIRA: *My Life On Stage*

Photo Credit: Jarrett Gaza

RICHARD STERBAN

CHAPTER EIGHT: *Brothers*

I 'm often asked in interviews to talk about the other guys in the group, which I gladly do. But that's mostly about the performers with whom I've shared a stage for the last forty years. The obvious reality is that we're performers for a couple of hours each day, but we're men—and we're friends—twenty-four hours a day, seven days a week. I think one of the reasons we've had success, and experienced the longevity that we have, is due to the foursome that we are. As Johnny Cash convinced us so many years ago, there's no denying that we have been blessed with something special. And part of that "specialness" is that we're so different, yet at the same time, we're able to come together as one group.

I think we realized more than ever just how special this foursome is during those years when Golden was gone. Steve Sanders, in replacing him, did a fine and admirable job, and we still made some Number One records with him in the group, but there was always that nagging realization—sometimes buried deep and other times just under the surface— that without Golden, something just wasn't quite right.

Though not anymore, for a long time, the most frequent questions we'd be asked had to do with the timeframe when Golden was no longer a member of The Oaks. Friends and enemies, reporters and fans all wanted to know what happened and why. While it was a very major upheaval in our lives, and while it became the most public of breakups, simply stated, it was about everything and nothing, all at the same time.

We were seasoned performers. We were all high strung. We were on top of the world, and were making more money than we'd ever imagined possible. We probably felt invincible, and thought that it was going to last forever, which probably contributed to our breakup. We all had egos, of course. We all had big personalities, and we all occasionally had ideas that might have differed from one or all of the other partners. We had always been able to work those out. For some reason, though, this situation just grew beyond what we could manage.

Looking back, more than anything else, we suffered misunderstandings caused by a lack of communication. It was really no different than a marriage. Troubles can be expected, but as long as communication exists, it can survive anything. When communication ends, too often, so does the marriage. The slights are less real and more perceived, but no less destructive. The love you have for each other gets clouded. It's still there; you just can't access it when it's most needed.

I've heard it said that in any marriage there will be times when the spouses love each other and times when they hate each other. It can survive these ebbs and flows as long as they never hate each other at the same time. While I can honestly say none of my partners ever hated the others, this sentiment describes what we went through. There were times when we thought Golden simply no longer wanted to be a member of our group—or any group—and, at the same time, I believe, he thought we no longer wanted him, and that just wasn't so.

If only we had talked our way through those situations, it would have, likely, saved us a lot of heartaches, but we just didn't do it. Instead, we walled ourselves off from each other and allowed our perceptions to take us over. I can remember at meet-and-greets with fans before shows when Duane, Joe and I would be standing together and Golden would be standing off by himself. Fans couldn't even get photos with all four of us at the same time. And I distinctly remember wondering why he wouldn't just come over to where we were and pose with us. All these years later, we have never discussed it, but I can't help but wonder if he stood there wondering the same thing about us: why were we choosing to stand away from him? Such were the misunderstandings that were taking us over at the time.

Ironically, even at the height of these misunderstandings, I don't feel that our shows suffered. It was certainly the biggest years we had ever enjoyed, and we were making some of the best music in our history. Our crowds were huge. Joe was jumping around and singing as strong as ever; Duane was as rock steady as always; and Golden was connecting with the audience like only he could. His appearance change—when he first took on his "mountain man" persona—also occurred at this same time, coinciding with our troubles, but I don't think that was a contributing factor to our problems. If anything, I think his new look might have been a manifestation of the fact that he was such an individual in his efforts, and in his ability to connect with an audience. In retrospect, I think we might have misinterpreted that individualism as proof that he didn't think of himself as a group member anymore. And, to further add to the confusing layers, he may have misread our perception, that he no longer wanted to belong, as evidence that we no longer wanted him with us. So, you see why I say the reasons were "everything and nothing" all at the same time.

There was just a great divide. With age and wisdom, I look back and realize that it probably wasn't nearly as expansive as we thought at the time. We could have easily patched our respective perceived problems and stayed together. In reality, the last thing we wanted to do was turn our lives upside down and mess up what we had going as one of the hottest groups in popular music, but we just reached a point where we thought we had no other choice. There was just too much unhappiness on our bus and in our partnership. So, in 1987, after many years of growing tension for all of us, Duane, Joe and I voted to remove Golden from the group. It was the most public—and the most painful—of breakups. It damaged our friendship, though I'm happy to say, not beyond eventual repair.

With Golden gone, we were faced with the immediate need to replace him. While Steve Sanders might not have been the most obvious choice, to us it made a lot of sense—and it was certainly convenient. The last thing we wanted to do was place an ad announcing a job opening; we didn't want to have a cattle call audition. Here was a guy, already playing in the band, who was a talented singer and knew the songs, so the easy thing to do was just move him a few feet forward and be done with it. And as I've said, we had several hits with Steve singing on them—in fact, we've just recently added those back into our stage show—but as good as the music was, we just knew inside that we lacked the same magic that we had with Golden. There was just something undeniable about us four being together.

In the months leading up to Steve departing the group, we could sense that the end was near. We knew he wasn't happy—and we certainly weren't happy. Though we didn't address it at the time, I think that Duane, Joe and I each had allowed ourselves to consider, in the back of our minds, if we made another personnel change, the possibility of a reunion with Golden.

Steve was a talented singer—and a heck of a showman—but he fought the demons of depression and drink. They were equal partners in his troubles, his professional demise, and, sadly, in his premature death in 1998. He had family issues at the time that he had to withstand and, unfortunately for him and for us, they became public and began to negatively impact the group. The stories appeared in print all around the country, each featuring "The Oak Ridge Boys" prominently in the headlines. We told him that things had to change and the negative publicity had to stop. As his troubles continued to mount, his battles with his demons continued to spiral more and more out of control, taking him with them. His drinking became worse, and depression seemed to envelope him. He would stay up all night in the front of the bus and worry about what his life had become. It never impacted our shows—he remained a professional on stage and in the studio—but it sure seemed to take a toll on his psyche.

We were in Ft. Worth, Texas, in late 1995, when Steve made his decision to leave us. Not only did he leave us; he left us hanging. He literally left on the morning of a show day. He called a meeting to announce that he was getting on a plane to go tape a tabloid television show so he could defend his wife and family against the negative publicity they were receiving. He said that his family was more important to him than The Oak Ridge Boys, and that his decision was final. I don't know if he thought we would accept this explanation and support his decision, but if he did, he was sorely mistaken. We told him, in no uncertain terms, if he followed through on this threat, he would no longer be a member of the group. If he walked out the door, it would never again reopen for him. He turned and left the room and, in that instant, The Oak Ridge Boys found ourselves a group of three, and only hours from a sold-out show.

We were incensed that he would allow his personal situation to negatively impact the group in that way. Each of The Oak Ridge Boys has always prided himself on not missing shows. Each of us has had to occasionally throughout the years, but it is amazing how few times it has happened. I missed one when my father died, one when my grandson died, and another for the funeral of my mother-in-law. The other three have missed a few with health or voice problems. But for Steve to leave us high and dry just hours before a sold-out show was inexcusable.

Fortunately, we were able to fly in Duane Allen's son, Dee, who, upon arrival, dressed, went on stage and performed a full show with absolutely no rehearsal. He really saved us that night—and for several shows thereafter, as did Duane's son-in-law, Paul Martin (now one of Marty Stuart's Fabulous Superlatives) until we were able to work out the details for Golden to come back home.

The venue where we were playing the night that Steve deserted us was next to another venue that was hosting a gospel sing on the same day. I can remember going over to see J.D. and The Stamps, who were performing next door, and sitting on the bus with J.D. I was very agitated over the situation with Steve and worried about whether Dee's flight would arrive in time. As he often did years before, J.D. tried to make me laugh in order to relieve the tension. When I told him what Steve had done, he simply said: "Well, son, what did you expect? He's a gospel singer isn't he?" That definitely broke the nerves for me for a little while, though I will readily admit that I was very relieved when I saw the car carrying Dee drive up before the show. The Oaks would survive that night, and the next few weeks, but something drastic and important needed to happen.

We finally got to the place in our individual lives when we were each man enough to set aside whatever differences we might have had with Golden and come back together as the group we always were destined to be. The reality was, since finalizing the details of the breakup we hadn't stood face-to-face or spoken to each other. As if by divine providence, we each began running into Golden around town. Joe would see him at the grocery store or Duane would run into him at an event. I was riding my bicycle one day and came up on him as he walked. I stopped, and we chatted. It was cordial but still somewhat strained; we rarely got past small talk about the weather and other inane topics. After a few similar occurrences, Duane, Joe and I each became aware that we hated the fact that we felt the way we were feeling. We'd had too many good years, and good times together, to feel so uncomfortable around each other. So, we decided to fix it.

With the encouragement of Jim Halsey, we each took turns getting together with Golden at his house, and we had our private conversations; we made our apologies, and we set things right. The more we talked, the more we began to focus on the things that had made us friends; soon we couldn't even remember the specifics about the things that had come between us. At that time we realized how insignificant, in reality, those disagreements really must have been. As soon as that was accomplished—on a personal level—we decided that, perhaps, it was time for us to make amends professionally. We invited Golden to come to our offices on Rockland Road in Hendersonville. We gathered around the piano in the studio and began to sing. If I recall correctly, the first song we sang was "Ozark Mountain Jubilee" and within the first few bars, we all had tears in our eyes. The magic was, indeed, still there. Now, some fifteen years later, it's really as if he was never gone. I don't mean that as any show of disrespect to Steve; rather it speaks to the depth of feelings that the four us continue to share for each other.

Golden is a thinking man. I couldn't count the number of times I've watched him sit silently in the front of the bus, stroking his long beard, and mull over something. He doesn't talk a whole lot but when he says something it's usually pretty profound. And it's often very funny. In 1994, we were at an event that was officially called "The Presidents' Summit for America's Future," but became known as the "volunteerism summit." Its purpose was to encourage people to be more active in their communities by volunteering to help others in some way. It was a noble effort much in the spirit of President George H. W. Bush's "Thousand Points of Light" campaign.

The festivities kicked off with an event in a high school football stadium featuring us, along with many of the top acts of the day. As we sat on our bus before the ceremony started, we could see, through the entrance gate, a large group of protestors. They marched back and forth on the sidewalk carrying signs painted with slogans like: "I'm Not Your Slave" and "Volunteerism Equals Servitude" and "You Can't Make Me Volunteer." We all sort of laughed at the ridiculousness of their anger. How could people object to volunteering? But Golden sat quietly in his big captain's chair at the front of the bus, stroking his beard. After a few minutes he said, "I was just thinkin'...don't you reckon some of those people out there volunteered to protest this morning?" That's the sort of simple brilliance that William Lee Golden can bring to a conversation.

At that same event later that night we found ourselves in the presence of Al Gore, the former Senator from Tennessee who, at the time, was serving as Bill Clinton's Vice President. For some reason, Gore completely ignored us that night; just refused to speak to us. As we walked away Golden said "He sure avoided us tonight, didn't he? But it's gonna make his head spin to see how easily we avoid that lever beside his name on Election Day."

Golden is a renaissance man. He's a talented painter and artist whose works have been exhibited in museums and galleries around the country. And, Golden is also a gentle man. He is quick to say hello to a stranger, and he's slow to leave a conversation with one. While we each have our core group of fans, in my heart, I believe he's probably the most popular of The Oak Ridge Boys. And I think, in some measure, that's because he's the best communicator. He cares deeply for the fans and has a way of showing it. Each of us has our own style of singing but I think nobody communicates a song the way Golden does. I think no one could have done the same justice to "Thank God For Kids," "Still Holding On," "Beautiful Bluebird," "Before I Die," or so many of the other songs that Golden has sung. Among his many talents, none is more amazing than his ability to deliver a song.

Golden remains the visionary he was all those years ago before I joined the group. When he listens to music—or watches another act perform—instead of just listening and enjoying, I think he's always studying them. He wants to understand what makes them tick and how they are successful (or what keeps them from being so.) It's like he's always in school—sometimes as the student and other times as the teacher.

Duane is the centerpiece of The Oak Ridge Boys. Not only do I think he's the best singer in our group, I think he's the best lead singer in country music. On a bad day, he's better than most singers are on their best day. He could be awakened at 3:00 in the morning and asked to sing a particular note, and he could do it; he is just that consistent. And there is no singer with more range and versatility than Duane. He can sing tenor above Joe's lead vocals and also get down into a bass register. Just listen to him on "Mama's Table." His range is really mind-boggling.

Duane has always been very involved in the music that The Oaks have recorded and performed. Among his many titles and traits, he is most definitely a "song man." He has a great ear for finding songs that fit our harmonies and our individual voices. He has spent years establishing a rapport, and fostering relationships, with songwriters and publishers, and it has paid off for us many times over.

The desire and ability he uses to stay in touch with the song people, carries over into his desire to stay in touch with the fans. In 2012, that often means doing so electronically. Duane is probably the most active of the group in staying in touch with our fans on the computer. With thousands of hits every day on our websites, this has become a big job, and no one asked him to do it; he is just drawn to staying in touch with our friends and fans by updating them on our daily activities. It is definitely just part of his caring personality.

He's the voice around which our sound is built but he not only offers stability to our sound, he adds stability to our corporation and to our lives. If any of us has a problem, Duane is always ready to listen. He'll offer advice if I ask for it, or he'll just be a sounding block if that's what I need; he's a very caring person. I'm proud to call him a friend; he's a good man.

If Golden brings the vision and Duane brings the stability, then Bonsall certainly brings the energy to our group. No artist can feel great every day; we all have good days and bad days. But I'd defy anyone to watch Joe on stage and try to determine if he is having a good day or a bad day, because he's always "on" no matter what. It's no accident that Joe represents us on stage (as the emcee, if you will); it's because he's so good at it, and part of the reason for that is his ability to leave behind any personal issues while he's on stage. He's the kind of person whose energy and enthusiasm is very infectious. If I'm having a bad day, all I have to do is get around Joe for a while and his positive energy will rub off on me. He's always been that way. We would not be The Oak Ridge Boys without Joe's spark.

The way Joe sings is also very important to us. He does not sing like a typical tenor singer. He has a quality that others do not. And his uniqueness is a big part of the Oaks' distinctive sound. Not long ago, while taping a Gaither Family video, we sang a song called "God Will Take Care of You," on which Joe sang the lead vocal. This is an old gospel standard that every quartet has sung, but as Joe sung it, I looked around that room and almost everyone—certainly every tenor singer—just sat there wide eyed and mouths open, caught up in his vocal performance. Many came to him after the taping to either comment on his singing or ask for tips. I'm not sure what he told them, but in my view, the rare quality that Joe has is letting the audience *have* a performance rather than making them *take* it. Too often a singer will force his performance on the audience, but rare is the singer who, like Joe, has the confidence in his own ability to not over-sing a song but simply sing it and allow the audience to receive it.

Likewise, Joe has the same quality as a person. He is fun and funny, he's smart and he's a sarcastic, but he is not overbearing in the least.

He respects those around him enough to allow them to determine how much they want to "receive." We can sit in the back lounge of the bus watching baseball, as we often do, and ride for miles and miles without even speaking. Other times we can talk so much that we lose track of whatever show or game we're watching. We have a good rhythm between us. My relationship with Bonsall, obviously, goes back a long way. We had a lot in common back in the days at Gimbels, and all these years later we still have a lot in common. He's my best friend, and has been for decades.

There are many factors that contribute to our success. We all thrive on the creative process. Over the years, the four of us have learned how to live with each other. With wisdom, we have grown from young men with a dream into men living our dream. Some of the things that we might have fought about—or wanted to, anyway—just don't seem relevant anymore. The group is more important than any of us individually. We've learned that it takes all four of us to make it work.

I can honestly say that there is no jealousy between us. We recognize that if one of us is getting a huge ovation, then it just makes the group stronger—and, besides, there is likely an ovation awaiting each of us somewhere along the line. I remember once many years ago, we were playing one of the first big dates we ever played after we'd started adding some country songs to our show. We were opening for Freddy Fender at the Arizona State Fair in front of a huge crowd. In the middle of our show, it came time for me to take the lead on a song. At that time I was singing the great old Bob Wills song, "Faded Love." As we sung that song, we absolutely tore down the house. The response from the audience was overwhelming—almost reminding me of the ovations Elvis would get. It should have put me on cloud nine but, for some reason, it had the exact opposite effect on me. I sincerely worried that my partners would somehow think I was trying to upstage them. (And let me say that this was totally in my head; there was nothing in our history that would lead me to think that they would react that way.) After the show, I was still shaken and I went to the guys and apologized. Of course, they thought I was crazy and they told me that the ovation had actually thrilled them because it was further proof to them that The Oaks were indeed on our way.

As much as anything, my reaction to the fans' reaction was probably the result of a sincere lack of confidence that can sometimes affect me. I remember once J.D. telling me—and I came to understand it later—that he never did any bass singing that he was really proud of until about the age of forty. While I certainly didn't want to wish my life away, as I've gotten older, I've found the same to be true. One advantage of singing bass is that the voice actually gets deeper with age.

A great piece of advice that J.D. offered me came during one of those relatively rare times he'd invited me back to his suite, during one of the endless bus rides with The Stamps. It was just the two of us: a fresh, young bass singer and a wise, experienced one. He said he could tell that I sometimes lacked the confidence that I should have. "There are singers and then there are bass singers," he said. "We're different from other singers—a different breed, a different animal. Bass singers have a little man inside our head that tells us there's no way we can hit that low note because it's just too low. For years I had to deal with that same little man, and I know you deal with him to. But what you have to do is stand up to that little man and tell him that he is wrong. He's not going to get the best of you. You can hit that low note. You're better than that little man."

That conversation meant more to me than J.D. could have known. He was so right; I had been struggling for years with that little man. Something that made the struggle that much more difficult, though, was the fear that I was alone in fighting it. I didn't know others—let alone a legend like J.D.—was fighting the same doubts that I was. As soon as I understood that that little man was a common enemy to other bass singers, I was more confident in my ability to beat him. I wish I could say that that realization solved any problems that I might face, but I can't. Even today, all these years later, that little man still makes an appearance every so often.

One thing every singer has faced—or will face—is a day when the voice is just failing you. And when you're having an off day vocally, there's no way you can fool yourself into thinking otherwise. As I've said about Joe, even on days when he's having trouble, he's been blessed with the ability to push through and "make it happen" without letting it show—and apparently without letting it get him down. Golden is much the same way. Even if he's having an off night, he is still right in there communicating to the audience as only he can do, and the audience is eating out of his hand. That is one trait I wish I had because when I'm having an off day, I'm pretty tough on myself. Incidentally, I'm not sure what Duane would do on an off night. I'll let you know if it ever happens. I've only been singing with him for forty years and every night, he just stands there and delivers as Mr. Consistency.

When Joe introduces me on stage each night he'll often point at me and say something like, "Nobody else has one of these." Also, through the years, many people have said very kind things about my singing. Of course, I appreciate those accolades (like anyone would) but some days

I'll wonder how they could possibly have heard my performance and still have felt that way. Obviously, I'm a good bass singer—or I wouldn't have the job that I have—but some days I just feel that I'm not as good as I could be—or should be. Many nights I feel like I'm letting my partners down because they're singing their tails off, and I feel like I'm not holding up my end of the bargain.

I know that the root of my "issues" lies in several factors: emotional, physiological and probably psychological. Our success, built slowly on the backs of each of us, proves our—and my own—abilities, so at some level, I know I'm a good bass singer. "Oom Poppa Mau Mau" is probably the most iconic bass line since The Marcels' "Blue Moon" so why can't I give myself a break and believe that I can consistently sing to the level to which I aspire?

Several years ago, I really felt like I was having some serious vocal problems; I even briefly considered retiring. (Perhaps not so ironically, this was during the time when Bowen was producing us.) A friend suggested I go see a man named Tim Adair who is a chiropractor who specializes in Applied Kinesiology (AK.) While many criticize AK as pseudoscience, I can only speak to my own experience with it. While I can attest to the results I've seen through AK, like anything else, it is a personal decision that each individual would have to research before deciding if it was right for them.

In my first consultations with Tim, he educated me as to the nature of the vocal issues I was experiencing. The first factor, as I came to understand, was stress. Stress brings down your adrenal glands and when they don't function properly, it impacts your lungs' ability to supply enough breath, and also impacts your thyroid glands, which try to compensate to help the adrenal glands' function. In so doing, the thyroid stops doing one of the things its supposed to do, which is to thin the mucous in the body. As a result your sinuses and allergy symptoms can increase—and that can be a killer for bass vocals.

AK focuses on certain muscle points that can affect the normal functions of the body, including the adrenal glands. Tim will target and massage those points, and the results, in my case anyway, have been quite impressive. Now, in addition to regular visits, I always go to see him prior to recording sessions. Skeptics might say that it's all in my head, but I know better, and I think my singing on recent records is a testament to the treatments.

I also understand that some of the potential throat problems that can affect my singing are emotional. If I start having sinus issues and feel like I have drainage in my throat, like everyone else, my inclination is to clear my throat, which is one of the worst things you can do. The more I do it, the more it hurts so the more I feel like I need to do it, which makes me worry about it, so it becomes a vicious cycle.

Tim also introduced me to a lady named Katina Robertson who has also really helped me. What she does is even harder to describe—and might sound even more unbelievable to a skeptic. She analyzes my voice to determine the acupressure points that could address whatever issues I'm having. After doing so, she'll assign what's called a protocol or code for me to follow. For example, a code might dictate two points—perhaps the bridge of my nose and my Adam's apple, or the temporomandibular joints of my jaw—onto which I apply varying degrees of pressure for a pre-assigned length of time.

Interestingly, Katina also delves into the emotional. While

analyzing my voice, she'll sometimes tell me that she thinks the root of my problem is not physical, but rather something that is going on in my life that might be worrying me. She'll say we need to "find the picture" and address it, and more often than not, she will be correct. Just recently, for example, she pegged a problem I was having as being tied to some personal stress that was bothering me. Though she couldn't have known it, my grandson was having surgery that day at Vanderbilt and it had my youngest daughter very upset—which in turn, was upsetting me. Emotions can indeed impact every aspect of our make-up, including the vocal cords.

I know that sometimes I simply think too much. I let my performance—or my doubts about it—get too much in my head. So, while it almost sounds like she is my shrink, the thing that Katina has helped me with the most is dealing with my emotions and psyche; helping me be more confident in my abilities. She's taught me a form of visualization: while I'm following the pressure-point codes, I focus on my upcoming performance, and visualize singing the very best that I can sing.

These things are clearly part of the "alternative medicine" or "holistic" methods of helping your body heal itself—and not recognized by the medical community—but, for me, they work. I've been to countless doctors and specialists, all of whom prescribed medicines like antihistamines and antibiotics or various treatments, and it seemed the more I took, the worse I felt. I'm certainly not opposed to standard medicine—in fact, I embrace it when it's called for—I just don't like the feeling of being "over prescribed."

There have been conventional doctors who have been quite helpful to me. Once, back during the days when Bowen was producing us, I had some serious physical throat problems (another coincidence?) For a time we thought it might even require surgery, but thankfully, it did not. In that case, I just had to go on complete throat rest for a period of time, writing things on a pad instead of speaking. For me, that wasn't so hard.

I've worked over the years to take care of my voice, and that's only increased, as I've gotten older and gained more wisdom. For years, part of my pre-show routine has been to get away somewhere by myself and stay quiet; I simply don't talk to anyone. I try to limit the number of interviews I have to do on show days, and I almost refuse to do any interviews on days when we have two shows. My Ear, Nose and Throat specialist, Dr. Richard Quisling has prescribed a regimen, of when and how to talk, that helps preserve my voice. One thing that has always been difficult for me to follow is his recommendation to speak in a much higher pitch than I sing, as doing so can prevent vocal cord fatigue. I've tried it, but it's just not comfortable for me, so I opt, instead, to just keep my mouth shut. In my experience, talking creates more strain on my voice than singing.

Of course my friends, my partners and my family have no problem with this because it also fits pretty closely with my personality anyway, as I've always been somewhat of a loner. It's like with a ballplayer— especially a starting pitcher. On game day, most starting pitchers are "in a zone" and not really interested in conversation. I guess I'm similar in many ways.

My singing style has certainly changed over the years, and it's largely been a conscious effort. Where I used to aspire to the smooth, fluid styling of bass singers like Armond Morales, over the years I've adopted more of a pointed tone like George Younce, of The Cathedrals.

In gospel music we, unscientifically, refer to it as having "raaah" (which rhymes with "man".) It simply means that like the point of a knife, it cuts through, or penetrates better. George has been the source, not only of much inspiration but also of valued counsel. He once told me that I should think of the word "green" when I sing. When you say the word out loud, it is automatically out front, bright and penetrating. Singing "green" is similar to what Dr. Quisling preaches to me about my speaking voice. Though he doesn't use the same words, he's trying to get me to talk "green" to open my voice and minimize the strain. The mistake a lot of bass singers make is trying to find their lowest tones way back in their throats, but that's not where the lowest notes are to be found. Besides, singing back there will wear your throat out very quickly.

While we're on the subject of low notes, bass singers are always asked what is the lowest note they can sing. I've recorded some pretty low notes in my years. On "First Step to Heaven," from the *From the Heart* CD I sing an F note below low C. But, the lowest note I've ever recorded is on "Working On A Building," from the same project, on which I sing an E below low C. I think it's no coincidence that both of those low notes came in recent years, after age forty, just like J.D. and George told me would happen.

☙☙☙

I can't address the issues associated with singing without mentioning the technological advances of recent years. One of the best things to ever happen for my singing has been the advent of in-ear monitors. When an artist sings onstage, he, of course, needs to hear himself. For years this was accomplished with speakers—called monitors or wedges—that sat on the stage in front of, and angled back towards, the singer, projecting the voices and band instruments so that he could hear himself and the others on stage. A few years back, we—all of us except Duane—moved away from floor monitors and began using small wireless monitors that deliver the sounds into our ears through ear pieces, similar to those that people use with their iPods or other music devices.

Since the first day I put those monitors in my ears, I found a new lease on my singing life. For me, it allows the re-creation of the atmosphere of a recording studio where every other voice and instrument is distinguishable and balanced to my own liking. The mix I have in my ears is certainly not a mix that anyone else would want to hear. I, of course, need to hear Joe, Duane and Golden, and I need to hear the band—especially the instruments that provide pitch (piano and guitar)—but I also need to have a lot of my own voice.

Physically, it's easier to sing higher tones louder than you can sing low tones, so the benefit that in-ears offer me is the ability to adjust the Equalization (or EQ), which means boosting or reducing the level of the different frequencies in a signal. Though it seems counter intuitive, as a bass singer, I don't want my EQ to be low-end and bass-y. I need it to be clean, with a lot of highs, so that my voice can penetrate and cut through the rest of the music I'm hearing. Chris Demonbreun, who has been our monitor engineer for a few years now, really has me dialed in nicely. I don't even have to do sound checks any more; he always has my mix perfectly in my ears, which allows me to concentrate on my singing, and takes away one more topic for that "little man" in my head to throw at me.

During our heyday when we were playing huge venues, floor monitors were the standard. I can remember the crowds were so deafening in their applause and screams, and we had so much going on onstage musically (and coming through the wedges), that I sometimes did entire shows without ever being able to hear myself. I just had to put it on auto-pilot and trust my instincts, and hope that I was singing on pitch. But now, I can hear every note of every song, and that's a very nice feeling.

As I've gotten older, and as is natural, I've lost some of my hearing. And the first thing that goes with hearing loss is the high tones. The beauty of the in-ears is that the monitor tech can compensate and re-place some of those highs. All of this converges to create a very comfort-able situation conducive to good singing—especially for a bass singer who sometimes has less confidence than he should.

I've mentioned that Duane has chosen to stay with floor moni-tors. That's just a personal choice for him, as the in-ears are for me. He's most comfortable—and gets his needs met—by using wedges. And the flawless performances he puts out there every night is a testament that it works well for him.

With age—and with the health issues that everyone will invari-ably face—we spend more time realizing that there will come a day when the four of us are no longer together. And, that is going to be a sad day. As a result, we're grateful for every day we spend together. While the prob-lems we once had are well documented, there have been many groups who never could learn to coexist. They might perform on stage together, and might have recording success, but they live completely separate lives. They travel separately, they arrive separately, they require sepa-rate (but equal) dressing rooms, they demand their hotel rooms be on separate floors, they don't speak off stage. I've never understood how they even exist that way; the pressure that comes with hating each other that much—or just having feelings of sheer indifference—must be crippling. That is something that will never happen with us. We still enjoy being together and we still enjoy performing for the fans. We've developed a good working relationship, and we've developed a true love for each other. We love what we do. If we ever stop loving it, we'll stop traveling. Until then, we're going to keep on going. It's as simple as that. We are brothers.

CHAPTER NINE: *Heading for Home*

When I was three years old my Uncle Pete—my mom's brother—changed my life. He took me to my first baseball game. We sat in the centerfield bleachers of Connie Mack stadium on a warm summer day in 1946 and watched the Philadelphia Phillies take on the Chicago Cubs. I couldn't believe my senses that day: the huge monument of a stadium, the concrete walkway, that brilliant green field spreading out in front of us, the Phillies in their bright white uniforms and red caps, the Cubs in their road grays, the smell of the cigar smoke and peanuts roasting, the hot dogs and popcorn. Uncle Pete had no way of knowing it, but on that day he introduced me to a love that would stay true to this very day. As James Earl Jones' character would say to Kevin Costner's in *Field of Dreams*: "It's baseball, Ray!"

Because he knew I loved it so much, Dad took me to several games as a child also. But as soon as I was old enough, I would go by myself. I had it down: I'd take the subway from Camden over to Philadelphia, get off on 21st and Lehigh, and then walk to Connie Mack. Every kid I knew was a Phillies fan—and we all wanted to be either Robin Roberts or Richie Ashburn.

I still remember 1950. The Phillies—the Whiz Kids—were in the World Series for the first time since 1915. Back in those days, of course, most World Series games were played during the daytime, and the region was so taken by the team that, with a permission slip from their parents', school kids were allowed to leave school early to go home so they could listen to the games on the radio or watch on TV. As I've already mentioned, at that time we didn't have a television, but my father's parents did, so I can still remember turning in my permission slip, leaving behind my friends whose parents didn't understand the beauty of baseball, and walking to my grandparents' to watch my beloved Phils.

Sadly, in the end, the Whiz Kids were swept by the hated Yankees that year but we were so strong, there was no doubt we'd win it next year. Of course, as a seven year old, I hadn't yet learned the painful truth that "next year" didn't always happen, and that, for the Fightin' Phils, it would take thirty "next years" before they'd bring home a world championship. On the other hand, I also could have never imagined that when "next year" finally did come, I would be there to experience it!

Since I couldn't know any of that then, and since dreams die hard, many were the nights I would lay in my bed with the transistor radio, and dial in the Phils on WIBG to hear Byrum Saam or Gene Kelly paint those glorious word pictures. When they were in the Midwest—or later, the west coast—I would turn the volume way down so my parents wouldn't hear me up so late past my bedtime. Somehow, deep down, I suspect they knew I was listening.

Years later, when I was living in Binghamton, NY, there was a minor league baseball team there called the Triplets (so-named for the triple cities of Binghamton, Johnson City and Endicott.) It's odd but I'd only known major-league baseball, namely the Phillies. I remember the first night I went to see the Triplets play at Johnson Field. Entering that little park, I felt much the same excitement that I'd felt some twenty years earlier walking into Connie Mack Stadium. I remember being shocked to realize that, though there were only twenty major league teams at that time, there were dozens and dozens of minor league teams around the country. It really excited me to think that there were games going on in minor league stadiums like this all over the country on that very night. I'll have to admit that, though I always loved major league baseball—and still do—that night in Binghamton kindled a love of, and a respect for, minor league baseball that continues still to this day.

Any time the tour schedule would allow, whether at home or on the road, any free night would find me at a minor league park watching a game between previously anonymous teams. It didn't matter that I'd rarely ever heard of any of the players—or that most of them would never make the big leagues—I just loved watching the games. It magnified my feelings, whatever they were. When things were going good, watching a game just seemed to make things better. When something in my life was going poorly, baseball provided a way to escape for a few hours. This remains true today.

Though professional baseball had been played in Nashville for nearly a hundred years, in 1963, the Double-A Nashville Vols had folded and left Nashville without a professional team, though colleges, of course, still played. In my early days in Nashville, if I was in town during the spring months, chances were pretty good I could be found at Vanderbilt University watching games. At that time, they were coached by a man named Larry Schmittou. By 1977, Schmittou had retired from coaching and put together a group of investors to attempt to bring back professional baseball to Nashville. He leased land to build a stadium, and soon began construction.

After reading about this in the Nashville newspaper, I got very excited. Though I wished I could have been a part of the ownership group, in '77, The Oaks were still very much a struggling quartet, not yet having found any widespread commercial success. With the release of "Y'all Come Back Saloon," however, things were beginning to look up. While construction was underway at the stadium site, Larry kept a little makeshift office in a small shed on the grounds. One day, out of the clear blue sky, I drove down there and knocked on Larry's door, and introduced myself to him. To my pleasure and surprise, he'd heard of The Oaks. I told him what a huge baseball fan I was, and that I had watched him coach at Vanderbilt. I explained that I couldn't afford to buy into the team but that I would love to somehow be involved. So, much like Bonsall had done with me back at Gimbels all those years ago, I started hanging around Larry Schmittou talking baseball (instead of gospel quartets).

Schmittou was a baseball man through and through—and he was a genius marketer. He was cut from the same cloth as legendary owner Bill Veeck, who, among other things was known for signing a 3' 7" player named Eddie Gaedel to be a pinch hitter for his St. Louis Browns, or the night, in Chicago, when he had the promotion to burn disco records, an event which became a riot that culminated with his White Sox having to forfeit the game. Well, Schmittou never had ideas that resulted in that kind of infamy but he certainly could be unorthodox in his approach. Once while coaching at Vanderbilt, in an attempt to delay the game until an impending rainstorm could arrive, he faked having a heart attack while visiting his pitcher on the mound. Other times he would rope off the warning track in the outfield to increase the capacity of the stadium. Once later, when I was involved with the Sounds, he ran a promotion where dollar bills were spread all over the infield and one lucky fan would be given one minute to pick up all of them that he could. I was selected as the official timekeeper, and just before the lucky fan was to begin, Larry pulled me aside and reminded me that this was my money out there on the field just as much as it was his. He looked me in the eye and said, "This guy does not get the full minute!" I don't remember how much time I might have shaved but if I'd ever doubted it before, I knew then that Larry was going to do whatever it took to make baseball successful in Nashville.

I continued hanging around with him in those early days, offering to do everything from paint the outfield fences to laying sod so that the stadium could be ready for opening day. Baseball did in fact make it to Nashville—in the form of the Double-A Nashville Sounds—even though it was delayed an extra week because the stadium wasn't quite finished on time. That first season, I was at every game I could make.

In the off-season, I received a call from Larry telling me that he might have found a way to work it out for me to become a part owner of the team. The General Manager, a man named Ferrell Owens, was interested in selling a small piece of what he owned, so I scraped together the cash to buy one share of the team, at a cost of $9,000. It was a way for me to put my money (that I didn't have) where my mouth was, and officially become part of the team that I'd adopted. I finally felt less of an outsider as I walked around on the field getting to know the players, coaches and manager. It became an exciting toy for me to play with. We were a Double-A farm team for the Cincinnati Reds at first, then the New York

Yankees, and eventually, in the middle 80's, we bought the Detroit Tigers Triple-A team from Evansville, IN (ironically nicknamed the Triplets) and moved them to Nashville. We later affiliated with the Chicago White Sox, then the Pittsburgh Pirates, and for the last six or seven years, the Milwaukee Brewers. We've seen many future major leaguers through the years, including Don Mattingly, Willie McGee, Prince Fielder, Aramis Ramirez and many others.

Through the years, I continued to buy additional shares—some more from Ferrell, as well as from some of the other owners. Because of the Music City connection, artists had always been part of the ownership group; Conway Twitty and Cal Smith had been there from the beginning and, later, Larry Gatlin and Jerry Reed would be owners.

My attorney, Gary Spicer, is also The Oaks' attorney in many matters. Through the years, he has represented many artists, athletes and actors. In fact, it was he who helped me increase my ownership in the Sounds. He represented Conway Twitty. In the early nineties, Conway needed some money for a deal he was working on, so Gary was able to put the two of us together to make the deal which allowed me to buy Conway's share of the team.

Spicer specialized in helping bail out artists from messes they had gotten themselves into. There was a time, in the late eighties and early nineties, when tax shelters were the hot commodity. Many artists found themselves sinking money into windmills or real estate, amusement parks or longhorn cattle. Most often those deals left a lot to be desired, and an expert was needed to sort out the details and salvage any good that existed—and Gary was that expert. Fortunately, for me, he was able to mostly keep me on the right path, one that led me to owning a larger share of the Sounds.

In 2008, the team was sold to a new ownership group, and since I was still only a minority owner, I had no choice but to sell my shares; I had to abide by the majority vote. So, for the first time in thirty years, I didn't own a baseball team. I still feel like a part of the team. In fact, I am; I was named Official Team Ambassador last season and will continue in that role this year. Our priority now is to get a new stadium built. The one that I saw go up when Schmittou first brought the team to town was a great park back then, but we're in dire need of a new one. I still go to a lot of games and hang out with the players on the field during batting practice. I even do some occasional color on their radio broadcasts—something that I also do regularly with the Vanderbilt University baseball team. Their coach, Tim Corbin, and I have become great friends. Baseball has always been—and remains—my hobby, a diversion from the music business.

In the summer of 2012, two baseball-related things are scheduled to occur that I must say I never dreamed would ever happen to me. The Sounds surprised me with a promotional night that will feature a giveaway of an official Richard Sterban Bobblehead figure. I must admit, in its own way, that means as much to me as one of the awards that sit on the shelf in my music room. It's just a very cool, quirky honor.

Another unexpected honor came to me by way of Davidson Academy, the private Christian school that both of my daughters attended. We knew that they were trying to update some of their athletic facilities, and like most parents, we donated towards their efforts.

Imagine my shocked pride when I learned that the school had decided to name the athletic fields *The Richard Sterban Athletic Complex*. Now don't forget, I, most often, found myself in the box, coaching first base, and yet I find myself, all these years later, with what I consider the great honor of being memorialized in such a meaningful way. It's a nice feeling to know that, long after I'm gone, kids who love sports just as much as I always have—and many who are far more talented at playing the games I love—will follow their dreams on fields situated on a complex bearing my name. What an honor!

☙☙☙

With The Oaks, through the years, there have been many times when my avocation and vocation converged, which, as expected, were great days for me. We have sung the National Anthem at countless games from Spring Training exhibitions, in front of a few thousand, to World Series and All-Star Games in front of millions.

We've had many good friends who played major league baseball; not only Phillies like Mike Schmidt, Tug McGraw, Greg Luzinski, Pete Rose and Ron Reed, but also other greats like Johnny Bench, Darrell Evans, Tommy Lasorda, George Brett and the late, great Hall of Fame catcher, Gary Carter.

We were welcomed on the field, and in the clubhouses, of some of our favorite teams. When Rose was playing for the Phillies, I remember him saying, "Do you realize how many lounge acts around the country are singing 'Elvira?' But, you guys are the reason for it; you guys are the ones who made it famous. You guys are big league, just like we are. You guys are welcome in this clubhouse anytime." In fact, that Phillies team used our song, "Dig A Little Deeper (In The Well)" as their theme song in 1980, and we were, indeed, in the clubhouse spraying champagne with them at the end of that season, the night "next year" finally came and they won the World Series.

One time, at a World Series, we almost missed our chance to sing the anthem. It was 1985 when the St. Louis Cardinals played the Kansas City Royals. We were scheduled to sing at Game Seven in Kansas City, if the game was played. I was at home watching Game Six on television, and it was looking like the Cardinals were going to win it all, taking with them our chance to sing. In the bottom of the ninth, the first base umpire, a veteran named Don Denkinger, blew a call that gave the Royals the chance they needed to comeback and win the game, forcing a Game Seven. Of course, this was long before the advent of the Internet and around-the-clock sports-talk, but the missed call was the main topic of conversation on the news. Many—especially Cardinals fans—were furious that such a travesty could occur in such an important game in front of a national television audience. I have to admit that I agreed completely that he'd blown the call—something that he would admit later—but for four guys sitting in Hendersonville, Tennessee, all we cared about was that we were going to sing the Anthem the next night at Game Seven. The Royals ended up winning that game and the Series. It was thrilling to be there, in their home park for the celebration.

Once when we were playing a show at the Philadelphia Spectrum, Joe and I were asked to play in a celebrity softball game to be held across the street at the Phillies' Veterans Stadium, just across the river from my hometown. I can still remember standing at home plate and looking out across the field to the big "jumbotron" video screen hanging above the centerfield wall. Seeing my face and name up there was, in its own way, as thrilling as seeing The Oak Ridge Boys name in lights on marquees in Las Vegas or Radio City Music Hall or the Forum in Los Angeles. It was impossible to comprehend how many miles I had traveled since seeing that first game, so many years ago, with my uncle—just up the street where the old stadium used to be. And now, here I was where the Phillies of the day played. To paraphrase what the Saturday Night Live character used to say, "Baseball had been very, very good to me!"

෩෩෩

Something else that has been very good to me (and for me) has been the fresh air of the seashore. That has long been my vacation of choice, whether it's Key West, or Jost Van Dyke, in the British Virgin Islands, or the Jersey shore. As much as The Oaks travel, you might think I'd be tempted to stay home any opportunity I have—and of course, I love to be home with my wife, Donna, and our girls, now—but I also love to travel to the ocean. For me, the first time I ever put my feet in the sand, the magic of the seaside got into my soul. It's just a wonderful place to find rest and relaxation. The sun, surf and sand rejuvenate me regardless of what has been going on in my life. Fortunately for me, Donna feels the same way about the ocean, so that's always our destination when schedules allow. Sometimes we'll sail, sometimes we'll snorkel, sometimes we'll hike, and sometimes, we simply sit in the sand and relax.

One of our favorite places is in Grand Cayman, called Rum Point. Many times I have sat there on the sand with Donna, each of us nursing some island concoction, watching the sun go down. And every time we're there, I have the same thought: Though I hope it's not tonight, whenever it comes my time to die, I hope it happens right here as I watch the sun dip beneath the horizon.

Another of my favorite spots is at Cane Garden Bay in Tortola. Here is where you'll find one of my favorite musicians you've probably never heard of. His name is Quito Rymer, and he is a terrific reggae artist; I just love to listen to him. In fact, I always thought if I were to do a solo album, I'd want Quito as a special guest. His fusion of music blends reggae instrumentation and style with almost gospel lyrics, very wholesome and meaningful. When he performs at his place on the beach there in Tortola, in addition to the tourists, the locals come out to listen and to dance to his cool island sounds.

For years I owned a beachfront condo in Atlantic City. It was close enough that we could get to it with some regularity, and was also near my Mom, so I could see her, as well. Nearby was one of our very favorite restaurants, a great little Italian place called *Angeloni's*. I still love it. In fact, when The Oaks appeared in Atlantic City in April of 2012, we went to *Angeloni's* for dinner.

I became good friends with the owner, a man named Alan Angeloni, because of a bottle of wine that I ordered. *Angeloni's* wine list is superb, and is an award winner on the *Wine Spectator* list. Once while dining there alone, I ordered a certain bottle of wine, and as it was delivered to my table, Alan came with it. He said he was so impressed with my selection that he wanted to meet the person who would order this bottle. We hit it off, and, with that, our friendship began. It has become a regular haunt for Donna and me when we are in the area.

Once, back in 1991, I believe, Alan and his girlfriend, Jackie, joined Donna and me on a trip to New York City to see Keith Carradine starring in the Broadway show, *The Will Rogers Follies*. We hired a limo to take us to the city. Before the show, we went to dinner at the famous restaurant, *21*. After we had been seated, there was a commotion at the front door and suddenly, in walked former President Ronald Reagan and his wife, Nancy, along with another couple. The Oaks had sung for President Reagan many times, but while I would have loved to have said hello, of course, we didn't want to disturb their dinner, so we went back to our conversation.

Later during dinner, I excused myself to go to the men's room. As I stood at the urinal, someone walked in whistling, and took the position next to me. As I moved to the sink to wash my hands, he did as well. At this point we made eye contact and there he was, President Reagan. I introduced myself, and he immediately remembered me, recalling the times The Oaks had performed for him. We had a nice chat, and on our way back into the restaurant, he even stopped by our table so that I could introduce him to our friends. Alan couldn't believe it. He said he thought it was going to be just a quiet dinner and a night at the theatre, and instead he ended up meeting a President.

After dinner, as we went to our limo to head to the show, we noticed a second one parked just in front of ours. As if on cue, President Reagan and his party exited the restaurant and got into the other waiting car. We both pulled out, creating an unofficial and spontaneous two-car motorcade. In an ending that seems too ironic to be true, we followed his limo all the way to The Palace Theatre; he was also attending *The Will Rogers Follies.* Needless to say, it was a very fun evening.

৵৵৵

The fact that Alan had taken notice of a wine that I ordered actually pleased me. For a long time, I was quite a collector of wines. I had a cellar built in our home, and enjoyed filling it with cases of our favorite vintages. I love to read about what makes one particular wine better than another; I've studied the art of winemaking, from the vineyards to the store shelves. My friendship with Alan has helped spur it on as a hobby, and I've become a pretty avid collector.

I like a bigger, bolder wine; I prefer reds to whites. My favorites are probably Cabernet Sauvignons or Red Zinfandels. I also love the challenge of identifying which wines were over-rated. I always thought it wrong, somehow, that people would brag on how much they paid for a bottle of wine. In my view, anyone could overpay for something— a car, a home, even a bottle of wine. I challenged myself to learn how, and where, to find a great bottle of wine that wasn't the most expensive in the store. It definitely can be done, and I've greatly enjoyed my time doing it!

Something that goes hand-in-hand with my tastes in wine was my enjoyment of a good cigar. Many don't understand the similarities between good wine and a good cigar: the aging process of both, the differences between a dark and lighter wine and a dark or lighter cigar. To me, one of the best ways to relax is to drink a nice glass of wine and smoke a good cigar. Though the places in which one can smoke a cigar are dwindling, I still enjoy one now and then.

These two hobbies led me to discover a simple pleasure that stays with me through today. As I've said, I'm probably a classic loner;

I just enjoy being by myself. While I've never really been a big drinker, I have long enjoyed the comfort and solitude of "bellying up to a bar" or sinking into a billowy leather booth at a cool club or sports bar. I might sample a local wine or sip a snifter of brandy, and, when possible, light up a nice Arturo Fuentes cigar, and watch a game on one of the televisions, or simply just relax in the darkened silence. In the beginning it might have simply provided an escape from the monotony of the road but as the years passed it became a haven away from the lights, the sounds, the demands of the road, the screaming crowds, the constant media respon-sibilities and the other blessings that curse a performer's life. Especially during the "Elvira" years, we would be met by screaming fans anywhere we went, and they were eager and willing to go to any lengths to meet us. They would camp out at the hotels at which they thought we were stay-ing or surround the buses, or sneak backstage. The ironic thing is that after almost every show, they could have found me in a quiet bar, sitting alone and drinking a glass of wine. Like with so many other aspects of life, it's the simple things that bring us the most pleasure.

Another hobby that allows me to feed my need for solitude is cycling, which also provides many other health benefits for me. Not only is it a way to relieve stress, it is just a great form of physical fitness. I used to carry a bicycle on the bus to ride while we toured, but I don't do that anymore. I still love to ride, but, as I've aged, my allergies have worsened to the point that I cannot ride on days when I have to sing. I've replaced it with the far less satisfying (for me, anyway) spinning, at the gym. While it's a good form of exercise, it's just not the same; it doesn't provide the same level of enjoyment. I really miss being outside.

Perhaps the hobby that brings the most chuckles is my interest in the weather. It's an interest that began when I was a freshman in college. I had to take a class on meteorology, and rather than it being a drag, I loved it. I was fascinated with cloud formations and fronts progressing, and the like. But the interest remained pretty latent until the advent of *The Weather Channel,* and then, with an endless supply of information, I developed a full-blown addiction. I watched it all the time; I knew the personalities, even felt like I knew them personally. One of their famous (or perhaps infamous) correspondents is Jim Cantore. He's the one who always reports live in the worst weather conditions. As people have joked, the last thing you want to see on TV is Jim Cantore reporting live from your neighborhood, or even your city! He's actually someone I'd like to meet. I'd love, sometime, to go out on assignment with him, go up in a hurricane-tracking airplane or something similar. I must admit, while I still love to follow the weather—and still watch faithfully—since the introduction of the MLB (Major League Baseball) Network, that channel now supplements my viewing habits.

My interest in the weather (along with my voice) has actually led to an unexpected career opportunity. For years, I've done public service announcements for the National Oceanic and Atmospheric Association (NOAA) weather radio network, the "voice" of the National Weather Service.

The hobby that has probably gained the most public attention, though, is my interest in fashion. As I've stated, it dates back to my days at Gimbels, long before I could really afford nice things. But it is something that has stayed with me all through my life, during the lean years as well as the heady times. I'm often asked how, and why, I started dressing the way I do onstage. I can't really say how it started but I can definitely point to the time when it started getting so much attention.

The National Association of Recording Arts and Sciences (the organization that presents the Grammy Award) used to hold an annual fashion show that featured artists as the models. Because of my interest in fashion, one year, I volunteered to participate. The day before, I had to go downtown for a fitting and to meet with Pieter O'Brien, the fashion consultant who had been hired for the event. For years, he had been the Fashion Editor for *Gentlemen's Quarterly Magazine* (GQ) so he was a pretty impressive guy. We hit it off from the very start, and he helped make the event a lot of fun. He even let me keep the outfit that I had worn on the catwalk, and I often wore it onstage with The Oaks, and in a photo shoot.

A few weeks after the fashion show, Kathy Gangwisch, our long-time publicist, called me and said that she and Pieter had been talking, and that she though it might be productive if he and I got together. I had always enjoyed dressing in my own style, and as The Oaks gained more success, my clothes had started to gain a certain amount of attention from the fans and the media. She thought he might be able to help take my own fashion sense to a higher level.

Pieter and I arranged to meet in New York. At our first meeting, he said that he'd love to work with me; I told him I would like that as well. He promised that he would never push me to the point that I would be uncomfortable, but his only caveat was that he was going to be "brutally blunt" with me, and that I had to agree to trust him and take his direction. I agreed, and with that, we were off. As we walked down Fifth Avenue, he looked me up and down, he tugged at the shoulders of the jacket I was wearing, he pulled at my cuffs, and then without warning, he stopped me. He pointed at my shoes and he said, "Those are the ugliest shoes I've ever seen. You need to take those off right now and throw them in that trash can right there." I looked at him and laughed, but he stood his ground and never cracked a smile. I knew he couldn't be serious but it turns out that he was. I assumed this must be a test of wills. I knelt down and began taking off my right shoe when he stopped me. He said, "OK, you can stop. You don't have to throw them away right now, but they will be in the trashcan before the day is over." With that, we were off again.

That day was the start of a relationship that would last for many years. Beginning with that trip, Donna and I would meet Pieter in New York City at least twice a year and I would buy a new wardrobe. Those trips, as well as his consultations, were a very expensive proposition for me, but I knew immediately that they were worth it. My reputation for fashion became widely known, and I was even fortunate enough to be named to many best-dressed lists through the years.

One December, Pieter invited me to his estate, just outside of New York City, for a Christmas party. This was going to be one of the biggest events of the season for the fashion world. The guest list included all of the top models as well as the fashion designers, and writers and critics from all of the top publications and trades. Donna was already there when my sedan delivered me from the airport. She and Pieter met me as I stepped from the car. I was wearing an outfit that he and I had chosen on my most recent buying spree. In fact, he had told me when I bought it that I should wear it to this party; that it would be perfect. The only accessory that he hadn't seen was the boots that I had bought to wear with the outfit. I don't know what it was with him and my shoes! As soon as he saw them, he rolled his eyes and told me there was no way I could go into his house to his party wearing these boots. Apparently, they looked "too new." As I stood in his driveway he knelt down and grabbed some gravel and rubbed them on the tops of these brand-new, first-time-worn (very expensive) boots. I guess it was my own fault; I'd said I would trust whatever he said.

That party was like something I'd never seen; we were surrounded by some of the most gorgeous women with perfect figures, and great looking men with chiseled features. It was like a television show full of beautiful people. At that time, The Oaks were riding pretty high, so many of the people there recognized me, which was gratifying. Even the fashion editor from *The New York Times* was interested to hear my thoughts and theories on fashion. It was a very cool night for me.

People often ask me where I got my style, and I think its fair to say that, although I definitely had some very distinct tastes already, and had developed my own sense of style, Pieter helped me sharpen it. He is an extremely talented designer, and he is still a friend. He helped me push the envelope, but true to his word, he never made me uncomfortable. Donna has always had a great eye for fashion also, and over the years Pieter helped her hone her own skills even more. I still consult with Pieter occasionally but we do not work together regularly anymore; Donna serves as my main advisor now. My oldest daughter, Lauren, even gets into the act now. Recently she has been going through the clothes I have in storage and pulling out the things that are suddenly hip and hot again, and I'm putting them back into stage rotation.

Pieter did just make a recent contribution to my look. He suggested that I shave, so after having it for a few years, I shaved the "soul patch," which has elicited a lot of comments from fans. One friend and fan who was happy when I shaved it was Barbara Bush. She didn't like it at all, saying that it made me look like the devil. She said it once in front of our long-time mutual friend, General Chuck Yeager, and, ever since then, he never fails to remind me of it every time we see him.

But I suppose no conversation about my style would be complete without a few words about my hair. I think the only story that might have surpassed the chatter that occurred when I grew my hair out was when Britney Spears shaved her head a few years ago. Some fans loved my longer style, and some acted as if I had run over someone's pet. All these years later, my own mother isn't happy about it. There were even news stories about it. And people still ask about it, almost nine years since I first grew it out. So here, for the first time anywhere, I'm going to, once and for all, answer the question of why I did it. I've never thought it was necessarily anyone's business, so I've avoided the question but there's no better place to finally answer it, so I'll do it here and now. I grew my hair out for only one reason: because I wanted to. Simple as that.

Donna and I ran into my old friend, Tony Brown, at a Grammy party. Donna complimented Tony on his hair, and he suggested I go see the lady that cuts his. As it turned out, I was looking for someone new, so I did. I told her I'd like to grow my hair out some, so to do that, she suggested first that we cut it very short, shorter than it had been since I was a kid. It then started growing, and the longer it got, the more I liked it (and the more Donna liked it, too.) So, I just let it grow. Will I ever cut it short again? Perhaps. I doubt that I'll ever go as short as it was for so many years, but I can see a time in the future when I might go a little shorter. Only time will tell.

As a loner, and as a very quiet person, the most personal of things is often the most difficult to talk about, but they are also, often, the most important. My family is vitally important to me—and they have lived through the best times and the worst times of my life and career. By virtue of that, they have seen the best and the worst of the effects of that success. Though my first marriage, to Sandra, fell prey to the pressures of life on the road, I know that she would agree that the three sons we had during our time together more than made up for any of the struggles that we had as a couple.

My first born, Rich, is a senior adjuster in the insurance business and lives just a few miles up the road from me in Portland, Tennessee. He's married, and has given me two wonderful grandkids: Mali and Nikalous. Doug, my middle son, is also married and is a chiropractor in the Nashville area. He has daughter, Madelyn, and a son, Matthew Tyler (the one who will be attending Southwestern Assemblies of God University, where I taught at the Stamps-Baxter School of Music.) Doug's son, Zach, was killed in 2010 in a car wreck. I still miss him every day. My youngest son, Chris, lives in Springfield, Missouri and has one daughter, Alexandra. He got his Bachelor's degree from Middle Tennessee State University, and, in May of 2011, he graduated from Southwest Missouri State

University with a doctorate in physical therapy. My three boys have been the source of much pride for me; they're good sons and they've all grown into good men.

I first met my wife, Donna, when she was working as a hostess for George "Goober" Lindsey at his celebrity golf tournament for the *Special Olympics,* in Montgomery, Alabama. Any interest I might have had in her was tempered by the fact that I was still in a marriage that I wasn't ready to give up on. Any interest she might have had in me was tempered by the fact that she mistook my quiet nature for me being an arrogant jerk. She couldn't understand why I said so little to her over the course of the day. I saw her again the following year at the tournament and, by then, I was separated, and she had just ended a serious relationship, so we talked about the possibilities of seeing each other sometime in the future.

Our first date was to see a minor league hockey game in Nashville. She wouldn't go with me, preferring instead to meet me there, but we had a nice time and agreed to go out again. For our first "real date" I picked her up in my maroon AMC Pacer (yes, seriously) and we went to see Emmylou Harris and David Alan Coe perform in concert at Vanderbilt University. Soon, we were seeing each other regularly.

A couple of years later, we were engaged to be married, but as the day approached I just didn't feel like I was ready to wed again; it just didn't feel like the right thing for me to do at that time. I really had serious doubts that I could be faithful to one woman, and while my spiritual life, at the time, might not have been strong enough to "force" me to do so, it was definitely strong enough that I knew it would cause me a lot of guilt and conviction if I'd married her but kept up my rambling ways. While it was one of the hardest things I've ever had to do, I broke it off. At about four in the morning on my to-be wedding day, I decided I had to get out of town—had to clear my head—so, for some reason still unknown to me, I decided I would drive the four hours to Gatlinburg, in the Great Smoky Mountains of East Tennessee. After less than an hour, a heavy snow began to fall so I checked into a hotel on the interstate and slept a few hours.

When I awoke, I was a jumble of emotions. I knew that by that time, the news had spread to Donna and everyone else. I was sad and worried and guilty and perhaps a little ashamed, but I was still resolute. Though I knew many wouldn't understand, I knew the feelings—the doubts—I was experiencing were real. In a strange way, I believed they were coming from God.

I was scheduled to fly to Orlando, Florida on the day after the wedding for a CMA board meeting, and for what was to have been our honeymoon, so I drove back to my condo to pack, and spend the night. When I arrived, Donna was there. I certainly hadn't expected to see her. She wasn't angry; she wasn't out of control. She just asked me why? I was honest with her to the extent that I could be. I couldn't bring myself to tell her that I wanted to see other women, so I just told her that it didn't feel right, and I didn't think our marriage could work at that time.

In an amazing show of maturity—and to demonstrate just what kind of woman Donna is—she gave me back the engagement ring. It was mind-boggling to me that she would do that. Though many of her friends advised her to keep it, it just wasn't in her make-up to do so. She told me that it no longer meant anything to her. While in retrospect that was certainly understandable, at the time it really hurt me. And in a strange way, her doing that immediately set my mind to thinking that perhaps she was someone for whom it would be worth my giving up other women. I recognized that there really was something special about her.

Ironically, after this happened, it seemed that the allure of the "single life," out on the road, no longer held the fascination—or, frankly, the satisfaction—that it once held. I wish I could say that God immediately turned me around but it didn't happen that quickly, but it did, definitely happen. Somehow through it all, Donna and I were able to remain friends and stay in close contact. Eventually, we were even able to comfortably date again. She came to understand that my concerns had truly been about my own life; they didn't have anything to do with how I felt about her. I came to believe that God had brought Donna into my life as someone that I needed at that time. I came to understand that I no longer had to live a lie. I could be faithful to one woman.

Another unintended consequence of this situation was, that it brought my personal life front and center in The Oak Ridge Boys' business, in the form of an article that ran in the Knoxville News-Sentinel about my aborted wedding. They got some of the facts basically right: that I had been engaged, that I had left my fiancée just days before the wedding; but the biggest thing they got wrong was the name of my fiancée. Instead of Donna Summers from Mobile, Alabama, they ran a headline and a photo of Donna Summer, the disco-music-recording artist. That caused quite the uproar in both the worlds of country and disco music. Our publicist, Kathy Gangwisch immediately contacted Donna Summer's people so that they would know we hadn't planted that story as a publicity stunt. Lord knows that that sort of publicity was the last thing I wanted at that time in my life.

Donna (Summers, not Summer) and I have been married now for twenty-four years and have been blessed with two daughters. Lauren, who was born in 1989, is a stage actress and director. She recently graduated the *International Academy of Design and Technology*, where she studied digital photography. Victoria (Tori) arrived in 1995 and is now a freshman in high school. She loves dancing and hopes to be a schoolteacher.

It's amazing to look back over my life and re-live all that I've been able to accomplish. It's like a ballplayer: he might dream of being the hero of a big game and of leading his team to a world championship, but the common thread for all greats is that they say they never even dreamed of being voted into the Hall of Fame—that just seems like too much to hope for. For me, I certainly wanted to be a singer, and even hoped to be famous one day, and win awards, but something I could have never imagined was the pleasure and pride I would experience by being a husband and father—and, now, a grandfather. I've been blessed with five great kids and seven grandkids. I wasn't always physically there— life on the road can do that—but I think they all know that, in reality, I've been "there" for them. To paraphrase the great Yankee, Lou Gehrig, I really do consider myself the luckiest man in the world.

CHAPTER TEN: *Boom Boom!*

Anyone familiar with The Oaks knows that we have a long of history of being active civically and politically. This was less a decision that we made over the years, and more of a reflection of our own beliefs and hopes for the country's future. While we've always understood, and respected, that our fans across the country come from differing backgrounds and political persuasions, we believe that there are times when we must stand up, whether for causes we believe in—things like the National Anthem Project—or for candidates we support.

Sometimes we worked for a candidate because he was the nominee of the party we supported, rather than someone with whom we had a personal history. Other times we set aside our careers in order to help someone who was a friend. Of course, The Oaks history books well chronicle the special relationship that we've forged with George Herbert Walker Bush, the forty-first President of the United States (or "41" as he's affectionately become known) and his wonderful family.

The first time we ever met him was when President Reagan invited us to perform at the White House for the annual White House Congressional Picnic in October of 1983. One of the highlights for us was when "The Gipper" said that The Oaks had more gold than Fort Knox. But more importantly, that was the day we realized what a true fan we had in President Reagan's Vice President. During sound check, he made a beeline to the stage to greet us, and over the next few minutes requested—and then sang along to—not just our hits but also our album cuts (including "Freckles" from our first country album.) Through the years when we've been with him, whether on campaign events, special occasions, official functions, private time in Houston or at his oceanfront compound, Walker's Point, in Kennebunkport, Maine. I'm not sure who has benefited the most from the relationship. I can say, unashamedly, that we love him and his family, and can also say, with humility and appreciation, that they have always been very good to The Oak Ridge Boys and our wives.

I remember many years after our first meeting, in 2005 at the second Inauguration of his eldest son, George W. Bush (the forty-third President or "43".) We were in D.C. to perform for some of the Inaugural guests. Before our show we were in the dressing room at the Georgetown Four Seasons watching TV coverage of the Inaugural Parade. As the parade was drawing to close, the network cameras caught the image of the 41st President standing up and leaning over and whispering into the ear of the 43rd President. They shook hands, and then 41 and Barbara departed. A few minutes later, we were being introduced onto the stage to perform. As we took to the stage, there was a small commotion at the entrance to the ballroom. Through the lights, we could make out the recognizable features of George and Barbara as they walked through the crowd, down to the foot of the stage. We each reached down and shook their hands and he told us to keep singing. So, sing we did while the crowd respectfully left them alone, and they stood listening (and yes, still singing along) to every song.

After the show concluded, we were backstage visiting with them. We told them how surprised and honored we were that they had come to the show in light of their hectic Inaugural schedule. He told us that he wouldn't have missed it. When we told him that we'd been watching the parade coverage, he told us that when he left, what he'd whispered to George W. was that he was sorry to leave but he and Bar "are going to see The Boys."

When not performing, one of the highlights of our year occurs in August, when we're able to take a little mini-vacation to stay at Walker's Point, the Bush family summer retreat in Kennebunkport, Maine. For about the last fifteen years, we've had a standing invitation to go, and though we wish it could happen every summer, we've been able to work it out about every other year, on average. It's always the four of us along with our wives. The days are filled with fishing and boating or cycling and tennis, cookouts, long conversations, good wine, and even a little singing.

If you've never seen it, Walker's Point is a beautiful home on the craggy Atlantic coast. The compound sits behind a wall for privacy but the curvy road leading to it from town allows for breathtaking views of the home and grounds. Because of the sightseers and photographers, there is even a wide spot in the road where visitors can pull over to safely take pictures and enjoy the view. It's a gorgeous place, and it's easy to understand why the Bushes love it so much.

When we're there, we'll usually eat meals at the house but one of the nights we'll always go out for dinner at one of their favorite local restaurants, and likewise, we'll typically go out for lunch a couple of the days. Over the years a little competition has taken shape where 41 or one of The Oaks will try to creatively pay the check without the other knowing about it. It became a tradition and a game. It started with one of us excusing ourselves from the table to pay, then progressed to calling ahead and trying to pay even before we arrived. One time I had the chance to outsmart him. Most of the gang went out on the President's fishing boat, but I skipped the trip so that I could take a nice bike ride on the breezy coast. We agreed to meet, at a particular time, at a local restaurant called "Yukon Jack's." I would bicycle there and the rest would arrive by water on the President's boat. We'd eaten there several times, so we knew the owner. I made it a point to arrive early, and went to the owner and gave him my credit card. I let him know that 41 was going to fight us mightily on this but that under no circumstances was he to allow the President to pay. After the boat arrived and we'd finished the meal, just as I'd predicted, President Bush protested the fact that the bill had already been paid. On our next visit, he proved that he still held some of the power as the former leader of the free world. At every restaurant we would visit, we'd find that no bill was delivered; he'd pre-arranged the payment all over town.

Our visits always conclude with a little mini, unplugged concert. President Bush has said it's the highlight of his summers. He'll invite several of their friends from Kennebunkport over for dinner. He says it's the hottest ticket of the summer and jokes that he holds the possibility of invitations over his friends all season. From year to year, we'd see many of the same faces. He'd always invite their pastor as well as some of their friends from Washington and Houston who also summer in Maine. Sometimes there might be a famous face or two. After the meal everyone moves from the dining room to the living room where the Boys gather in front of the fireplace and sing a few acapella songs. We'll take requests, which always include "Elvira" and some gospel songs—especially "Amazing Grace," which is always a favorite—and, perhaps, "Thank God For Kids."

One year, he invited so many people that we had to move the informal gathering outside on the front lawn, and even set up a small sound system. Even though it was much bigger and almost like a real show, it was still a lot of fun; however, the next year we were back inside and there were fewer guests, so I think the Bushes decided that they preferred the more informal gatherings.

For meals, Mrs. Bush always insists on making sure the four of us are spread around—we're not even allowed to sit with our wives. I've come to understand that that is a holdover from her days in the White House where couples are separated when seated so that everyone is encouraged to meet and have conversations with people they don't know.

Barbara even turns it into a little game. Prior to dinner, each guest draws a playing card from a deck. The number on the card will correspond to a number at the table, so that is where you're to sit. One year, the seat I drew was next to Senator Olympia Snowe. Though she's a Republican, I would have to say that our views on many subjects are radically different. We both survived the dinner—and political conversation—unscathed, and in the end, she was a very nice lady.

While the dinners primarily consisted of non-celebrities, occasionally there would be some famous folks there too. Over the years, we've dined with Vice President Dick Cheney, Brent Scowcroft and James Baker. The very first time we were there, we met a very stunning woman, a professor at Stanford who had served on the National Security Council for 41 as his Advisor on Soviet and East European Affairs. I remember them saying that she not only spoke several languages fluently but also spoke several dialects of each. Amazingly, she also loved to talk football, and was excited because the NFL season would be starting in about a month. A few years later she could come to national prominence as the Secretary of State for President George W. Bush. Of course it was Condoleeza Rice. She was so impressive, obviously brilliant, but very unassuming.

The Bushes attend the Methodist Church in Kennebunkport. It's perhaps the most beautiful setting I've ever seen for a church, sitting on a group of rocks jutting out in the ocean. On the Sunday morning of our first visit there, we all decided to go to church. While the church sits only a couple of coves away from Walker's Point, there were too many of us there to go over by boat so we rode over. The informal motorcade consisted of several cars and a couple of secret service vehicles. Condi drove the car in which Donna and I rode. We got to know her very well over the course of that weekend, and liked her very much.

For us, Walker's Point has become a periodically recurring once-in-a-lifetime vacation. Ironically, prior to making the decision to run for President in 1980, 41 had considered selling the compound as they didn't really use it, and it had somewhat fallen into disrepair. Because of his memories, however, of being there as a young man, he decided to keep it. Though his campaign for the presidency wasn't successful that year, he soon realized that as Vice President, he would appreciate having someplace to which he could escape for much needed rest and relaxation. All these years later, it seems almost unthinkable that he might not have had it; it has become a place that is almost synonymous with him and his family. For everything else it is, for us it has been a beautiful place to enjoy precious time with wonderful friends. And, for me, it just doesn't get any better than that.

༄༄༄

In January of 1994, Donna and I were on vacation in Key West, FL. We were lying on the beach with our favorite books of that day. I forget what I was reading—probably a baseball biography or Rush Limbaugh's latest shot across the bow of liberalism. Donna was reading Barbara Bush's memoir. At one point she commented to me that the Bush's fiftieth wedding anniversary was coming up in January of 1995. "We, the Nashville country music community, ought to throw them a celebration to thank them for all of their support of us," she, very innocently, said. Neither of us said much more about it, though we later learned that each of us had continued to think about it, realizing that it actually was a pretty good idea.

The Bushes—specifically George H. W.—had probably done as much for country music as any radio station or concert promoter in recent years. Having the leader of the free world promoting the music and its artists had a huge, positive impact on the business. He talked about his favorite artists in media interviews; he invited acts to the White House and to events around the country. He was a fan and didn't mind letting it be known. In fact, in 1991, he'd become the first sitting

President to attend the annual CMA awards. If any national figure deserved a show of gratitude from Nashville, it was this man and his wife of fifty years.

Some time later Donna called the former President's office and introduced herself by pitching the idea to his Chief of Staff, Jean Becker (who soon became Donna's very close friend.) Almost immediately they agreed it was a great idea and one that could, and would, happen. At that point we called on a couple of friends and colleagues for assistance: Kathy Harris, who has worked with The Oaks almost as long as any of us have, and Steve Robinson, an event producer that we had known and worked with, at that time, for a couple years (and the same friend who all these years later helped me write this book).

Over the next several months they worked on turning this innocent idea, and noble concept, into a full-fledged event worthy of the occasion. With the efforts of so many people—including the former President's staff, (most notably, Ron Kaufman who had been the Political Director of 41's White House,) the Gaylord Opryland team, The Nashville Network and so many others, on January 6, 1995, *"With Love from Nashville: The 50th Anniversary Celebration of George and Barbara Bush,"* was held in Nashville at The Grand Ole Opry. The black-tie affair raised money for The Bush Library Foundation, The Barbara Bush Foundation for Family Literacy and NARAS' MusiCares. The show, a special for The Nashville Network, featured many friends of the Bushes including Vince Gill, Loretta Lynn, Chuck Norris, Amy Grant, Eddie Rabbitt, Lee Greenwood, Lorrie Morgan, Tommy Lasorda and many others. Of course, The Oaks were proud to host the event.

The whole family was there—including the newly elected Governor of Texas, George W., and Jeb, fresh off a defeat in his first bid to become Governor of Florida. (Of course, the future would make Jeb a very successful two-term Governor of Florida and would hold even bigger responsibilities for George W., as he would preside over some of the toughest challenges ever to face an American President.)

As the family took their seats, and the lights dimmed, my partners and I each made our way down a darkened aisle from the rear of the Opry House. With no introduction, we began an acapella version of "Amazing Grace." For reasons that will be explained later, it was a song that had taken on deep meaning in our relationship with this family. It was a poignant and exciting way for us to start a show which, two hours later, ended with nearly twenty artists, entertainers and friends standing onstage singing a love song: the great Irving Berlin's "Always" to the first couple. "I'll be loving you, always. With a love that's true, always."

One of the most memorable moments of that night came when one of the graduates of the Barbara Bush Foundation for Family Literacy, who, as an adult, had learned to read, took the stage to read a letter from someone who could not attend. I should say here that this event occurred just two months after President Reagan had written his extremely poignant farewell letter to the American people, announcing that he had been diagnosed with Alzheimer's. On this night, the graduate read a letter from Mrs. Reagan. It was not clear to the audience, who the letter was from until the young lady read the line that opened the last paragraph: "Ronnie and I wish we could be with you tonight." With that, you could have heard a pin drop in the Opry house. By the time the letter signed off, "from my roommate and me" there was hardly a dry eye in the house. It was quite a moment in a night filled with wonderful moments.

Later, in a private reception, in the Presidential Suite at the Opryland Hotel, the Bushes cut a wedding cake that was an exact duplicate of their original cake. The whole night was a beautiful once-in-a-lifetime experience. Not only was I proud of Donna—and everyone who had worked so hard—but, also, I was amazed how the idea for an event that would gain such world-wide media coverage could have been hatched lying on a beach where the Atlantic and Gulf of Mexico meet.

Two years before the fiftieth anniversary celebration, on January 13, 1993, President George H. W. Bush presented the Presidential Medal of Freedom to former President Ronald Reagan. That date is etched in my memory because the night before that, on January 12, The Oak Ridge Boys and our wives spent the night in The White House. We had never had that opportunity before (and haven't again). It was quite an honor. Donna and I slept in the East Bedroom, which had served as Caroline Kennedy's bedroom, Nancy Reagan's Study and, later, as Chelsea Clinton's bedroom.

The Medal of Freedom ceremony occurred in the East Room of The White House, and was one of 41's last significant acts as President. I thought it was very touching that he would honor the man he served as Vice President. We didn't perform; we were simply there as guests, which made it very special for us. The personal thing that I remember about that day was seeing President Reagan after the ceremony in the official receiving line. We had met and performed for him on several occasions, but on this day, he couldn't quite place us, for some reason. Mrs. Reagan had to reintroduce us to him and remind him who we were. It seemed odd to us, but she dismissed it by saying that her husband was suffering from a touch of the flu. While his Alzheimer's diagnosis had not yet been made, years later it was revealed that Reagan had become increasingly confused during 1993. I can't help but believe that we witnessed a little foreshadowing of that on that day in The White House. He was the first candidate for president for whom I'd ever voted (after my experience in the Soviet Union). We had gotten to know him over the years. He was a good man and a great President. The revelation of his illness was a sad day.

Something humorous happened later on the same day. At a reception, the Reverend Billy Graham, who was in attendance for the ceremony, saw us and came over to say hello. We shook hands and said hello, but as my wife, Donna, reached out to shake his hand, someone from behind him called his name. He turned away without shaking her hand, became distracted and never returned to us. Though it wasn't an intentional snub, Donna was a little taken aback by it. Just for a moment, the feeling was a little uncomfortable but, as he so often does, Joe broke the tension by suggesting the reason for the snub had been that, "Reverend Graham sensed sin." We all laughed, and Donna hasn't yet lived that one down.

We've been blessed with many once-in-a-lifetime experiences. I have to admit, though, that there is one in particular that might have been the one least expected by me. In the summer of 2004 we were in College Station, Texas at the site of the George H. W. Bush Presidential Library for an event called "*41 @ 80*," the celebration of the eightieth birthday of the Library's namesake. It had been a weekend of wonderful activities, including a barbecue and concert at the Houston Astros' Minute Maid Park, and another skydive by the tough former leader of the free world. The Oaks would perform after his parachute jump, and we presented him with a custom made jacket crafted by famed designer, Manuel, which featured various depictions of the president's life in public service.

The great CBS sportscaster, Jim Nance, hosted the event, and the President was joined on stage by the former leader of the Soviet Union, Mikhail Gorbachev. We were standing backstage, having finished our performance. As the event ended, we heard someone backstage saying—very loudly—"BOOM BOOM! BOOM BOOM!" We didn't know what it was about, but all of the sudden a circle of people started moving towards us. The front line parted, and we could see that President Gorbachev was in the center of the group. He walked right up to me, and he threw his arms around me. Then he stepped backed and took both fists and pounded them on my chest, saying over and over, "BOOM BOOM!" It was a little confusing to us—me especially—but it seemed okay because he was smiling broadly as he did this.

Soon, 41 walked up and joined us. He introduced us as "the Boys." Gorbachev said something in Russian. (Interestingly, despite Gorbachev's long history with the west, he still only spoke Russian—even in private.) So, in this case, Gorbachev's aide and translator tried to explain to us what his boss was trying to say. It turns out that Gorbachev was a fan of singing groups, and he especially loved bass singers. Apparently there was no word in Russian that corresponded to the word "bass" so he adopted the word "boom" conveying the booming sound in the speakers when a bass singer sings low. So, I can honestly say, while I have been honored with many friendships and opportunities I could have never imagined would come our way, the most surprising among these would be to learn that the former leader of the Soviet Union—the man who was forced into democracy, in no small measure, by the exhortations of President Reagan's, "Mr. Gorbachev, tear down this wall,"—was not only a fan of quartet singing, but of the bass singer of The Oak Ridge Boys. I could have never seen that one coming!

Another political event that produced a surprising reaction was a few years before that, in April of 1997, at General Colin Powell's *"The President's Summit for America's Future"* held in Philadelphia, PA. Also known as the "Volunteerism Summit," this event was designed to promote a spirit of volunteering and neighborhood across the country and featured many stars including: Oprah Winfrey, Tony Bennett, LL Cool J, Wynonna, Michael Bolton and others, as well as former presidents Bush and Carter and the sitting president, Bill Clinton, along with their first ladies. After the opening ceremonies, at which we sang the National Anthem with the R&B group, All-4-One, we headed out into the streets of Philadelphia with George and Barbara Bush to clean up vacant lots, and repair and paint dilapidated buildings. It was a cool experience, to say the least (though, actually hard work!)

Later that night, we attended the gala finale after which we found ourselves back stage with the principles including President Clinton. Despite being a lifelong conservative and someone who had worked hard, on behalf of the elder President Bush, to try to keep Bill Clinton from becoming president, I have to say that meeting then-President Clinton was quite a thrill. I'd heard people say that he had a magnetic personality, so much so that some even called him Elvis. Well, at the risk of paraphrasing what another democratic politician, Lloyd Bentsen, said a few years back to my friend Dan Quayle: "I knew Elvis Presley. Elvis Presley was a friend of mine. And Bill Clinton was no Elvis Presley." Having said that though, shaking his hand and talking with him was actually quite memorable. Bill Clinton did have a way about him that must have served him very well in his life.

I remember once, though, when we were campaigning with 41 trying to keep Clinton from becoming President. In fact, it was in Cleveland, Ohio, and the first time we campaigned for him that year. The campaign had flown us in on a private plane the night before. The next morning, we were onsite awaiting the arrival of the presidential motorcade. Of course, there's a warning system of sorts because just prior to his arrival the Secret Service helicopters patrol the skies. Soon, the motorcade pulled through the gates and screeched to a halt directly in front of where we stood waiting. The back right door on the first limousine opened and we were expecting to see the President, when, who pops out but the actor, Bruce Willis. He came over to us, and we all shook hands. By that time, the President had walked over from his limo, and we had a few moments to visit before the event began. We each took the stage and did what we were there to do: we sang, Bruce told some funny stories, and the President campaigned.

We had a couple of more stops that afternoon, so we all hopped on the plane and flew on to Indianapolis (where another actor, Arnold

Schwarzenegger joined the team.) On the flight to Indianapolis, we had some time with Bruce Willis. He told us that this was the first time he'd ever publicly campaigned for a candidate but he had been compelled to do it by what he called the other candidate's "lying eyes." He said that a lot of Americans—especially of his parents' generation—didn't like some of the stuff that Clinton had been doing in his personal life. Then he laughed and said that some of it didn't offend him, but he had to support 41 for the folks, like his parents, who were bothered by it. I'm sure many people felt that way, though, of course, Bill Clinton, indeed, became President.

శ్రీశ్రీశ్రీ

Throughout our careers we've often been either compared or paired with many other quartets. None was more surprising—and, admittedly, more fun—than our association with The Singing Senators. Originally Republican in their affiliations, the Singing Senators consisted of Trent Lott, of Mississippi; John Ashcroft, from Missouri; Jim Jeffords of Vermont; and Larry Craig, from Idaho.

Beginning in 1996, we had many opportunities to sing with them. If we were performing in Washington, DC, and the Senate was in session, we could almost always count on seeing them backstage or on the bus—and many times we would invite them to sing onstage with us. Of course several other times we would be in D.C. for private events—sometimes for a political cause or, other times, for charity or a corporation—and it would be pre-arranged for us to perform together. They even came to Branson and sang onstage with us. We would usually sing some gospel songs, and of course, we'd always have to sing "Elvira."

We'd heard that whenever they would do a show by themselves, "Elvira" was their closer; they even sang it on the Today Show once.

Prior to one event in DC, in late 1997, as I recall, we hung out with the Senators all day long. We ate with them in the Senate Dining Room, they gave us tours of the Capitol—including all the way to the top of the dome—we relaxed with them in their offices, and we went onto the floor in the Senate chamber. It was a great day for us all. At the end of the evening, we walked to the center, right under the rotunda—where passed Presidents and Members of Congress lie in state—and we started singing. I don't remember how many songs the eight of us sang, but I know that we did "Amazing Grace" and "Sweet, Sweet Spirit," and a few others. As we would do whenever we performed onstage, we stood paired with our vocal counterparts: Duane with Senator Craig, Joe with Senator Jeffords, William Lee with Senator Ashcroft and I with Senator Lott. The way it sounded that day in the rotunda—the way our voices blended and echoed throughout that stately building—gave us all goose bumps.

Goose bumps were a condition that we've almost come to expect because of some of the amazing experiences with which we're continually blessed. They weren't always happy moments, but they were all so very memorable. One that tops this category for me occurred on Air Force One. We were campaigning for George H.W. Bush in his 1992 bid for reelection, and flying between somewhere in Ohio and Louisville, KY, which was scheduled to be the final stop of the campaign.

Air Force One is divided into several separate sections. The President's private quarters are, of course, up front, and there are additional compartments for senior staff and staff, secret service and military aides, and the press. The Oaks were sitting in our own private compartment, each of us lost in his own thoughts of the day, when George W. Bush walked in. At that time he was the owner of the Texas Rangers baseball club, and also working on his father's campaign for reelection. He asked if we'd mind to come with him because, as he put it, "Dad would like to see y'all up front. We just got some final polling information, and it's bad news. It's over." We could hear the hurt in his voice, and I must admit to suddenly feeling a little kick to my stomach. Countless times in my Christian life, I've felt that God either placed someone in my life at a particular time for a specific reason, or I've felt that I was placed by God in a particular situation to be of some service. When this day began we thought we were simply filling a slot for our friend who happened to be the President. He needed someone to entertain his crowd of supporters, and we were, of course, thrilled to oblige. We're all political junkies, watching the news and reading newspapers and books, the Internet and magazines. We knew that Bill Clinton was giving our guy a tough time and that it wasn't looking promising, but we'd continued to hold out hope—just as he had. So to hear this decree from his son—what was tantamount to a political death sentence—hurt us, as well, on behalf of our dear friend and his family.

We followed George W. to the front of the plane. Despite the somber nature of the visit, it was still an awesome feeling to be in the President's private cabin on Air Force One. When we arrived, the President was there along with Mary Matalin, who was one of his closest advisors on the campaign. Almost immediately, he said that he was feeling a little down and could use some inspiration. He asked if we would consider singing "Amazing Grace" one last time. Of course, we obliged, and the moment was truly magical.

We were sitting on a couch, the President was sitting on the edge of his bunk, Mary was in a seat and George W. stood against the door. With the first notes of harmony, Mary reached for the box of Kleenex on the table beside her and began to weep. Next tears formed in President Bush's eyes and began falling down his cheeks. Soon after, George W. completed the circle. To this day I don't know how we managed to sing the song without breaking. In some ways it was like singing at the funeral of a friend, as we had done for Johnny Cash when his June died. For us to cry would have seemed somehow disrespectful. At a time like that, they need strength from us, and our song. Something inside of each of us gave us the strength to get through the song. It was a moment that is etched into my soul. I can honestly say that I will take the memories of that day with me to the grave. It was very special. At that moment, I realized why God had placed us on that plane, on that day. An all-knowing God knew that this President, whose political journey would soon end, would need the encouragement and comfort that our song could bring him. It was an humbling feeling. And I know it made a deep impression on George W. Bush as well, for he would always ask us to sing that song when we were with him. Over the eight years of his presidency, we had the opportunity to be with him many times—including his last campaign event in 2004 staged in Milwaukee. Of course it had an entirely different feel as the polls looked positive that night and the next day he would march to a sound victory over John Kerry. But even at what amounted to a pre-victory rally, with all of the excitement and hoopla surrounding it, he requested, and we sang, "Amazing Grace" once again.

But after that "command performance" in the President's cabin in 1992, there was still one more event to do; there was still a throng awaiting our arrival at the Louisville airport, most of whom did not know that the cause was lost. The President met them like the hero he was. He never let them see the pain he was feeling. He knew they were there to see him, their President, and the man they wanted to vote for the next day. So he gave them what they wanted. It was as fine an example of the old adage "the show must go on" as I had ever witnessed.

At the conclusion of the event, we were back on our bus—which had met us on the tarmac—and I remember that we did not want to leave to head home to Hendersonville until we saw Air Force One take off into the southwestern sky to return our friend to his home in Houston. We all shed tears later that day: tears of fatigue, tears of sadness, and tears of respect and love for this man and his family. By that time, they had become very special to us, of course, and I'm proud to say, continue to be.

One funny story about President George H. W. Bush involves my oldest daughter, Lauren. She met him around the time of the fiftieth anniversary celebration when she was four. Donna had always taught her that a young lady should address grownups as "Mr." or "Mrs." She often bypassed the last name and simply used the person's first name, as in "Mr. Steve" or "Miss Linda." When it came time for her to meet the Bushes, I told her she should refer to him as Mr. President. She was a little confused that the rules changed. When she met him the first time, she called him "Mr. George." Donna corrected her that she was to call him "Mr. President." He jumped in and told her that he would like it if she would call him "Uncle George." While this should have been easier, in her young brain it all got scrambled and it came out as "Uncle Mr. President Bush." He enjoyed that so much; he laughed and laughed. It stuck for a while, a very nice memory.

❧❧❧

We also had funny experiences on airplanes. Sometimes they occurred in the midst of torturous circumstances. In 1996, the American war hero and patriot, Senator Bob Dole, was running for president against Bill Clinton—and trailing badly. He needed to shake up the last days of the campaign, so he came up with the idea of campaigning, non-stop, for the last ninety-six hours of the campaign—visiting fourteen states in all. As had become our sense of duty, we agreed to spend many of those hours flying to campaign events with him. The plane would land, and the candidate, his wife, his staff, the press and the traveling artists would file off of the plane and onto a stage that had been built on the tarmac. On the good events there would also be a big crowd there waiting on us. Lee Greenwood or Larry Gatlin and we would go out and warm up the crowd with a couple of songs, and then Senator Dole would give his stump speech, shake a few hands, take a few pictures, and then we'd get back on the plane and fly off to the next event.

I remember the last event of this ninety-six-hour marathon. I believe it might have been somewhere in Colorado, and I know that it was sometime in the middle of a very cold and very snowy night. The traveling press corps was grumpy, the staff was overworked, we were missing the bunks on our own bus, and the candidate—a wounded veteran of World War II—was, of course, very tired. The events had long since been running together, distinguished only by whether it was sunny and cold or nighttime and cold. As we slowly stutter-stepped up the aisle of the plane, like sheep heading to be sheered, the silence was suddenly shattered as the grumpiest of the traveling press yelled "Bob Dole has lost his (bleeping) mind!!" Though shocking at first—and though it might not have been their intention—the off-color remark actually served as a welcome relief from the tension. Everyone laughed—including the Senator, if I recall correctly—and we, then, went out and did the last event of the campaign, and got back on the plane to fly home.

Another time we were doing a bus tour with Senator Dole. We were in the Midwest, riding the bus with the Senator. We would roll into some town where there would be a stage and sound system set-up, we would jump off and sing a couple of songs acapella, or to tracks, and then the Senator would come, speak, shake some hands, and then we'd all jump back on the bus and do it all over again in the next town. On one of the rides between the stops, Ted Koppell, of *Nightline* fame, was riding with us. While we had never especially been fans of his, after spending some time with him—and ignoring his politics—we realized that he was a nice guy with a good sense of humor, and fun to be around. Once between stops, Koppell was dozing in the back lounge of the bus, and we got the idea to sneak back there and awaken him with a song. We chose the old gospel number, "Feelin' Mighty Fine." We eased our way back and gathered around the snoozing newsman. He was really out cold. With a silent count off, Bonsall launched into the first verse in his best "gospel high lead" voice, and we fell in behind him in harmony: "Well, I woke up this morning feelin' fine, I woke up with Heaven on my mind!" We finished the verse and then moved right into the chorus with echoing harmony: "Well I'm feelin', feelin' mighty fine, I got Heaven, Heaven on my mind. Don't you know I want to go, where the milk and honey flow..."

I'm not sure exactly what we were expecting from Ted, but what happened is the one thing we were not expecting. He seemed to sleep through the first verse, hardly even noticing, let alone being startled by us. By the time we moved into the chorus, he began to stir, then as we finished, he was rubbing his eyes and trying to focus on us. As if he was awakened every morning by a Southern Gospel alarm clock, he smiled and said, "Gee, fellas; that was just terrific." So while our little joke didn't turn out exactly like we'd planned, at least Ted didn't get upset with us. And the best part was, after that, we actually became closer and really enjoyed spending time together.

On another leg of that same trip—with Koppell still on the bus— another funny thing happened. Joe has written about this before, but in addition to the stops the bus would make, sometimes as we would pass through towns too small to host rallies or events, there would still be some Dole fans or supporters standing along the roadside. In these circumstances, the Senator would get on a microphone and greet the crowd, and encourage them to vote, as the bus slowly passed. One time, Dole was in the back lounge taping an interview with Koppell. As we rode through one town, there was another crowd gathered but the Senator was tied up with the interview, so he couldn't address the crowd as we passed. We were sitting in the front of the bus and all of the sudden Bonsall grabbed the microphone and gave his best impersonation of Bob Dole's stilted, staccato delivery so as not to leave those roadside supporters disappointed. We still don't know if they believed it was the Senator, but that night when that interview ran on network television, as Bob Dole answered the questions in the back of the bus, in the background you could hear the distant sounds of Bonsall impersonating the candidate. I've always wondered what people watching on TV thought about what they heard.

Of course, history tells us that Bob Dole did not become President. In the wake of the election, as Senator Dole made the rounds on late night television, many pundits remarked that had the affable and funny Bob Dole who appeared on those programs shown up on the stump, the election might have turned out differently. Of course we'll never know if that is true but I can say that, in all of our interactions with him, he was a gentleman, always good to us, and also quick with a funny joke. All of us Oaks were proud to have served a man who had so unselfishly served his country.

೧ೕ೧ೕ೧ೕ

Another funny experience happened when we sang at The Republican National Convention in New Orleans in 1988—the one that confirmed George H. W. Bush as the nominee for President. After we'd performed and the nominee made his acceptance speech, they brought us back onstage to close the event by singing "God Bless America." The Bush family stood onstage waving and smiling, soaking in the applause as the balloons fell and the confetti began to fly. George Bush walked over to us and waved some more, then he stood beside me and for the entire last chorus of "God Bless America" he attempted to sing bass with me. Patriotism and friendship prevents me from critiquing his bass-singing chops, so I'll simply say that I'm confident he was a better bass singer than I would have been a President!

᷇᷇᷇᷇

I mentioned Dan Quayle earlier. Because of his serving as Vice President for our friend, 41, we also had many opportunities to spend time, and become friends, with the Veep from Indiana. He is another man who was far different in private than he was portrayed or perceived in the media. I always enjoyed the chance to sit with him and hear him talk about politics around the globe, He was very well read and had the great ability to explain things in a way that was very easy to understand. And, he has a great sense of humor.

A few years back, when his son was attending Vanderbilt Law School, the former Vice President visited Nashville pretty often. On one of those occasions, Donna and I joined him for dinner at *Mario's,* one of our favorite Nashville restaurants, that has since closed. We arrived a few minutes early and were already seated, enjoying a nice glass of Cabernet. We saw him arrive, and as he made his way through to the back of the restaurant to our private room, the other diners recognized him. People applauded, some stood to shake his hand as he passed, many shouted greetings: "Hey Dan, youdaman!" "Mr. Vice President, we love you!" "We miss you!" "Four more years!" Watching him react was like watching Dean Martin work a room. He was suave, he was funny, he was cool: "Thank you." "No, you're the best." "I love you too, but you're not getting my Bud Lite," (a slogan from a popular television commercial at the time.) It was really cool to see him so relaxed and comfortable. He had received such a bum wrap, it was nice to see he had rebounded and stayed true to himself—so comfortable in his own skin. In a business (both politics and music) where so many people are different (and not in a good way) in private than their public personas, it's always refreshing to find a public figure who is better, smarter, nicer, more approachable than even his public reputation.

દ્જર્જ

For five years during the mid-eighties, I even got a small taste of the political, when I served on the Board of Directors for a couple of great organizations. I was asked to sit on the board of the Elvis Presley Memorial Foundation, which was quite an honor. More recently, they've changed their name to the Elvis Presley Charitable Foundation, and they work to continue the spirit of Elvis's generosity, and to help continue some of the charitable work that he started during his lifetime.

Around the same time, I also served on the board for the *Country Music Association (CMA),* along with other artists and industry leaders like Charlie Daniels, Brenda Lee, Joe Galante and Vince Gill. We were there to offer some insight and our own unique perspective on the trends of the business. During my tenure, we traveled all over the world, to places like London, New Zealand and Australia, with the idea of promoting country music around the globe. We would have a series of meetings and press interviews, all designed to bring country music to a broader audience, both domestically and abroad. Unfortunately, the board's by-laws were written that a member was only allowed to miss one meeting per year in order to maintain membership. Because this was during The Oaks' biggest years, finally our schedule precluded my attendance at two meetings one year, so I had to relinquish my position on the board. I must say that I greatly enjoyed my time there and I might even do something like it again (as long as I don't have to run in an election!)

❧❧❧

To kick off 2011, The Oaks had the honor of performing for the Inauguration of Bill Haslam, the 49th Governor in our home state of Tennessee. It was our second time to do this, having also done so in 1995, for then-Governor, Don Sundquist. In addition to singing the National Anthem at the official swearing-in ceremony, Governor-Elect Haslam also asked us to sing "Amazing Grace" (there's that song again!) at the Inaugural Prayer Service held earlier that morning at Nashville's famed Ryman Auditorium. Though I hadn't known him well prior to the Inaugural, I had supported Haslam in the election. One thing that I really appreciated hearing him say was, prior to the Prayer Service, when he told us that, while there were a lot of things he had to do that weekend as part of the Inaugural festivities, that Prayer Service was the one thing he most wanted to do. He's a good man, and, in his first term, he's proven to be a good leader for our state.

❧❧❧

The most recent time that "Amazing Grace" was at the center of an emotional event for us was on August 6, 2011, the night we were inducted as members into The Grand Ole Opry. The Opry is similar to the Hall of Fame for a performer or an athlete. It's something you know exists—and it even might be something you dream of being a part of—but, at the same time, it's something to which you can never quite imagine ever being invited as a member. Since 1925, it has been home to the most venerable of all country singers; legends like Hank Williams, Patsy Cline, Marty Robbins, Eddy Arnold, Minnie Pearl, Ernest Tubb, Bill Anderson, and later, Dolly Parton, Roy Clark, Barbara Mandrell, Randy Travis, Garth Brooks, Reba McEntire, Blake Shelton, Brad Paisley, Carrie Underwood, and so many others.

On July 8, we'd been asked to perform in a guest slot, as we had done many times before. Though I noticed several old and important friends milling around backstage, I still didn't quite sense that anything different or special was about to occur. After our first song, as Joe was addressing the audience, we heard a ripple of laughter from the crowd, and turned to see ninety-year-old Opry legend, "Little" Jimmy Dickens, standing amongst us dressed as Golden, complete with long beard, cowboy hat and sunglasses. We still weren't sure what was happening but, after a few jokes, he floored us by announcing that the following month we would become the newest members of the Grand Ole Opry.

The next month passed quickly and, in addition to tour dates and photo shoots and recording sessions, it was filled with many interviews to talk about the honor. When the night finally arrived, I couldn't help but notice that I was nervous. I asked my partners about it and discovered that we each were feeling the butterflies of the moment. After all these years that's a pretty rare occurrence; it emphasized how special this night was for us. We attended a reception, did more interviews—with our good friends, Charlie Chase and Lorianne Crook, and for several other outlets—and then, at 8:50 pm, during the Cracker Barrel portion of the show, it was time to be introduced onto the stage, by one of the grand ladies of the Opry, Jeannie Seely.

We hit the stage running and opened with "Bobbie Sue." For some reason, the house lights were up—something else that doesn't often happen—so, we could see the sold-out crowd, and they were all up and dancing, fueling us even more. Next, after a few words from Joe, we went straight into "Elvira," and again, the crowd was on its feet. After "Elvira," Pete Fisher, the Opry's general manager, joined us onstage and said some kind words. He, then, introduced Little Jimmy again, and, together, they made the official induction. I know my partners well enough to know that, like me, they were all trying to keep their emotions in check.

The point at which it became a losing battle was when Pete directed our attention to the huge video screen onstage, for there was "our president," George H. W. Bush. He had taped a video message to honor our induction. Among his remarks, he said: "I cannot think of any group or any person who deserve this honor more. I think of the Opry and the Oaks, both as American icons, beloved from coast to coast and known around the world. I can't think of a better union. I love you boys, and my best to everyone at the Grand Ole Opry, one of my favorite places in America."

It was more than we could take. The most difficult part was that, at its conclusion, the audience was expecting one or all of us to say something. In his usual role, Joe stepped up, and expressed his gratitude to God for the blessings of our lives and our career, and to the many people who had played a role in our being here. He choked back tears as he thanked President Bush, and as he made mention of the thirty soldiers who had been killed that very day in Afghanistan, many of them Special Forces. He pointed out that even the freedom to gather at a place like the Opry, and sing our songs, was possible because of the sacrifice of so many like those fine young soldiers, who had paid the ultimate price.

All four of us said a few words—again, a very rare occurrence on any stage, but something that seemed appropriate on this special night. Golden honored the history of the institution of the Opry by talking of listening as a child in Brewton, Alabama. Duane told some personal stories that outlined the intersecting histories of The Oaks and the Opry. As fate would have it, his wife, who for years has been a background singer on the Opry, was in the audience, as a six-month-old baby when The Oak Ridge Quartet made their debut on the Opry All-Night Gospel Sing, as her father sang, as part of the group that opened the show. He also recalled the night, in 1967, when he and Golden first sang on the Opry with The Oaks. It was a terrific story. As could probably be expected, I said only a few words of thanks and appreciation. While I'm often accused—deservedly so—of being stoic, on this night, my struggle for words had only to do with my emotions. The Opry had always been a gig we were proud to do as guests, but the honor of becoming an official part of the family really moved us.

After a commercial break—because, after all, the Grand Ole Opry is still the longest running live radio show in history, this night being the 4,466th consecutive Saturday night broadcast—it was time for another song. Earlier in the week, we had decided that we would close with "Amazing Grace." We thought it would best speak to our feelings about the evening since God's grace is what had made it possible, and because it was so meaningful to us. We, of course, had no way of knowing the added poignancy it would take on after the video appearance of our dear friend. Isn't it amazing (no pun intended) how that great old hymn is woven into the fabric of America and The Oak Ridge Boys? Joe has always said, "It's all about the song," but it's astounding to me how many times "the song" has been that song.

రుురుురు

Another cool Opry moment occurred for us in the spring of 2012. For the last four years, Keith Urban and Vince Gill have hosted a tremendously successful event called "All for the Hall," which is a concert to raise money for the Country Music Hall of Fame. Late in 2011, Keith had invited us to be a part of the show—and what a lineup it was:

Keith, Vince, Rascal Flatts, Lady Antebellum, Diamond Rio, Alabama, Miranda Lambert and her group, Pistol Annies, The Band Perry, Little Big Town, Thompson Square and surprise guests, Merle Haggard and Don Williams.

The crowd of 16,000 strong, at Nashville's Bridgestone Arena, roared their approval for every performance—and none more so, I'm thrilled to say, than for us. Their applause was like being immersed in a flood of water. We were, arguably, the oldest group on the show, but we absolutely rocked that house. It was an exciting and wonderful night, raising more than $475,000 for the Hall of Fame.

At one point in the night, a large black duffel bag was brought onstage and Vince directed Keith to open it. He did, and, in it, he found a microphone stand from The Grand Ole Opry. The members who were there that night, Vince, Diamond Rio, Rascal Flats and The Oaks, came out on stage and surprised him with his official invitation to become a fellow member. He was overwhelmed. He hugged each one of us on-stage and thanked us. For the rest of the night, he sang into a micro-phone on that Opry stand. It was quite a night for him, and also for us. A few weeks later he was officially inducted. As I've said, I'm proud to be a member of that family, and I'm glad to now have Keith as a brother.

෨෨෨

We've been blessed with many political friends from both sides of the aisle, good men and women with whom we might not all agree politically, but who love America just the same. Having said that, it probably wouldn't surprise many to know that we usually work and campaign for our friends on the Republican side; I've already mentioned many on the national level, but there are others closer to home, includ-ing my own State Representative, Debra Maggart, and former State Sena-

254

tor and now-Congresswoman from Tennessee's Sixth District, Marsha Blackburn. Many of my friends have campaigned their way to victory while others have failed. We've never taken our stands lightly. We know that, on paper at least, half of our fans could potentially disagree with any decision we might make to campaign for someone. But for us, we see it as our civic duty. In many ways it's like some of the charitable endeavors we've undertaken. We feel a responsibility not only to give back but also to support those things, and people, in whom we believe. It's one of the reasons we spent so many years active in great organizations whose mission was to help protect, feed, or educate children.

The Boy Scouts approached us in 1981 to ask if we would be the official spokesmen for the organization. Though none of us had ever been Scouts, we jumped at the chance. We believed then—and still do today—that the Boy Scouts is one of the finest organizations for the development of boys into young men. One of the hit songwriters, who was writing for The Oaks publishing company at that time, was Jimbeau Henson ("Fancy Free" and later "Colors," among others) so we approached him about writing a song that could be used as the centerpiece of our support of the Boy Scouts. He wrote a great little ditty called "Check Out the Boy Scouts," which became their theme song for a while, and was used in the public service announcements.

We performed the song live for the first time in 1981 at the quadrennial Boy Scouts National Jamboree at Fort A.P. Hill in Virginia for more than 25,000 scouts. Burl Ives, the great folk singer who had long been involved with the Boy Scouts, was also on that show. At the next gathering, in 1985, we performed again, this time for nearly 33,000 scouts. Those were unforgettable experiences for us.

We really enjoyed our involvement with the Scouts—and, admittedly, we basked in the prestige that came to us as a result of the association—but we couldn't help but wonder if it really made any difference, or had any positive influence on any of the kids. I can say that our experience has proven that the answer is yes. A year never passes that we don't come into contact with someone who tells us that they were there and remember singing along with us when we sang "Elvira," or, they'll say, they became fans because they saw us at the "Jambo." There was a ballplayer named Lenny Harris who played for the Nashville Sounds before moving on to the Cincinnati Reds in the Major Leagues. He had been a Boy Scout, and every time he saw me at the ballpark, he would sing "Check Out the Boy Scouts" to me.

In the spring of 2011, The Oaks were honored with our portraits being hung at the Nashville location of The Palm Restaurant. During the event, Golden and I were interviewed by music reporter, Storme Warren. In the middle of the interview, he thanked us for our involvement with the Boy Scouts. He said that he'd been a scout at one of those Jamborees, and had always tried to live up to the image we'd espoused. That really made us feel good. Like the song we later recorded "Did I Make a Difference?" it's always nice to know that we did.

In 2001, The Oaks received one of the highest honors of our career so far, when The Boy Scouts of America awarded us with *The Silver Buffalo*. Prior to us, the award has been bestowed on nearly every U.S. President since Harry S. Truman, along with such luminaries as Hank Aaron, Neil Armstrong, Colin Powell, Jimmy Stewart and Douglas MacArthur.

We always had a special place in our hearts for kids who needed help. We were the official spokesmen for the *National Committee for the Prevention of Child Abuse* (now *Stop Child Abuse America),* and for five years, we hosted a series of benefit concerts in Dallas called "Stars for Children." We enlisted the help of many major acts including The Commodores, The Gatlin Brothers, Johnny Cash, Roseanne Cash, Kenny Rogers and many others. Joe was really instrumental in getting us involved and, over the years, enough money was raised to open eight homes to help battered children. On our most recent Christmas tour, we partnered with "Save the Children" to raise awareness and much-needed money to help feed, clothe and educate children in the United States and around the world.

In 2006 we became the National Music Ambassadors for an initiative called *The National Anthem Project,* sponsored by the Music Education National Conference. They commissioned a study that revealed that two-thirds of the American people either didn't know the words to the first verse of the "Star Spangled Banner," or didn't know the story behind its writing. So they set out to educate the public on our National Anthem. They felt that they needed to have an artist who could help them carry their message. As it was later told to us, they compiled a list of some two hundred names of artists that they might target. Through research and feedback, they culled the list to one hundred, then fifty, then ten.

From there, they redoubled their efforts to scrutinize, not only the artists' history and image but, very importantly, their version of "The National Anthem." They were less than impressed with the recent trend towards modernizing the song, or an artist using it as a vehicle to show off some perceived stylistic tweaks, "vocal acrobatics," as it has been termed. Of course, the song is known to be difficult to sing, anyway, with lots of range, but one of the main goals of the project was to return the anthem to a song that was sung—and to which people could sing along—instead of a song to be performed or simply heard. It's similar to the way I earlier described Joe's ability to allow the audience to receive a song rather than forcing them to take it.

When, after all of their deliberations, they asked if we would consider serving as the Official Musical Ambassadors of *The National Anthem Project*, we enthusiastically accepted. Before our involvement—and since—we have had the opportunity to sing the Anthem at dozens of events, everything from World Series games to political conventions, NASCAR races to the dedication of the 9/11 Memorial at the Pentagon; we even recorded and released it on our album, *Colors.*

In the Spring of 2011, while The Oaks were in Atlantic City performing at Caesar's Palace, we were asked to sing the National Anthem at the first annual Atlantic City Boardwalk Rodeo, the largest rodeo on the east coast. It was held in Boardwalk Hall, at the Convention Center. As we stood in the ring singing the for the cowboys on horses and the huge crowd, I was struck by the irony that this was same building where I had sung so many years ago, in high school, while performing with the All-State Chorus. Back then, it had been the biggest stage I'd ever appeared on, and now, while my group was in town to headline one of the finest casino showrooms in the country,

I was, again, in this great hall, blending harmonies with friends, singing our nation's anthem. Pretty cool, indeed.

One of the most frequent comments we hear is that people appreciate the way we sing The National Anthem, which, for us, is the highest compliment. In our role with the project we have sung, spoken, taught, and been interviewed countless times in an effort to help return our nation's song to its rightful place of respect and honor. As I look back on our career, if we have helped in that cause, even a little, then that's a legacy of which I am most proud.

CHAPTER ELEVEN:
Reinvention: The Boys Are Back

One of the most important words in The Oak Ridge Boys pantheon is, no doubt, "reinvention." From the earliest days of The Georgia Clodhoppers, who became The Oak Ridge Quartet, to the hard-charging Oak Ridge Boys that shook up the gospel world and led to the four of us, who have comprised the group for the last forty years, reinvention has always been a constant, and, in many ways, has been the key to our continued success. Too many artists believe that reinventing themselves requires them to change what they do and the way they do it. For The Oaks, though, it's always been how to maintain our foundation and keep doing what we do, but make it fresh and different, new and exciting.

Arguably, our most significant reinvention was when, maintaining our strong four-part harmonies, we transformed from a gospel mainstay to a force on the country charts. While, later, losing our way with Golden, forced us into a reinvention we would have preferred to avoid, it nonetheless led us into one that served us well, even if borne of necessity. The most welcomed reinvention, of course, occurred with William Lee's return. But there have been many others in our career; so the biggest lesson to be learned about reinvention is that, while it can sometimes come by choice or sometimes be forced upon you, it can be necessary, and it can be very positive.

As I've mentioned already several times, one of the constants in our professional lives since 1975—and a major force behind our various reinventions—is the Godfather, Jim Halsey. Beginning with those two pickup dates in the summer of '75, Jim has always worked to promote us in ways that, quite often, were bigger than even we thought we deserved at the time. From the headlining gig at The Landmark, to the Soviet tour with Roy Clark, to festivals and shows he got us on, he constantly encouraged us to succeed by putting us in the position where we had no other choice.

In those early days, he would insist on us getting equal billing with the headliners with whom we were appearing. That created the perception that we were not just an opening act but rather that we were co-headlining. This was vital in our evolution.

We appeared at the American Song Festival; the Wembley Festival, in England; the Montreaux International Jazz Festival, in Switzerland; and The Acropolis, in Nice, France. We performed with Johnny Mathis at Royal Albert Hall, in London. We even did a command performance for Princess Caroline of Monaco, in Monte Carlo.

෨෨෨

A side note and funny story: also on the show in Monte Carlo was Roy Clark and the "Gentle Giant," Don Williams, a great singer and a nice man. It was the first trip to Monaco for all of us, and to say that this was a formal country would be a gross understatement. Anywhere we went, it was hard not to feel underdressed—even for me. At no place was this truer than the famous Monte Carlo Casino. While we didn't perform there, it was located right next door to the fabulous hotel in which we were staying, the Hotel de Paris, so I think each of the acts visited it just to see what it was like inside. Joe and I went together and walked around, taking in the sites. It seems everywhere we looked were male patrons in tuxedos and females in formal gowns. Believe me when I say that it looked nothing like Circus Circus, in Las Vegas, on a Friday night! After an hour or so of taking in the scene, we were ready to go back to the hotel. As we were leaving through the front entrance, we saw Don Williams about to enter. As was his signature look, both on and off stage, he wore jeans, a denim jacket, denim shirt and his brown floppy cowboy hat. He didn't see us because he was in a conversation with the guard/host/maitre d' at the front door who was explaining to him that he wasn't dressed appropriately to enter the casino. Don started out calmly explaining that he was in town to perform for the Princess, but it was having no affect on the host; he simply refused him entrance. After two or three rounds, Don was getting visibly angry and more persistent. "I just want to go inside and see the place," he insisted, "I won't stay long." At this point, we were glad he hadn't seen us because we didn't want him to be further embarrassed by this indignity happening in front of us. We weren't the problem; we knew he was a huge star, but contrary to what happened to us all those years ago at the National Quartet Convention when the guard refused to let us in, Joe and I could be of no help in Don getting inside the casino. In the scheme of things we were far less important than he was; after all, he'd headlined the show for the Princess. After a few minutes, the guard had finally had enough of the Gentle Giant, and in the stodgiest and most sarcastic French accent we'd ever heard, the last thing we heard him say to Don was: "Sir, I do not know where it is you have left your horse, but I would strongly recommend that you go to him and ride back to wherever it is you came from." I still don't know if Don ever made it in—or if he even really cared. With that, we quickly did our best to blend in with the crowd and pass by, unnoticed, and return to the relative security of our hotels rooms, where, at least, we knew who we were, and nobody cared how we dressed!

હ્જ હ્જ હ્જ

Halsey had long ago impressed upon us that television would always be a major component in our career plans. Through the years, we appeared on a varied assortment of shows including: *Don Kirshner's Rock Concert*, *The Merv Griffin Show*, *The Midnight Special*, and *The Dinah Shore Show*. We appeared on *The Tonight Show* more than thirty times. We were even one of the lucky performing acts that was invited to join Johnny at the couch for some conversation. To the best of my recollection, however, we never accepted that invitation, instead requesting the opportunity to use that time to perform a second song. The Godfather had made us understand that we could make more of an impression on the huge television audience by singing our songs than by talking about them. Johnny always seemed impressed with that approach as well.

In 1982, The Oaks taped a special for *HBO*. We were performing in Pine Bluff, Arkansas, and other guests included Charlie Daniels and Roseanne Cash. It was a huge success for us, and in those years, it was still a rare occurrence to find country music on a prestigious channel like *HBO*. That was the night, as a matter of fact, that "Thank God for Kids" made its debut. Of course, it went on to become a smash hit for us, and is still one of our most requested songs. Nobody could sing that song the way Golden does.

Throughout the nineties and into the first decade of the twenty-first century, with national exposure ranging from our own TV show, *Live from Las Vegas,* as well as our regular syndicated charity specials, television helped keep us relevant in a music business that was rapidly changing. While many other acts saw their touring schedule drastically cut, or saw smaller crowds at the shows they did play, The Oaks maintained a heavy touring schedule, and our crowds stayed consistent. Over the last several years, The Oaks have averaged between 160 and 170 concerts per year. That is a staggering number for an act of our caliber. For two years, we had a very successful and lucrative sponsorship deal with BluBlocker Sunglasses (for what we called our *Red, White and Blu-Blocker Tour.*) This was around the time that *Colors* was our current release. Our buses were wrapped with a graphic that included a huge photo of us wearing our custom designed Oak Ridge Boys BluBlocker sunglasses. It was just another manifestation of the power and value of television exposure.

Our TV show, *Live from Las Vegas* was a great experience, but I think our timing was just off. The original intent of *The Nashville Network (TNN)* had been to do a long-term deal with us for the show. They hoped we would become a replacement for *The Statler Brothers Show,* with which they'd had a good run. Unfortunately—for us and for them—TNN soon changed formats, and the focus and the name of the network changed—first to *The National Network*, then to *Spike TV*—so a long run was simply not in the cards for us. But the one season we did was very well received and featured many exciting moments with great guest stars. The caliber of talent that producer, Sherman Halsey (Jim's talented and award-winning son), booked to appear on that show was varied and impressive, including Tim McGraw, Jo Dee Messina, Engelbert Humperdinck, Kenny Rogers, Little Richard, Penn & Teller, Merle Haggard and our old friend Roy Clark. If nothing else, we learned who some of our friends were with that show!

Television is still vital to our continued growth, and we continue to be blessed with lots of exciting recent appearances including: *Imus in the Morning*, MSNBC, several shows on The Fox News Network, The Food Channel, *Late Night with David Letterman*, and The History Channel.

When we recorded our *Voices* CD project, we had been away from radio for about seven years. Halsey had the idea to do a one-minute version of our song "Baby When Your Heart Breaks Down," and release it as a single to radio under the marketing tag "Got a Minute?" It was a gimmicky idea, but the beauty of it was, it was not a gimmicky song; it was a great country song that sounded just like The Oak Ridge Boys. We hadn't sold out to gain attention; we'd simply looked for a new way to market our new music. And though it didn't become a hit, it received lots of airplay and coverage in the media. We appeared on several television shows including *Donny & Marie* and *The Tonight Show,* and also, *USA Today* wrote a feature about us. That's the kind of publicity that never gets old! I'm convinced that our continued reinvention is the reason we've been afforded these opportunities.

Another source of reinvention has come with the emergence of social media. I can remember when the extent of "social networking" was our bus and truck drivers talking with truckers and others on the CB radio (remember those?) Now we not only have websites, but Facebook and MySpace pages, Twitter accounts and podcasts, Vimeo and YouTube pages, and Smartphone applications (apps). It's a brave new world, and it's one that artists must embrace if they're going to stay viable. If nothing else, I think The Oaks have long since proven our intention to remain current by embracing the new technologies of the time.

As I've already mentioned, while still doing gospel, we broke the mold on how gospel quartets dressed, we incorporated some movements on stage, and we used stage lights. When things started happening for us in the country field, we were the first touring act to use many production elements that are now common. We were the first to carry moving lights (called Vari-lites)—at a cost of $10,000 per week, which was a huge amount of money for us to commit—but we thought it was worth it in order to take us to the next level. We were the first to use fog machines, lasers and flash pots, all of which added to the excitement of our shows. We were the first to utilize wireless microphones, which allowed us to roam (or in Joe's case, to run) all around the stage.

We don't seek some sort of credit for these things. Had we not started using all of these modern production elements, some other country act would have, but the fact is, we did use them first. In that way, with our continual reinventions, we blazed the trail. Just as many groups influenced and inspired us, I know that we influenced others, sometimes in small ways and sometimes in larger, career-defining ways.

We did a Christmas tour with Kenny Rogers once, and a young, mostly unknown artist from Oklahoma named Garth Brooks opened for us. On the first night when we met, he already knew our names, but I remember he referred to each of us as "Mister," as in: "Mr. Sterban, it's an honor to meet you; Mr. Golden, I love your singing," and so on. He was the most polite kid we'd ever met, and, while he wasn't in awe of us, it was obvious that he was grateful to be on the same tour with two acts like The Oaks and Kenny. After his opening set—when we performed, and later when Kenny was on stage—Garth never moved from his seat just offstage; and, it was obvious that he was studying us, soaking up everything that happened onstage.

Now, I don't claim that we deserve any of the credit for Garth's stage presence—God obviously blessed him with enormous star power—but, I definitely think we made an impact on him. On the first night of the tour, he walked out on stage and quietly moved from one song to the next. On the second night—after watching our show the night before—he literally ran out on the stage and slid on both knees to a stop in front of the microphone at center stage, and he never slowed down for the rest of the show—or maybe for the rest of his career. Whether or not he got his ideas from us, I think he definitely learned something on that tour, and, as we all know, he took what he learned and turned it into something the country music world sorely needed, and had never seen before.

That's really one of the great, untold secrets of the music business: no matter who you are—or how much success you've had—if you want to, you can still learn something from other acts. In 1985, we were in Las Vegas to perform on the annual Jerry Lewis Labor Day Telethon for Muscular Dystrophy. As that is always a big show filled with lots of entertainment, there were many stars backstage over the course of the time we were there. Among them was the great Sammy Davis, Jr., whom we had met a few times before—either at industry events or backstage when we were performing in Las Vegas.

On this night, Sammy was not in very good shape. He was walking on a cane and with a pretty bad limp. He said he been struggling for a few months with his hip. (A couple of months later, in November, Sammy would actually have hip replacement surgery.) I remember standing backstage watching some of the other performers as Sammy regaled us with stories from the Rat Pack—the legendary group consisting of him, Frank Sinatra, Dean Martin and others over the years. He was quite charming and very funny but with each movement, he would wince in pain, as if it would almost take his breath. He never complained but it was clear that he should have been someone resting instead of preparing to perform live in front of a television audience of tens of millions.

Finally one of the production people came and informed him that he was the next scheduled performer. He limped towards his dressing room relying heavily on his cane as well as his friend and valet, Murphy Bennett. A few minutes later, he reappeared, polished even more than before—Sammy's level of "bling" would shame any rap star currently on the scene. On this night, he wore tuxedo pants with a cropped, white jacket over a red shirt with white trim. He eased towards the wings of the stage, where he stood. As the star of the show, his best friend Jerry Lewis, was introducing him, he turned to Murphy and tossed him his cane. I caught his eye as he turned back towards the stage. He winked, flashed that ten-thousand watt smile, gave us the thumbs-up signal and bound out on the stage.

He sang three songs—including his signature "Mr. Bojangles" in which he dances—and it was as if he were Superman. There was no indication of a limp, no hesitation, no unsteadiness in his gait. He tapped and pranced and twirled like a machine. After he finished—to a well-deserved standing ovation, nonetheless—he strutted towards backstage, gave one final turn and wave to the crowd and came through the curtains. As soon as he was in the darkness of the wings, Murphy, who carried his cane, met him, and the limp returned with full fury. He grimaced as he walked towards the dressing room, stopping only to bid farewell to us. It was perhaps the greatest, single example of showmanship that I have ever witnessed.

That experience was the epitome of the old showbiz axiom that says: "the show must go on." Those people in the studio audience, as well as the television audience, were expecting him to perform, and it didn't matter that he hurt. He was going to give them what they wanted to see. There have many nights over the years when one of us has sat on the bus or backstage, feeling less than "stage-ready" whether suffering from the flu or some other infection or virus. At times like that, we always remember Sammy. Sam is gone now, but all these years later, he still serves as an example to which we aspire.

Another grand example of bravery occurred in June of 2011 when Glen Campbell announced that he was suffering with Alzheimer's disease. He and his wife Kim had seen the gradual signs, and Glen faced it the way any artist would like to: he created more art. He recorded his final studio album, *Ghost On the Canvas*, which was released to rave reviews, and he set out on his farewell concert tour, dubbed "The Goodbye Tour," (in homage to his long-running "Goodtime Hour" TV show).

Though we'd never appeared on his network series, we knew Glen for years and did many shows and TV appearances with him. We first worked with him in the early 1980s on some network television specials. Two of those shows provided vivid memories of two sides of the man. On one of them, there were several big artists of the day on stage at once. We were to share lines of a song. There were other artists with us that I don't recall but I do remember Glen, Alabama and Barbara Mandrell. During rehearsals, the producer and musical director were onstage with us, trying to find a key that would fit each voice. Everyone weighed in—some more forcefully than others—with which key would be best, but Glen stood by silently. After a few minutes of bickering and negotiating, the producer turned to Glen and asked, "What about you? What key do you need?" Glen smiled, shook his head and said, "It doesn't matter to me. I can sing it in any key." And he was right. He wasn't bragging; he was just blessed with a beautiful voice, and an incredible range.

The second television experience that stands out in my memory was for a network Christmas special, probably in 1981. Marty Pasetta (who had produced Elvis's *Aloha from Hawaii* worldwide broadcast in '73) was the producer for this show. We had worked with him the previous year on another Christmas special that had been filmed in Texas, and, let's just say, the fake snow didn't fool too many viewers. To rectify that situation, for this special, we were flying up to Banff, Alberta, Canada, where the snow was real, and plentiful.

Also on the show were Glen Campbell and Tanya Tucker. At this time in their lives, Tanya was a twenty-two-year old wildcat of a country singer and Glen was twice her age, three-times divorced, and sowing his wild oats. They've admitted that their short-lived relationship was a volatile mix of love and hate, drugs and drama; and while we didn't witness the drugs, we certainly got an eyeful of the rest. We filmed this Christmas special in several locations in Banff, so to move from place to place, we rode on a bus together. On those mostly short rides, Glen and Tanya would go from hugging and kissing to screaming and fighting. It was the most amazing display I'd ever seen. They had no self-consciousness about doing either in front of us. It made for quite a memorable trip. Not long after that special, Glen and Tanya broke up, and he soon met, and fell in love with, Kim, the lady who would become, and remains to this day, his wife.

We became close with Glen in the early days of Branson, in 1992, when we both performed at The Grand Palace Theatre. After the first season, he came into the dressing room one night to tell us that he was opening his own theatre the following year, and he asked us if we would consider appearing at his theatre on the days he wasn't working. We jumped at the chance, and never regretted our association with this class act.

James Keach, who produced the great Johnny Cash biopic, *Walk the Line*, decided to chronicle Glen's "Goodbye Tour" in a documentary film. In addition to following Glen on the tour across the United States and Europe, James wanted to conduct interviews with some artists who had been close to Glen. Of course, we were honored when he asked us to participate. As happens so often, our talking turned into spontaneous singing. After we shared some memories, we broke into an acapella version of "Farther Along." It touched even us, and the words took on an even more poignant meaning. Alzheimer's is such an insidious disease, striking people from all walks of life; the famous and those who will never receive any credit for their brave battles. Hopefully, as the song says, "we'll understand it all by and by."

I was proud of my friend for the way he chose to face this challenge: on stage in front of his adoring fans, doing what he loved most to do. And though he was all but completely reliant on on-stage prompters for even his most familiar and famous lyrics, somehow those synapses that control the melodies and the guitar breaks were still firing and remained at the ready for him. It was an amazing thing to witness.

Another inspiring moment related to a dear friend occurred in 2010, but in this case rather than simply witnessing it, we actually played a role. It was when Jim Halsey was being honored by the Oklahoma History Center. Roy Clark was there, along with the Governor; football coach, Barry Switzer; us, and many others. In recent years, Roy's health had been somewhat failing; he was walking with a cane and he had not been performing live, which certainly was his prerogative but also was a real shame because he's such a phenomenal talent. We were all seated on the stage taking turns to say a few words in tribute to the Godfather. After Roy spoke, The Oaks came up to perform. Almost immediately, Joe started having some fun with Roy, kidding back and forth. The more this went on, the more Roy seemed to transform into the Roy Clark of old. The twinkle came back in his eyes and the jokes came easier. They even started trading memories from the Russia trip, with Roy laughingly reminding Joe that he "shouldn't tell the whole story!"

After several minutes of this we all but forced Roy to get up with us to perform, and the first song we sang was "Just A Little Talk With Jesus," just like we did in the Soviet Union, and on so many other stages around the world. By the time we got to the verse that he sang, Roy had dropped his cane and was doing the little dance that he always used to do during the song. It really was a great moment for us. Later, after the event had concluded, his wife, Barbara, came to us and thanked us for encouraging him to get up and sing. And, as it turned out, after that, Roy even began doing some dates again on the road. It seems that that old spark was still inside him just waiting to be reignited. After all that he had done for us through the years, we were thrilled to think that we could play even a small role in getting him back out there to share his talents.

ॐॐॐ

In the mid seventies, we recorded with Paul Simon and Jimmy Buffett, toured with Johnny Cash, appeared at Carnegie Hall, and won our fourth gospel Grammy. In the mid eighties, we headlined two nights at New York City's Radio City Music Hall, with The Judds as our special guests; served as the official spokesmen for the Boy Scouts of America; and our family broke apart. In the late-nineties, Golden came home, we appeared at B.B. King's club in New York City, won the prestigious American Eagle Award from the National Music Council, and hosted our own weekly television show from Las Vegas. A decade later, we recorded a long-form gospel video with Bill Gaither, cut a White Stripes song with a thirty-year-old rock-and-roll producer, performed at *South by Southwest,* in Austin, sang in the Rose Bowl Parade, appeared with The Mormon Tabernacle Choir, recorded a gospel record with the legendary Blind Boys of Alabama, put a song on the charts for the fifth consecutive decade, and were made members of the Grand Ole Opry. As diverse as those may seem, the one constant through them all was that, though each could be classified as "reinvention," we always remained true to what it meant to be The Oak Ridge Boys. We may have branched out, but we never sold out.

The reinvention of the Oaks has never been more obvious than in our recordings of the last decade or so. In that time, we've recorded nine new projects: three gospel, two Christmas, one patriotic, two country and one cross-genre. The one thing in common they all shared? As disparate as their styles might have been, they all featured The Oak Ridge Boys singing Oak Ridge Boys music.

From the Heart was our first all-gospel project in twenty-five years. It was nominated for a Grammy and won a Dove Award from The Gospel Music Association. We recorded it fresh off of our induction into the Gospel Music Hall of Fame, which was, of course, quite an honor for us. Our patriotic release in 2003, *Colors,* was a labor of love, as much as anything—a reflection of our personal love of the country—but we were rewarded with a Grammy nomination for Best Country Performance by a Duo or Group. We received another Dove Award in 2007 for Country Recorded Song of the Year (for "Jonah, Jacob and Moses."). All of these projects were produced by Michael Sykes and Duane. In 2010, we won our ninth Dove when *A Gospel Journey,* the concert performance we taped for Bill Gaither, won Best Long Form Video.

Since 1988, we have ended every year with a Christmas tour. Each November, we start in Branson and do about a week's worth of performances and then pack up the decorations and lights, reindeer and sleigh, and we head to a different region of the country where we spend the next five or six weeks spreading a little Oak Ridge Boys Christmas magic. I'm not going to lie; it's a grueling tour. We come out and do about an hour's worth of hits, then we take an intermission while the stage gets transformed into a winter wonderland, then come out and do an hour's worth of Christmas songs, ranging from tradition-al carols to some of our Christmas hits through the years. It's grown into a spectacle that features Santa Claus, elves and children; it really is a wonderful way to spend our holiday season. What began as just another way to reinvent ourselves, and bring to the fans some of the Christmas music we had recorded, has expanded into a major part of our touring year, with almost every night bringing another sold-out crowd. It's a good thing we enjoy it because we realized long ago that the Christmas tour is here to stay!

One day in early 2007, out of the blue, we got a call from Shoot-er Jennings, Waylon Jennings' and Jessie Colter's son, who was making some noise in Music City by bringing back some of his dad's outlaw coun-try. He asked if we would consider recording with him on his album, *The Wolf*. Of course we did it, and the result was, not only, a cool song, "Slow Train," but, also, the decision to collaborate with him and his producer, David Cobb, on our next CD, the 2009 project that became *The Boys are Back*. This was, perhaps the reinvention that got the most recent atten-tion for us—some of it good and some of it negative.

We recorded *The Boys Are Back* at Compass Studios (dubbed

"Hillbilly Central" in the mid-seventies) located on Nineteenth Avenue, on Music Row, in Nashville. It used to be Waylon Jennings' offices and studio. Ironically, it was situated next door to a building that Duane once owned, where the Oaks offices were when I'd first joined. Because of the proximity, we would get to know Waylon over the years. And that was where we'd first seen his little boy running around and playing. Of course, that little boy, Shooter, was now heavily involved in this project—in fact, having written the title cut especially for us.

With *The Boys are Back,* we went down some roads that we'd never really traveled before, but while we did—reinventing ourselves, again, in the process—we did so without changing ourselves. You can listen to anything we've ever done—including recent material like "Seven Nation Army," "Boom Boom," or "Hold Me Closely"—and you can still know it's The Oak Ridge Boys singing. The songwriter and recording artist, Jamey Johnson, who has been setting Nashville on fire with his music, wrote a song for the project called "Mama's Table." The moment we heard it, we knew it had been written for us. Jamey said that hearing us sing his song was surreal and that hearing our voices sing his words was a culmination of a dream for him. There's something unmistakable about us. As producer, David Cobb challenged us to grow and stretch, to record songs we might have never considered before, and to record in ways that we'd never tried, and the results were astounding.

Just as some fans didn't understand or accept it when we began adding some country songs to our gospel repertoire, some of the music from *The Boys are Back* also raised some eyebrows. It, definitely, received lots of national attention, and gained us a whole new generation of younger fans—and our regular fans recognized it as just another vehicle to deliver Oaks' music. In many ways, it was recorded in the same raw, scaled-down style of Rick Rubin's sessions with Johnny Cash. Collectively and individually, we recorded some of our freshest vocals on that project. Many major reviewers across the country—including some who had, seemingly, forgotten we even existed—reviewed the project. Whether they liked it or not, it was nice to be back on some of the relevant news pages again—and, by the way, we don't think we've been there for the last time!

We worked with Jamey again in 2011 when we sang on the title cut of a record he produced, the new CD from The Blind Boys of Alabama called *Take the High Road*. This was a great cut, and gave us the opportunity to make several appearances around the country with them.

As I write this, we have two new recording projects in the works. One of these studio projects, which released in May of 2012, for the Gaither Gospel Series, teamed us with producer, Ben Isaacs. The concept for this project was originally for us to do another straight-ahead gospel album, but it transformed into a more general acoustic-driven release ("gospel-friendly," as Duane termed it) for which we recorded some familiar covers in addition to a new title or two. Golden sang a beautiful version of John Denver's "Back Home Again," which became the title track of the project. We also recorded "Coat of Many Colors," from Dolly's catalogue (with Joe singing lead), and the Kris Kristofferson classic, "Why Me Lord" (on which I sang the lead.) We're looking forward to adding some of these songs to our stage show.

In support of this project, in late 2011, we appeared on another of the Bill Gaither television tapings—this one, in Charlotte NC, a throw-back to the old tent meetings that Billy Graham used to host, in his early days. Reverend Graham's son, Franklin Graham, was there, as was Billy's long time song leader, Cliff Barrows. Also in attendance was the great George Beverly Shea, then 102 years old. It was almost shocking, when he opened his mouth, to hear that he still had that amazing set of pipes; he still sang in that strong low-register voice. I have to admit, it encour-aged me to hear him singing so strong at his age. It gives me hope that I might be able to do the same!

There were so many artists participating in the taping, we were supposed to perform only one song from the CD: "Lead Me to The Rock." As we took to the stage, Gaither instructed the pianist, Gordon Mote, to play a little bit of "Elvira." I'm not sure if he'd intended for us to sing more than a chorus, but, not being ones to miss an opportunity, after the chorus, Joe launched right into the first verse, and we ended up doing the whole song. We even led the congregation in the singing of the "Oom Poppa Mau Mau" lines. It was quite a spectacle.

In April of 2012, we went into the studio—again with Ben Isaacs—to record a new Christmas CD. This one, scheduled to be titled *Christmas Times 'a Comin'*, will feature a mix of familiar classics, along with some new (hopefully, soon-to-be) classics. The producers wanted me to sing an Elvis Christmas song, so we decided on "Here Comes Santa Claus," which turned out to be very fun. Duane and Ben also found me a wonderful new Christmas love song called "All I Want for Christmas is You." I really like it, and enjoy singing it. I hope it finds its way into our Christmas show.

As hard as it is to believe, this will be our thirty-third release—and our sixth new Christmas project. As Joe likes to joke, we've recorded as many Christmas records as Andy Williams and Perry Como. It might be true!

I'm sometimes asked in interviews if, after all these years, we get frustrated with the demands or expectations of record companies, and, I can honestly say, we do not. The industry is so tenuous; nothing is as it was anymore. Sales that, twenty years ago, would get an artist released from a label are now producing Number One records for artists. With very few exceptions, no one—not the artists, the record labels, the distributors, or the retailers—are making money on record sales, the way they once did. The days of a label signing any act that can sing, and putting out a record to see if it hits, are long past. With the current environment in the music business, the fact that a label in town has offered us a new deal to record our music is something for which we are very grateful. It excites us to, again, get into the studio with a producer who is a fan of The Oaks, and who has some fresh ideas for a project.

In early 2011, Cracker Barrel Old Country Stores surveyed customers, in their 603 locations nationwide, about the artists that they would most like to see on the stores' CD shelves. I'm proud to say that The Oak Ridge Boys topped that list. As a result, we began talking about the possibility of producing a CD for exclusive release in their stores. As often happens, there was an ebb and flow to the negotiations. At one point, we had all but given up hope that the deal would happen, but—to his credit—Duane decided to call our contact at Cracker Barrel directly, and, as a result of that conversation, the deal came back to life—so in early July we found ourselves back in the studio under the direction of three producers: Michael Sykes and Duane Allen, and in an exciting turn of events, Ron Chancey.

This project, titled *It's Only Natural,* included, in addition to new material, re-recordings of some of The Oaks songs from the late eighties and early nineties. During those years when Steve Sanders was with us, we had five Number One hit records—songs like "Lucky Moon," "Beyond Those Years" and "Gonna Take a Lot of River," that we'd recently put back in our live shows. Even though they're songs we recorded nearly twenty years ago, because of the new vocals and arrangements, they feel fresh and new. We also cut "Red Dirt Highway," a song that Golden had a hit with while he was gone. We agreed to re-cut Elvira, in honor of her thirti-eth anniversary. Since the original release, we've re-cut it only once, and that was for a 2011 project with the Dukes of Dixieland, done, of course, in the Dixieland style. It was a very cool cut but it was sort of a novelty. When we learned that Cracker Barrel wanted "Elvira" on this project, we just couldn't resist the opportunity to rerecord it with Chancey at the board. And once he agreed, we all got excited at the prospect of record-ing some new material with him, so, just like he'd done so many times for us in the past, he went out and found some great songs, two of which are on this project.

On our first day in the studio, we had already recorded five songs during two sessions. Michael Sykes and Duane had presided over those and spirits were high. We knew we were recording some good music. After dinner, Chancey arrived to produce the last session of the day, at which we would record the two new songs referred to above and "Elvira."

Jim Halsey was there, along with Sherman, and Jon Mir and Kathy Harris were there from our office. Donna had been there with me throughout the day. Raymond Hicks, who had been our road manager throughout our biggest years, and was now a music publisher, stopped by. We'd all had a great visit but a night which already seemed destined to be special became even more so when through the door walked Jim Fogelsong and his wife Toni. In that instant, in addition to so many people who had played important roles in our lives, the three most significant individuals in the history of The Oak Ridge Boys were, once more, with us in the studio. The promising future that now also comprises our rich history began when the four of us came together with Jim Halsey, Jim Fogelsong and Ron Chancey, and now, all these years later, we were together again at a recording session where great music was being made. It was an awe-inspiring evening.

As fate would have it, Cracker Barrel had sent a camera crew to that session so the gathering was memorialized for all time, and like a blessing from God, what the cameras captured might well be some of our most magical moments in recent history. "Before I Die," with Golden singing lead, was the first song on that session. It may be one of my favorite songs we've ever cut. Some of the lyrics are just so beautiful, I have to admit, I got a little bit emotional while singing it. The other, that featured Duane on lead with all of us sharing vocals, was called "The Shade (Comes Free With the Tree)." It, too, was just a terrific song. With those two complete, it was time to cut "Elvira." We discussed with Chancey some options: cutting a straight-ahead version that paid homage to the original, or bringing a completely new sound to the song. In the end, we unanimously agreed to keep the spirit of the original cut, which had been so good to us, but to update it using the sounds of today's contemporary country music.

It was 10:00 at night on a day that saw us begin twelve hours earlier; we had sung all day long, but no one wanted to leave the studio. I can't say the excitement matched that of thirty years earlier because it was a different phenomenon. I can say that it was just as special in its own way. Here we were, less than two years away from celebrating forty years spent together as a group; thirty years since "Elvira" first came to us. There is no way to calculate how many times we have sung it over those decades; but with a studio full of some of the finest musicians that have ever created recorded music, we sang the song with a new energy that shocked everyone who heard it that night—maybe even ourselves, just a little bit.

It's Only Natural was released in the fall of 2011, and was an immediate success for us. Sales were strong—it was the highest debuting album in *Billboard* for the week of its release, entering the country chart at Number Sixteen—and the promotional tour we did was a whirlwind. From Florida to New York City to Houston, Texas and beyond, we seemingly spent any day we weren't performing promoting the release. We made several television appearances on which we performed the first single from the project, "Whatcha Gonna Do?" (which was published and pitched by Raymond Hicks, which made it especially rewarding to us) as well as our new version of "Elvira." It was professionally satisfying that the feeling we experienced in the studio shone through on the recordings and was recognized by the fans.

So simply stated, the project became another Oak Ridge Boys release featuring the kind of music we've always done—just another opportunity to reinvent ourselves while remembering who we are.

The relationship with Cracker Barrel also led to them sponsoring our 2011 "The Boys are Back for Christmas Tour." The stage featured the iconic storefront, for which Cracker Barrel is famous, all decorated for Christmas, and included four rocking chairs sitting in front of a huge roaring fireplace. We did thirty-nine shows in thirty-one cities and nineteen states, in just over a month-and-a-half. In fact, from Thanksgiving until December 21, when the tour ended, we had only two days off. On top of that, we also did several lunchtime appearances at Cracker Barrels in the cities in which we were appearing.

For this tour—and for the first time ever on stage—we featured a segment in which each of us shared stories from our lives, especially memorable Christmases from our childhood. As we sat in our rockers and reminisced each night, I think we learned something new about each other. It was not only a nice way to share something private with those in attendance, but it also offered us a peaceful, intimate few moments, in an otherwise grueling schedule, in which we could just breathe and think about what makes each of us love Christmas so much. And in so doing, it also served as a reminder for why we each love being members of this Oak Ridge Boy family.

As an exciting extension of our relationship with Cracker Barrel, in 2012, one version of our new Christmas CD will be sold, exclusively, at Cracker Barrel. That version will feature two additional songs (on both of which, I sing the lead) from earlier Christmas releases. We're extremely grateful for the relationship we've built with Cracker Barrel. It's very ful-filling to be associated with a brand that is so loved around the country, and we're proud if they feel even a little bit the same about us.

ॐॐॐ

I'm always asked how we've been able to keep touring all these years. The reality is that, as the years have passed, we've developed wis-dom. We all eat better now, we exercise, and we make sure we get plenty of rest. We've learned to remove the things that brought us stress. I can't say we always took care of ourselves, but I can say that we've all learned from our past mistakes and corrected them.

While nearly every year takes us to a venue or a town we've never played before, we also still visit many places at which we've been perform-ing for decades. In August of 2011, we performed on the main stage at the Kentucky State Fair for the thirty-sixth consecutive year. As the Louisville Courier-Journal stated in a pre-event column, that is a record that will never be broken—until we break it in 2012 (if the good Lord's willing). I'm happy to say, it's already on the schedule.

In February 2012, we appeared at Don Laughlin's Riverside Ca-sino in Laughlin, Nevada. It marked the thirty-second consecutive year we've appeared there. Even during our biggest years after "Elvira" we never missed a year in which we took a week away from touring arenas to return to the showroom at the Riverside.

Our normal schedule there has always been Tuesday through Sat-urday. In recent years, we've taken to extending the run to seven days and even adding matinees on four of the days; eleven shows in seven days. We have almost the exact same history at John Ascuaga's Nugget Hotel and Casino, in Sparks, Nevada, where we've done a three-day engagement there every year for more than three decades. In Branson, Missouri, where we've been appearing since the early nineties—for the last three years, in a theater that bears our name—I'm proud to say that, any night we're appearing there, we still draw some of the biggest crowds in town.

I'm always asked in interviews how long we plan to keep touring and recording. As Joe likes to say on stage most nights, while other groups like Alabama and The Statler Brothers have retired, The Oak Ridge Boys simply buy new buses and keep adding shows! The realities of life are certainly catching up with The Oak Ridge Boys, just as they are to everyone. There's no doubt we've got more life—and career—in our rear view mirrors than in our windshield. But how could I ever quibble about that?

I got to sing in the Atlantic City Convention Center when I was a kid. I wasn't sure I'd ever have a greater thrill. I got to make my living singing in a quartet. How could I have been so lucky? I fell in love and had five wonderful children. My name and my spirit will live on through them and their children long after my time here is done. I was fortunate enough to know the king and have him call me his friend. How much cooler can it get? I've been blessed enough to know The King and have Him call me His child. Thank you, Lord. I've toured the world with my brothers and had more success than I could have ever imagined. I know we've made a difference in the lives of many, by simply bringing some, a smile and a song, and by bringing others something more tangible like food or shelter.

A preacher friend of mine once said something that speaks directly to how I feel. If I were to stand in front of God, and He reached back and pulled out a box that was labeled "Richard Sterban's blessings" and then opened it to reveal an empty box; and if He said to me, "Richard, I'm sorry but every blessing I was going to give you in your life has already been given. There's nothing left." I could smile, shake His hand, and walk away knowing that I had received much more than I ever deserved.

And as I walked away, there is no doubt that I would be singing a song. After all, it's all I ever wanted to do.

Acknowledgements

From Richard Sterban

Writing a memoir is a daunting task. Living a life is a wonderful, sometimes difficult and exciting adventure. Reliving it, remembering every high and every low, and committing them to written words on a page for anyone to see, is both exhilarating and sobering. The good fortune and heartache, the love and loss, the victories and the defeats that come our way as the days and the years fly by, are the lyrics and the melody to the songs that become our lives.

Just as the living requires the contribution of countless others, so, too, does the writing. Just as I have, no doubt, unintentionally omitted the mention of people who played a significant role in some aspect of my life, giving special mention to some here may result in the same sort of failing. But there are many I must thank, and, first and foremost, thanks to the Lord for never forgetting about me even when I might have acted like I'd forgotten about Him. I'm living proof that Proverbs 22:6 is true. To Donna, my wife and partner; to my two daughters and three sons, and my five grandchildren: my life would be incomplete without each of you. Thanks to my parents who taught me not only right from wrong, but also the work ethic and lessons that every son should know.

I've already written much about my partners in song, but again, here I must thank Joe, Duane and Golden for forty plus years of friendship and successes the likes of which we could have only dreamed. Thanks also to: Kathy Harris and all of the Oaks staff; Jon Mir; my friend and counselor, Gary Spicer; the Godfather, Jim Halsey; Darrick Kinslow, for

ACKNOWLEDGEMENTS

minding the business on the road and for being my friend; Billy Smith for driving us safely every night, and for the good late night conversations as I ride in the jump seat; Paul Moore and all of the agents at William Morris Endeavor Entertainment, for keeping our datebooks full for all of these years; Billy Dean for some enjoyable and helpful conversations on the road; Terry Calonge, for your friendship and for believing in this project; Pam Lewis, for your ideas and enthusiasm; David Brokaw, Kirt Webster and Kathy Gangwisch, thanks for all of the efforts in spreading the word about The Oaks; and Sandy Brokaw, your efforts have reached beyond publicity. Thanks for your friendship and for the many hours of conversation about baseball and life. As 41 said to Rusty Staub all those years ago: "You're the man!"

A special thanks to my friend, Charlie Neglia, the owner of one of my favorite neighborhood restaurants, Avanti Gourmet, for allowing us to spend so many afternoons in a booth doing interviews for this book. As usual, the food was wonderful, and the hospitality was greatly appreciated.

Thanks also to my long-time friend, Steve Robinson, for helping me get the thoughts and memories out of my head and onto these pages.

Finally, thanks to you who might be reading these words. To have been blessed with friends who call themselves fans of what we do—whether it be our music or writing or something else—is a gratifying and humbling feeling. I've never taken that for granted and it gives me just as big a thrill today as it ever has over the course of my life. Thank you for caring about a kid from Camden and for sharing my memories within these pages.

From Steven Robinson

Most of the pages of this book were typed on a MacBook on my lap in the middle of the night as I sat propped up in bed. All my life, I've been my most creative in the wee hours. I was born at 3:00 a.m., so maybe it all started then and there. My wife, Heather, and our golden retriever, Colt, deserve much credit for not kicking me out of the room all those nights as I pounded away at the keys (sometimes, apparently, very loudly). They tried their best to sleep through it all. So, thanks to them.

Thanks to my parents, Jackie and Nina, for, among other things, making sure I had all the books I wanted as a child so that my love of words could grow. Thanks, also, to my big brother, Roy, for, among other things, always being there to watch out for me.

Many people were so very helpful to me in the researching and writing of this book. They include: Kathy Harris, Felicia Squires, Jon Mir, Ron Chancey, Nick Bruno, J.R. Damiani, Joe Moscheo, Gary Buck, Donna Sterban, Amanda Luedeke, Darrick Kinslow, Joe Bonsall, Duane Allen, William Lee Golden, Terry Calonge and Jeremy DeLoach. Thanks also to Donnie Sumner, Ed Enoch, Jimmy Blackwood, Kieran Davis, Don Robinson, and John Stoj. Special thanks to Gary Hovey, at Elvis Presley Enterprises; and Julie Heath, at Warner Brothers Entertainment.

Finally, I want to express a heartfelt thanks to Richard Sterban for entrusting to me the memories of his life. I've been fortunate to know him and Donna for the last seventeen years and it was an honor to work with him on this project.